Your Guide to the Family History Library

your
guide
to the
Family History Library

Paula Stuart Warren and James W. Warren

BETTERWAY BOOKS
CINCINNATI, OHIO

www.familytreemagazine.com

Facilities, services, and other businesses listed in this book are included only as a service to the reader. Information listed is subject to change at the discretion of the facility or service and is beyond the control of the authors. We appreciate notification of any changes to update future editions of this guide or for articles.

James W. Warren, Paula Stuart Warren, and Warren Research and Publishing are not affiliated with the Family History Library, Genealogical Society of Utah, Salt Lake Convention & Visitors Bureau, hotels, restaurants, or the other businesses and services mentioned in this book. We do appreciate input from any of these services and businesses, and also their efforts to make Salt Lake City and the Family History Library a great place for genealogists to visit.

The five city and area locator maps included in this book were prepared by Carol Barrett, CRG Digital Design, 1756 Eleanor Avenue, St. Paul, Minnesota 55116. Phone (651) 698-0552. Maps © 2000 by Paula Stuart Warren and James W. Warren.

Some material in this publication is reprinted by permission of The Church of Jesus Christ of Latter-day Saints. In granting permission for this use of copyrighted material, the Church does not imply endorsement or authorization of this publication.

Other fine Betterway Books are available from your local bookstore or on our Web site at http://www.familytreemagazine.com.

05 04 03 02 01   5 4 3 2 1

Library of Congress Cataloging-in-Publication Data

Warren, Paula Stuart
    Your guide to the Family History Library / by Paula Stuart Warren and James W. Warren.—1st ed.
      p. cm.
    Includes bibliographical references and index.
    ISBN 1-55870-578-3 (alk. paper)
    1. Church of Jesus Christ of Latter-day Saints. Family History Library—Handbooks, manuals, etc. 2. Genealogical libraries—Utah—Salt Lake City—Handbooks, manuals, etc. 3. Genealogy—Library resources—Handbooks, manuals, etc. 4. Genealogy—Bibliography—Catalogs—Handbooks, manuals, etc. 5. Genealogy—Research—Methodology—Handbooks, manuals, etc. 6. Salt Lake City (Utah)—Guidebooks. I. Warren, Jim. II. Title.

Z733.C55 W37 2001
026'.9292'0973—dc21
                                              2001035498
                                            CIP

Editor: Sharon DeBartolo Carmack, CG
Production editor: Brad Crawford
Production coordinator: John Peavler
Cover designer: Karla Stover
Interior designer: Sandy Conopeotis Kent
Icon designer: Cindy Beckmeyer

Family History Library cover photo and photos for part openers and chapter openers are reprinted by permission of The Church of Jesus Christ of Latter-day Saints. © 2000 by Intellectual Reserve, Inc.

Downtown Salt Lake City photo © Richard Cummins/Corbis.

DEDICATION

*A special dedication to the folks from around the United States who,
for nine trips, joined us on weeklong excursions to the Family History Library.
Their questions, suggestions, and friendliness formed the basis for the
annual short books we did on the library and the city.
We are ever grateful for their participation and friendship.*

*We can't forget Ann Peterson, a friend from the Minnesota Genealogical
Society, who guided Paula on her first trip to the Family History Library.
Ann, we miss you and thank you for your able assistance on that trip.*

About the Authors

The authors don't live in Salt Lake City, but for many years it has been like a second home to them! Paula Stuart Warren and James W. Warren are professional genealogists whose research and lecturing take them on the road for much of each year. Paula and Jim spend many weeks each year in Salt Lake City doing client research at the Family History Library. They led group trips to that library for seven years, giving special one-on-one assistance to registrants. Participants came from all over the United States.

Working together full-time, they operate Warren Research and Publishing in St. Paul, Minnesota. They provide on-site research and consultations, specializing in the upper-Midwest states and research at national repositories. A major focus of their research for many years has been the history and genealogy of an American Indian community. Their writing includes research guides and family histories for clients.

Paula is a Certified Genealogical Records Specialist, certified since 1988, and has been a full-time professional researcher for almost twenty years. She served as a national officer of the Association of Professional Genealogists and for six years on the Minnesota Genealogical Society Board of Directors. The author of several publications, Paula's *Research in Minnesota* was published in 1992 by the National Genealogical Society. Her subsequent *Minnesota Genealogical Reference Guide* is in its fifth edition. Her own Midwestern family history traces back to seven different nationalities, thus giving her a lot of exposure to different records at the FHL.

Jim has worked full-time as a researcher for almost twelve years. He has served since 1992 on the Federation of Genealogical Societies (FGS) Board of Directors, and is currently FGS vice president-administration. Jim is a former president of the Minnesota Genealogical Society and of the Irish Genealogical Society. He transcribed *Minnesota 1900 Census Mortality Schedule,* the only known surviving portion of a 1900 mortality schedule. Jim's personal research focuses on his maternal Minnesota Irish lines and his paternal lines in Arkansas, Indiana, Kentucky, and the Carolinas. Alas, he can currently claim only two nationalities, English and Irish.

The unique combination of a couple who work together full-time but with different styles and approaches brings a special strength and humor to their writing and teaching. The Warrens have lectured in more than thirty states and at the annual conferences of both FGS and the National Genealogical Society since the early 1990s. They are the intermediate course coordinators for the annual weeklong Salt Lake Institute of Genealogy. They teach the "Discover Your Family History" series at the Minnesota Historical Society, and were National Conference Cochairs for the 2001 FGS Conference, held in the Quad Cities in Iowa and Illinois.

Paula and Jim are active volunteers in genealogical, historical, and professional organizations. They were the corecipients of the 1992 Grahame T. Smallwood Jr. Award of Merit from the Association of Professional Genealogists.

The Warrens have passed on some of their wanderlust to two sons, a daughter, and four grandchildren. They are among the reasons that, although Paula and Jim enjoy their travels to Salt Lake City, they love to come home again.

Acknowledgments

This book would not have been possible without the help of many other people. Some helped directly on the book, and others lent their expertise about the Family History Library (FHL) over many years. We thank them for sharing so that all of us may know more about the FHL and about our ancestors. Many researchers responded to our requests for suggestions for the book. Some responses were unique, but many were duplicates.

The present and former staff at the FHL have always welcomed us. Their friendliness and sharing were big factors in the compilation of this book. Thank you to all the staff and volunteers of the Family History Library, and of the Family and Church History Department of The Church of Jesus Christ of Latter-day Saints, for the work you and your predecessors have done for the past 107 years. A special few of those people who over the years have unfailingly helped us and expressed a true interest in what we were doing are June Calder, Elaine Hasleton, Dawne Hole, Cheryl Howland, Dean Hunter, Irene Johnson, Debbie Latimer, Glade Nelson, Ken Nelson, Jimmy Parker, David Rencher, and Stephen Young.

To the registrants, too numerous to mention individually, over the years on our Salt Lake City group trips, a special thanks. You taught us with your questions and suggestions, and it was always a joy to assist you with the library and the city and an even greater joy to see you help one another and become, in many cases, good friends.

The professional research community in Salt Lake City—a number of whom have been generous in their suggestions and sharing over the years—deserves our thanks. Over many years other colleagues have suggested updates to our annual Salt Lake City guides, and we are thankful for their assistance: Carol Ekdahl, Gary Mokotoff, and Eileen Polakoff.

Jason Mathis of the Salt Lake Convention & Visitors Bureau has been an ongoing source of support and information for this and other projects.

The people listed below are others we need to thank personally for tips and information provided while we compiled this guide. If we have neglected to mention someone who generously shared, please forgive us.

Carol Barrett, Kyle Betit, Lynn Betlock, Claire Bettag, Tony Burroughs, Sharon DeBartolo Carmack, Karen Clifford, Jill Crandell, Madilyn Coen Crane, Kathy Deiss, Carol Dye Ekdahl, Nancy Emmert, Ann Carter Fleming, Dixie Hansen, Patricia Law Hatcher, Kathleen W. Hinckley, Harold Hinds Jr., Birdie Holsclaw, Linda Huss, Sherry Irvine, Jill Johnson, Roger D. Joslyn, Brenda Kellow, Sue Kratsch, Sandra Hargreaves Luebking, Anita Lustenberger, Alan Mann, Rhonda McClure, Gary Mokotoff, Eileen Polakoff, Dwight Radford, Joy Reisinger, Gordon Remington, Barbara Renick, Marsha Hoffman Rising, Vaughn Simon, Patricia Walls Stamm, Nancy Carlsen Stanger, Deborah Swanson, Duane Swanson, Loretto Dennis Szucs, Elizabeth Thorsell, and Donna and Roman Turbes.

A special thanks goes to Bill Brohaugh of Betterway Books for his initial contacts about working with Betterway. Bill, you understood the constraints of our family and other commitments and did not pressure us. Because of this, we chose to work with Betterway when our schedule allowed. We missed the opportunity to work with you directly, but we think we ended up with a pretty special editor in Sharon Carmack. Sharon was a friend and colleague before we began this book project. She has become an even closer friend and more respected colleague as a result of working with her. We have appreciated her patience and flexibility all through the project. We, and this book, have benefited greatly from Sharon's experience and suggestions.

Our gratitude goes to a few key people for the very special roles they played in the final months of this book: to David Rencher, director of the Family History Library; to Dean Hunter, collection development specialist-British Isles at the library; to our production editor, Brad Crawford, for whom the changes never seemed to end; to Carol Ekdahl, who has been our eyes and ears in Salt Lake City between our trips there and who keeps us on our toes; to Carol Barrett for the excellent maps she prepared; and to our eldest son, Jim, and daughter, Katie, whose assistance and support down to the wire were invaluable, as always.

Our parents and grandparents set the tone for us. Their memories of family and events helped spur us on to keep researching. That brings us to today's generation, our children and grandchildren: our son Jim and his family (Michelle and our grandson Marc and granddaughter, Kaylene), our daughter, Katie, and her family (Dean and our grandson Ryan and a grandchild to be named about the time this book appears in print), and our son Patrick. They are what all those ancestors have come down to. We're pretty proud of that family history.

Over the years our three adult children have been a part of our business and have spent time at the Family History Library with us and their input and other help have been valuable. They are the best proofreaders anyone could find— after all, think of the pleasure they took in finding mistakes their parents made. Seriously, we love you all and couldn't have done this book without your support.

Paula and Jim

Abbreviations Used in This Book

DAR	National Society, Daughters of the American Revolution
FGR	Family Group Records
FGS	Federation of Genealogical Societies
FHC	Family History Center
FHL	Family History Library
GRC	Genealogical Records Committee (for DAR)
GSU	Genealogical Society of Utah
ICAPGen	International Commission for the Accreditation of Professional Genealogists
IGI	International Genealogical Index
JSMB	Joseph Smith Memorial Building
NARA	National Archives and Records Administration
NGS	National Genealogical Society
PAF	Personal Ancestral File
PERSI	*Periodical Source Index*
PRF	Pedigree Resource File
UTA	Utah Transit Authority
WPA	Works Projects Administration

Icons Used in This Book

 Case Study — Examples of this book's advice at work

 CD Source — Databases and other information available on CD-ROM

 Citing Sources — Reminders and methods for documenting information

 For More Info — Where to turn for more in-depth coverage

 Hidden Treasures — Family papers and home sources

 Idea Generator — Techniques and prods for further thinking

 Important — Information and tips you can't overlook

 Internet Source — Where on the Web to find what you need

 Microfilm Source — Information available on microfilm

 Money Saver — Getting the most out of research dollars

 Notes — Thoughts, ideas, and related insights

 Oral History — Techniques for getting family stories

 Printed Source — Directories, books, pamphlets, and other paper archives

 Quotes — Useful words direct from the experts

 Reminder — "Don't-Forget" items to keep in mind

 Research Tip — Ways to make research more efficient

 See Also — Where in this book to find related information

 Step By Step — Walkthroughs of important procedures

 Supplies — Advice on day-to-day office tools

 Technique — How to conduct research, solve problems, and get answers

 Timesaver — Shaving minutes and hours off the clock

 Tip — Ways to make research more efficient

 Warning — Stop before you make a mistake

Table of Contents
At a Glance

Table of Contents

PART FIVE
**Making the Most of Your Trip to the Beautiful
Salt Lake City Area...166**

Introduction

Who is this book for? We led group research trips to the Family History Library (FHL) in Salt Lake City for seven years. Each year we updated a booklet with the basics of the city and the library. Everyone who joined our group trips thought we wrote the booklet just for them. Being the good genealogists we are, we actually wrote it as a reference for ourselves! A bit selfish, maybe. We are still writing from a somewhat selfish viewpoint—we want a guidebook we will use. We are also writing from the perspective we know best—a U.S. viewpoint. On an unselfish note, we want to let many people know about the Family History Library, Salt Lake City, and the surrounding area.

Many folks in Salt Lake City have made us feel welcome and have become our close friends over the years. We hope they don't mind our telling more people to come to this beautiful area. We also hope our professional colleagues who work in the library regularly will forgive us for increasing the number of users.

This book is not directed at the professional researcher who lives in Salt Lake City or visits the library regularly. It is written for the researcher who is just beginning the research process, for the person who visits Salt Lake City and is enticed to find out what the genealogy library is all about, and for the person who just never takes the time to learn more about the city and the library. For everyone, though, we hope to impart at least some new information or ideas. Even if we just steer you toward a new guidebook or a different restaurant, we have succeeded.

This was a difficult book to write, as the library and the city are undergoing constant changes. We tried to be current and also a bit futuristic. If the TRAX (light rail) line does not open on 400 South in late 2001, please forgive our references to that! Some of the projected library changes may not yet be in place the first time you use this book.

This is not a book to read and put away: It is meant to be consulted frequently. Still, we know there will be some readers with expectations that exceed the reality of a book this size. It is not a guide to all the records or all the countries represented at the library. Imagine the size of that book! Such a guide would be a multivolume work. Through the classes, conferences, institutes, audiotapes, and guidebooks we mention, you have many opportunities to learn more. We also offer you some resources you can use without going to Salt Lake City.

Many abbreviations are used throughout the chapters, but the first time the terms are used in a chapter, they are completely spelled out and the abbreviated version appears in parentheses. For a quick reminder, a page of all the abbreviations follows the Table of Contents.

Tourism in Utah is a good business, and the number of visitors to the FHL places it in the top ten attractions in Utah. The FHL is located directly west of Temple Square in downtown Salt Lake City. Many of the distances and directions mentioned in this guide are from the vantage point of the library and Temple Square and are based on a researcher's staying at a hotel close to the library. Lots of TV shows and movies are shot in Salt Lake City. *Touched by an Angel*, filmed on location in Salt Lake City and the metropolitan area, is just one example. Beyond the FHL are a big, beautiful city and state, and we hope you take time to enjoy them too.

When you visit the FHL in Salt Lake City or your local Family History Center, take time to thank the staff that keeps the facility open for you to use. Thank them for helping us indulge our compulsion to find out as much about our families as we can.

We thank the FHL staff and others for graciously sharing information for this book. We appreciate their cooperation. However, any misstatements, errors, or omissions in this book are ours.

See you in Salt Lake City!

Paula and Jim

PART ONE

Starting Points and Basic Information

ONE

What Is the Family History Library?

T he Family History Library (FHL) in Salt Lake City houses the largest collection of genealogical and family history materials in the world. Thousands of people discover every year that learning more about their family history adds a new dimension to the present and future. Many people find much of their history in this library and its collections, which are open to anyone at no charge.

WHY DO SO MANY PEOPLE GO THERE?

People go there because the world's ancestors are there—including yours! The scope and depth of the library's collection are unmatched, and the library's location and facilities are convenient. That attracts experienced researchers from around the world. The library has a wealth of databases, indexes, and published resources, but much of the collection consists of original records on microfilm. Sound family history connections are usually made only through the use of original records. People visiting Salt Lake City for various reasons also find their way to the library for a few hours, and that often begins an exciting ancestral search for them. Members of The Church of Jesus Christ of Latter-day Saints research their ancestors as part of their religious beliefs but make their facility available, without cost, to anyone who wishes to use it. This huge collection and genealogy's phenomenal growth in popularity make the library an irresistible destination and resource for people worldwide.

The World's Ancestors Are There—Including Yours!

While the FHL's collection certainly does not include everything, more people are likely to find ancestral information there than at any other major research facility. The collection includes birth, death, and marriage records; census schedules; military files; church registers; cemetery transcriptions; immigration lists; and many other types of records from all over the world. The collection concentrates on records of deceased individuals (pre-1920 records), so personal privacy issues are not normally a concern.

Important

The Scope and Depth of the Library's Collection Are Unmatched

The library collection includes records from every U.S. state and Canadian province and from more than sixty-five other countries. Not everything for every locality is here, and some locality collections are far more extensive than others. Many of the records the library has microfilmed still exist in their original form in the church or courthouse or archive where they were created or filmed. Theoretically, you could accomplish much of the same research by going to all the places your ancestors lived and visiting all the pertinent churches, courthouses, cemeteries, libraries, and local, state, provincial and national archives. Most of us would need five lifetimes to travel to all those locations and do that research on-site. The library, however, provides many of the records of the world in one central location—a pleasant, efficient facility in which to do research.

Nowhere else can you jump in your research from one U.S. county to another, from a local to a national repository, or from one country to another the way you can at the FHL. Where else, in one place, could you

1. locate your Midwestern or Southern ancestors in filmed county records . . .
2. use the federal census and local probate records to track their migration in reverse to the eastern United States . . .
3. find their U.S. arrival in the filmed National Archives passenger arrival records . . .
4. then use Swedish police registration records, German church registers, or British census records to locate the ancestral families in the old country?

There simply is no other research repository anywhere with a comparable worldwide collection of research material for genealogy and family history.

The Library Is Convenient

The library is ideally located in the heart of vibrant and comfortable downtown Salt Lake City, the "Crossroads of the West." It is directly across the street from Temple Square, Salt Lake City's number one tourist attraction. Hotels, restaurants, and two major shopping malls provide all the conveniences within easy walking distance. The library is just a few blocks from the interstate and less than a ten-minute ride to the Salt Lake International Airport. Thousands of researchers fly to Salt Lake City each year to research for days or weeks at the library and never need a car or cab. (As you read on you'll see that Salt Lake City has a lot to offer in addition to the library.)

Within a few blocks of the library are many other attractions, including Abravanel (Symphony) Hall, Mormon Tabernacle Choir concerts, and professional sports, including the NBA's Utah Jazz. The city offers an enjoyable, diverse experience for researchers and many attractions for family and friends.

The Library Is a Wonderful Place to Work

Genealogists often spend time in cramped, crowded, old facilities that are understaffed, have limited hours, and are not geared to help researchers. The FHL is a modern, comfortable, well-equipped facility with extended hours and lots of

Quotes

VOICES OF EXPERIENCE

"The FHL is the best specialized research library I've ever worked in, and I've worked at most of the outstanding research libraries in the U.S. It's simply fabulous."

—Harold Hinds Jr., Ph.D.

reference and volunteer help. It is closed only on Sundays and a handful of holidays each year. The facility is intended to make researchers effective, productive, and comfortable.

Each floor of the library has a reference counter staffed by a combination of volunteers and professionals specializing in the records housed on that floor. Some of those professionals are among the most knowledgeable in the world in their areas of specialty. Each floor has modern, well-maintained equipment. Five hundred microfilm stations provide a film reader, electrical outlet, and working space for papers and a laptop. Computer workstations are being expanded and upgraded to provide access to the FHL electronic collections as well as to the Internet. At some workstations, library patrons will also be able to retrieve e-mail.

People Visit the Library When They Are in Salt Lake City for Other Reasons

Many visitors to the FHL are in town for other reasons: conventions, business trips, family visits, skiing, or just driving through. Shuttle buses at the airport can even bring folks with a layover to the Temple Square area for a quick visit between flights.

Whatever brings you to Salt Lake City, a short or extended visit to the FHL can augment your family history research. The library is a wonderful place to trace some of your genealogy and a resource you're not likely to exhaust in a lifetime of research.

Much of the Collection Consists of Original Records on Microfilm

Microfilm Source

You may have already spent time at libraries in your area or researched your family using online resources. Libraries and the Internet are filled with wonderful resources for genealogists, but most of those resources are "secondary" sources: research compiled by someone else or material copied, abstracted, or indexed from other sources. The FHL collection includes many secondary sources, **but its real strength and depth is the volume of original records on microfilm.** Birth, death, and marriage records; civil and church records; probate, land, tax, and court records; and many others that document specific events and information on ancestors and their contemporaries around the world are available in the library. Experienced genealogists know that genealogical connections and events are most reliably proven using those original records.

QUESTIONS ABOUT THIS UNIQUE LIBRARY
How Are These Valuable Filmed Records Preserved?

The master film copies of the library's 2.5 million rolls of microfilmed records are housed in the Granite Mountain Records Vault, a storage facility and extensive microfilm lab literally dug into a mountainside in Little Cottonwood Canyon, about twenty-five miles from the library. It was constructed to withstand any foreseeable disaster, natural or man-made. The FHL can make copies from

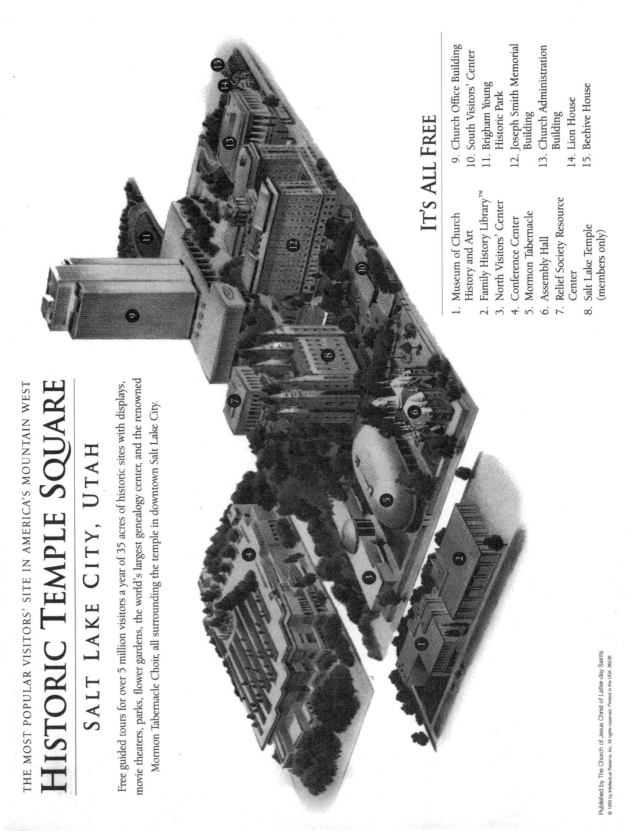

THE MOST POPULAR VISITORS' SITE IN AMERICA'S MOUNTAIN WEST

HISTORIC TEMPLE SQUARE

SALT LAKE CITY, UTAH

Free guided tours for over 5 million visitors a year of 35 acres of historic sites with displays, movie theaters, parks, flower gardens, the world's largest genealogy center, and the renowned Mormon Tabernacle Choir, all surrounding the temple in downtown Salt Lake City.

IT'S ALL FREE

1. Museum of Church History and Art
2. Family History Library™
3. North Visitors' Center
4. Conference Center
5. Mormon Tabernacle
6. Assembly Hall
7. Relief Society Resource Center
8. Salt Lake Temple (members only)
9. Church Office Building
10. South Visitors' Center
11. Brigham Young Historic Park
12. Joseph Smith Memorial Building
13. Church Administration Building
14. Lion House
15. Beehive House

Published by The Church of Jesus Christ of Latter-day Saints
© 1999 by Intellectual Reserve, Inc. All rights reserved. Printed in the USA. 36236

Figure 1-1

Reprinted by permission. Copyright © 1999–2000 by Intellectual Reserve, Inc.

the film masters kept here to replace worn or damaged library film copies or to circulate to the Family History Centers (FHCs).

What's *Not* in the Collection?

Reminder

There are limits to the collection. **Not *everything* you will need for your family research is at the FHL.** Not all records, and not all places. Even when a set of records is filmed, it may cover only a part of the time period for which records exist in a county courthouse or national archives. Have patience, and make the most of what is there. In general, pre-1920 records have been the focus of the filming. The library has microfilmed records all over the world, but only in locations where it has been able to obtain permission to film original records. While many types of records from many areas are available at the library, they represent a fraction of the records that exist worldwide. It is a well-selected fraction, however, focusing on original (primary) source material and the kinds of records that link generations. In other words, it focuses on genealogically useful and valuable records.

In some cases, the library purposefully excludes certain types of records. U.S. newspapers are an example. These are already widely microfilmed and available in each state, so the library makes no attempt to duplicate those resources. The library concentrates instead on records not yet filmed. In general, the library continues to film in areas not yet filmed and returns to areas filmed earlier to add more records and resources. For many localities, you have hands-on access to large collections of microfilmed records whose original records may not be open to researchers on-site.

Why Does Such a Library Exist?

Members of The Church of Jesus Christ of Latter-day Saints (often called the "Mormon" or "LDS" church by non-church members) are encouraged to actively seek information on their ancestors. Their religious beliefs stress that families, including deceased ancestors who have been identified, can be bound together in family units for eternity through sacred LDS Temple ordinances. To facilitate their members' family history research, the Church founded the Genealogical Society of Utah (GSU) in 1894. For more than a century, this organization has pioneered the collection of genealogical records worldwide. Access to those records is based in the FHL in Salt Lake City. The library and its collection exist primarily as a tool for Church members to do their genealogical research. In reality, however, a large percentage of the 2,400 people who use the library each day have no connection to the Church. They are simply interested in researching their family histories, which they are invited to do at the library with no charge, no obligation, and no "recruiting" by the Church.

How Has the Library Come to Be the World's Largest Genealogical Collection?

The collection and the scope of operations have grown steadily over the past century. In the early years, the pace of growth was gradual. By 1944, the library collection consisted of forty-two thousand books and two thousand rolls of film and was used that year by fourteen thousand patrons. The library has always accepted donations of genealogical materials, and it extensively purchases books, as well as records preserved by others in microform. The pace of filming and acquisition has increased rapidly in recent decades. Most of the microfilm collection is the result of the library's own worldwide filming projects. GSU was a pioneer in microfilming, beginning to utilize in 1938 that then-revolutionary technology. Courthouses, archives, churches, and other institutions welcome the GSU microfilming teams, whose work preserves the information contained on original records while making it more easily accessible on microfilm. **Today the microfilm inventory, the heart of the library's collection, has grown to more than 2.5 million rolls.** The collection also holds roughly 750,000 microfiche; 300,000 books; and 4,500 periodicals.

Notes

If Anyone Can Use the Library Free, Who Pays for All of This?

The members of the Church worldwide provide the financial resources that support the library and the worldwide acquisition and access to these records. It is no small expense! The GSU presently has more than 240 microfilm cameras filming records in more than fifty countries. Approximately 5,000 rolls of film and 1,000 books are added to the library collections *each month*. The library staff has about 230 full-time professional staff and 200 volunteers who provide services to visitors and FamilySearch Internet users. The library is now used by more than three-quarters of a million patrons annually. More than 3,400 FHCs around the world provide local access to much of the library's microfilm collection. At least 100,000 rolls of microfilm circulate to FHCs monthly. In addition, the library makes an increasing number of computerized indexes and sets of resource information available on its free Web site and on inexpensive CD-ROMs and library publications.

Today, the library is a division of the Family and Church History Department of The Church of Jesus Christ of Latter-day Saints. To most researchers, however, it is known simply as the FHL. (We use *Family History Library*, or *FHL*, throughout this book. In your research, you may also come across other terms, including Genealogical Society of Utah or Family History Department. We have chosen to use *Family History Library* generically in this guide.) Its role as part of the Church is fairly apparent to most library visitors, but the role it plays in our own genealogical research is uniquely important.

What Should the Rest of This Book Do for Me?

This book is designed to help you effectively use the library's resources as you research your family history. Use the "In a Nutshell" sidebar that follows to help you use the book most appropriately. If possible, read the whole book to get the full picture and hints; you don't need to read through it all at once. But it is organized in a way that we hope will help you methodically learn about and use the many resources of the library.

This book is intended for beginning and intermediate researchers, researchers who have never been to the FHL, and researchers who haven't been there recently. It contains many suggestions that should also be valuable for experienced researchers.

IN A NUTSHELL: USING THE LIBRARY AND THIS BOOK

What is the Family History Library?

- The largest genealogical research library in the world.

- A central repository for published material, electronic information, and microfilmed original records from more than sixty-five countries worldwide.

- A facility used daily by more than 2,400 enthusiastic, friendly, idea-sharing researchers from around the globe.

Why go there?

- Because most well-prepared researchers can accomplish as much research there in a week as they could in many months almost anywhere else.

- To research in a comfortable, modern, well-equipped facility.

- Because you can quickly (or at your own, more comfortable pace) move from indexes to original records, from one geographic area to another, and from one era to another with self-service films and books.

- Because the odds are excellent that many of *your* ancestors' records are in the library collections.

What should I do before I go there?

- Organize what you know about your family, and ask questions of your family members to learn more.

- Read this guidebook thoroughly. (What may not be clear to you in one chapter might make more sense when you've read what's in other chapters. It all ties together.)

- Make use of information on the FamilySearch Internet site (see chapter three).

- Visit a nearby Family History Center. Ask questions. Use their on-site resources. Order microfilm from the FHL to use at the Family History Center (see chapter six).

- Take advantage of genealogical society activities or seminars in your area.

- Accomplish as much research as possible at repositories close to home.

- Prepare specifically for a trip to Salt Lake City (see chapter seven).

What if I'm in Salt Lake City but didn't really prepare for a trip to the FHL?

- Read chapter two, "Basics of Family History Research."

- Read chapter fourteen, "I Only Have a Few Hours!"

- Visit the FamilySearch Center in the Joseph Smith Memorial Building to get started.

- Visit the FHL. Take the brief orientation, ask questions of reference staff, and use the finding aids and informational handouts in the library. Check some basic sources, such as U.S. census records, for your family.

- If you have more than just a few hours to research, read chapter thirteen, "Working in the Library."

- Make plans to return to the library, and get organized first.

What if I can't go to Salt Lake City?

- Do the same things listed above under "What should I do before I go there?" You still have tremendous family history resources available to you without a trip to Salt Lake City.

- Maximize your use of local repositories, genealogical societies, and published and online sources.

- Your local FHC provides you close-to-home access to the majority of the Family History Library microfilm collection.

- Don't give up—you may someday find a way to make that trip to Salt Lake City!

TWO

Basics of Family History Research

his chapter is designed to help those just getting started with researching their family. This brief introduction does not replace reading the all-important how-to guides or attending classes to broaden knowledge of sources and techniques.

WHERE DO YOU START?

Begin your family history research with yourself. No one else knows as much about you as you do. Have you kept a diary or journal that lists key points of your life? Begin your own chronological time line that tells when and where you were born, began school, learned to ride your first bicycle, went out on your first date, got your first job, and more. After you have begun to document your life, branch out to your family. This includes your children, parents, grandparents, brothers, sisters, aunts, uncles, cousins, nieces, and nephews. They are all part of your family history and might hold clues for further research. Ask for information on dates and places of birth, marriage, death, divorce, adoption; places where the family has lived; and names and addresses of other relatives. **Ask them to share copies of pictures, old letters, certificates (such as birth, marriage, death), and those very important family stories** (even about the painful family events—we all have them).

These starting points are important, regardless of your family's ethnic or religious background. We all need to start with the present and work back in time, linking and proving one generation at a time.

Hidden Treasures

Your Family's Names

A key part of your research is knowing the various given names and surnames of your ancestors. Remember that spelling doesn't always count! If you only look for what you determine is the "right" spelling of the name, you may miss an index or record entry where the clerk misspelled the name. You might miss the U.S. census entry where your Norwegian immigrant ancestor did her best to spell the name and the census enumerator did his best to write it down. Then there are the records written in a language you don't speak or understand. Whether the record is in Latin, English, Spanish, or French, many people will have difficulty reading the correct name. Writing styles have changed over the years, so you may not recognize a name even if it is spelled as you think it should be.

Keep Track of What You Gather

Before long you may find your house or apartment filling with stacks of papers, file folders, and computer disks. **How can you make sure you will keep track of the important information and can find it easily?** Using file folders or binders categorized by family surname and by topic—such as interviews, birth records, death records, obituaries, census records, or probate records—makes record retrieval much easier. Use ancestor charts or family group sheets. Ancestor charts depict the direct ancestry of an individual. Family group sheets show a picture of all members of a specific family, parents and children, with births, marriages, and deaths among other details. The lines you can't fill in point to information you still need to discover. These forms can be purchased at genealogical seminars and conferences and at historical society gift shops, and they are available online at some of the major commercial sites.

Supplies

Take a tip from those who have preceded you in this pursuit. Many lectures, guidebooks, and software programs—genealogical or not—might prove helpful for organizational techniques. Sharon DeBartolo Carmack's *Organizing Your Family History Search* is one book you may need. Another helpful book is William Dollarhide's *Managing a Genealogical Project*.

Be sure to note the source for every piece of information you find or are told. You may need to check the resource again or remember which relative told you the story about a 1921 family event.

Begin to create time lines. Make a time line for each individual or family. Include event dates and places. It might help to include an entry that in 1866 the Brown County courthouse burned to the ground or that the Green City birth records begin with 1865. See chapter seven for an example of a time line.

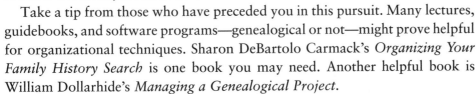

**WHERE TO FIND FAMILY GROUP SHEETS
AND ANCESTOR CHARTS**

- Vendors at genealogical seminars and conferences sell these.

- Genealogical vendors offer these via their catalogs and Web sites.

- Historical and genealogical societies and museum gift shops may sell these.

- Some genealogical guidebooks have forms you may copy.

- The Family History Library and its Family History Centers have forms for sale on-site and online.

- Check the Web sites at the end of this chapter for sites to print and download forms.

Supplies

Some researchers prefer to do all of this using charting or genealogical software such as Family Tree Maker, The Master Genealogist, Personal Ancestral File (PAF), or a database program. Genealogical periodicals, especially those with a computer bent, often have reviews and comparisons of these. Whichever format you choose, be sure to make backups and store them safely away in case of loss.

Finding More Family Background

Reminder

After you have begun to write down details about yourself and gather the details your family has to share, it's time to venture out to libraries, archives, and genealogical and historical societies, which have additional information. You can find these in the areas where you or your ancestors lived and at the local, county, provincial, state, regional, and national levels. **There is no one place where you can do all your research, no one place which will have all the information on your family.** Many sources are in book form, many are now on microfilm or microfiche, and many remain in the original, manuscript form. Many of these records for your family may be found at the FHL.

Learn about these records. Maybe you can't find the christening record for Great-Grandma in the Swedish church where her sisters were christened because the church did not start keeping such records until after her christening. Maybe there is no death record for Great-Granduncle Horace because the state where he died did not require death records until twenty years after his death. Fortunately, some guidebooks, articles in genealogy periodicals, and lectures from the experts share information on record-keeping practices and beginning dates for records.

Keep some type of research log as you work in the FHL and other places. It is important to know which church records, county histories, censuses, and other records you have checked and what the results of the search were. Examples of research logs are in chapter thirteen.

REAL RESEARCH

Research Tip

Most of us will not find a "magic" index, Internet site, or document that tells us what we want to know about all our ancestors. One birth certificate, one passenger list, one naturalization record, or one christening record doesn't stand alone and prove our ancestry or solve our research problems. **We have to gather all the pieces of the puzzle, all the clues, all the indexes, and all the records and put them together.** We have to gather these for the greater ancestral family (this includes your second cousin Mary and Great-Grandma's brothers) to trace the family backward in time and learn who they were, how they were related, and where they came from. You can't find one record and assume you have found your ancestor, regardless of whether the surname is Anderson or Smith or Wojtowicz. You need to find, analyze, and put together all the pieces of that big puzzle.

Is the Information Correct?

As you find details on your family, be sure to prove the facts. If Aunt Mary said that your family left Germany in 1888 to live in Indiana, learn which German and U.S. sources will help to substantiate this date. She also told you that Great-Grandfather John Griffin was born in Arkansas in 1888. You will find that birth records were not kept that early in that state; your task is to learn what other sources will help to prove his 1888 birth date and locate them. If you have a death date for a relative, look for a church record, death certificate, family Bible, cemetery record, tombstone, and an obituary to verify the date.

What Has Already Been Done on Your Family's History?

In several chapters of this book we cover sources to look for what has already been compiled on your family's history. Don't forget to check the FHL Catalog for a published genealogy or manuscript concerning one or more of your ancestral lines. Be sure to check at other libraries for these. You will find databases of names, indexes to records, queries about individuals and families, and information about continuing your research in both published and online formats.

Basic Places for Genealogical Help and Information

We can easily sit at a computer or a microfilm reader or copy all the work done by Cousin Jane in Tallahassee. But we all need assistance to really understand what we find or copy, to fully glean the clues contained, or learn about more records and keep up-to-date with new indexes, record discoveries, and techniques. Do you know if there is a difference between a marriage license and a marriage record? If someone mentions Soundex, do you know what they mean? Do you fully understand that tool and how to use it?

What sources offer additional help in researching your family? Fortunately there are many such sources. Classes, lectures, and seminars, as well as published, online, and one-on-one help are available. Follow the lead of other genealogists. If you attend a national-level genealogical conference you will find professional genealogists attending lecture sessions to continue their education. Due to the specific nature of this guidebook—focusing on Salt Lake City and the FHL and its resources—we mention only some selected educational outlets in the paragraphs that follow.

CLASSES AND EDUCATION

Check with area genealogical and historical societies and the FHCs to see if classes are offered. The National Genealogical Society and Brigham Young University present two opportunities for long-distance education. Classes are also offered at community education departments and via colleges and universities. For class listings check genealogical and historical society publications; local newspapers; and college, university, and community education course brochures. You may find one-session presentations or multiple-session courses on one or more topics. The latter usually allow for more interaction with the instructor. Most classes provide handouts, and some multisession classes have homework.

State and Local Seminars

State, provincial, county, or city genealogical and historical societies hold one-day or longer educational seminars one or more times a year. Some feature one main speaker and others have several. For information on many genealogical societies and their events check out FGS Society Hall <http://www.fgs.org>, Cyndi's List <http://www.cyndislist.com>, or *The Genealogist's Address Book*.

National and International Conferences

In the United States and other countries you are likely to find these major educational opportunities. These largely annual events feature multiple sessions (some over one hundred) on various genealogical topics. The sessions may include lectures on genealogical software use and updates or on school, church, probate, census, birth, and other records. Lecturers may share ideas on finding, using, and interpreting records in the place where you live and in other localities. Many of these events host a thousand registrants or more and have a large area where genealogical vendors display their wares. Some of these conference opportunities are listed below

- **Brigham Young University Genealogy and Family History Conference:** held each August in Provo, Utah; http://ce.byu.edu/cw/cwgeneal
- **Federation of Genealogical Societies:** annual national conferences with lectures on a variety of genealogical topics; held in a different U.S. city each year; http://www.fgs.org
- **GENTECH:** annual conferences with computer/technology-related lectures; held in a different U.S. city each year; http://www.gentech.org
- **International Association of Jewish Genealogical Societies:** Annual conferences held in a different city each year; locations have included New York, Salt Lake City and London; http://www.jewishgen.org/ajgs
- **Irish Genealogical Congress:** held every three to four years in Dublin, Ireland; http://indigo.ie/~irishgc/
- **National Genealogical Society:** annual conferences and some regional seminars; held in different U.S. cities; http://www.ngsgenealogy.org
- **New England Historic Genealogical Society:** Regional conferences held around the United States; http://www.nehgs.org

Audiotapes

Conference logistics, your budget, and your everyday life may prevent you from attending all the national-level conferences. The alternative is to purchase audiotapes of lectures from Repeat Performance <http://www.audiotapes.com>. This firm tapes most sessions at many larger conferences. Many genealogists listen to the tapes while walking, jogging, driving, or taking a long-distance research trip.

For More Info

AUDIOTAPES OF GENEALOGICAL LECTURES

Audiotapes of lectures by researchers with expertise in that subject or geographic area can also give you greater insight into specific records and repositories. Check the Repeat Performance Web site <http://www.audiotapes.com> to see what audiotapes are available.

Institutes

Many genealogical education institutes are available for researchers. These institutes usually last from three to six days, and classes are offered all day; some may include evening sessions. The same group of students attend class together for the length of the institute. Homework may be involved. These are a good way to learn in an environment that takes you away from your daily chores. You can immerse yourself in education and interact with other genealogists. Some U.S. institutes are

- **Genealogical Institute of Mid-America:** Springfield, Illinois; http://www.uis.edu/continuinged/genealogy/index.htm
- **National Institute on Genealogical Research:** National Archives, Washington, DC; http://www.rootsweb.com/~natgenin
- **Salt Lake Institute of Genealogy:** Salt Lake City, Utah; http://www.infouga.org/institut.htm
- **Samford University Institute of Genealogy and Historical Research:** Birmingham, Alabama; http://www.samford.edu/schools/ighr/ighr.html

Continue Your Education

One day at our state historical society one of the librarians saw Paula walking into a class. The librarian asked why on earth Paula, a longtime genealogist, was attending the class. Paula answered that each instructor taught her something new or reminded her about some basic information that she might not have used in a long time. The moral? Don't stop learning if you plan to keep researching your family history. An instructor just might be the one to tell you about an obituary index hidden away in the office at the public library in your ancestral hometown.

PUBLICATIONS

Attend one of the genealogy seminars or conferences and you may find genealogical book, supply, and software vendors galore. The explosion of genealogical material online has not stopped the production of genealogical books. Imagine row after row of books on Swedish genealogy, Germanic genealogy, Minnesota genealogy, New York City genealogy, naturalization records, and more. Many of the publishers have online catalogs; these and others have catalogs available at the genealogy conferences and seminars. **Genealogists today are fortunate that mainstream bookstores, both the independents and the national chains, carry genealogy books.** Check appendix B for complete citations to the following books and for other helpful titles.

Printed Source

Genealogical Research Guides—General

- Allen, Desmond Walls. *First Steps in Genealogy: A Beginner's Guide to Researching Your Family History.*
- Carmack, Sharon DeBartolo. *The Genealogy Sourcebook.*
- Croom, Emily Anne. *Unpuzzling Your Past: The Bestselling Basic Guide to Genealogy.*

- Rose, Christine, and Kay Ingalls. *The Complete Idiot's Guide to Genealogy.*

Ethnic Resources
- Brandt, Ed, et al. *Germanic Genealogy: A Guide to Worldwide Sources and Migration Patterns.*
- Chorzempa, Rosemary A. *Polish Roots.*
- Colletta, John Philip. *Finding Italian Roots: The Complete Guide for Americans.*
- Carmack, Sharon DeBartolo. *A Genealogist's Guide to Discovering Your Immigrant & Ethnic Ancestors.*

Locality Resources
- Merriman, Brenda Dougall. *Genealogy in Ontario: Searching the Records.*
- Guzik, Estelle M., ed. *Genealogical Resources in the New York Metropolitan Area.*
- Hogan, Roseann Reinemuth. *Kentucky Ancestry: A Guide to Genealogical and Historical Research.*
- Leary, Helen F.M., ed. *North Carolina Research: Genealogy and Local History.*
- Szucs, Loretto Dennis. *Chicago and Cook County: A Guide to Research.*
- Warren, Paula Stuart. *Minnesota Genealogical Reference Guide.*

GENEALOGICAL SOCIETIES

If you live in Iowa, join the Iowa Genealogical Society. If you live in Sweden and have family that came to Iowa, join the Iowa Genealogical Society. Next see if there is a local society in the county or counties where your family settled. For a Swedish ancestry, find a Swedish genealogical society both in the United States and in Sweden. If you have Jewish ancestry, find a Jewish genealogical society. If you have African-American ancestry, join one of the many African-American genealogical and historical societies. These organizations offer classes, seminars, and publications.

The Iowa Genealogical Society features, of course, items related to Iowa genealogy. Some members have family who never lived in Iowa, so the annual seminar also may feature sessions on doing genealogy in such general subjects as census records and vital records and in other states or countries. The publications of many of these societies have articles on research for a particular ethnic group or locality and frequently include information for research beyond the society's locality. Many genealogical societies and libraries house many years of genealogical periodicals. The *Periodical Source Index* (PERSI) is a topical index to thousands of issues of genealogical periodicals. (See the discussion in chapter nine for more details.) If you don't take time to read both current and back issues you may miss an article that refers to a family Bible for your Griffin family or a special newspaper index for your ancestral hometown. You should read the periodicals that are specific to your ancestors' places of residence, but

Internet Source

WEB SITES

These sites are just a few of the many that offer education, links to other sites, record abstracts and indexes, forms to print, guidebooks and software for sale, and more. There may be a fee to use specific parts of some commercial sites.

- USGenWeb Project: http://www.usgenweb.net or http://www.usgenweb.org
  Provides links to information about, and sources for, many counties across the United States.

- RootsWeb: http://www.rootsweb.com
  A volunteer site with many record abstracts, indexes, educational items, and links.

- Cyndi's List: http://www.cyndislist.com
  Provides categorized links to thousands of sites. Examples of categories are Passenger Records, Church Records, Scotland, and Libraries.

- Ancestry: http://www.ancestry.com
  Many databases, books, and electronic resources for sale; online censuses; educational articles.

- Genealogy.com: http://www.genealogy.com
  Databases, books, and electronic resources for sale; educational articles; genealogical software.

- Family Tree Magazine: http://www.familytreemagazine.com
  Links to many resources and databases, forms to print, books for sale, educational articles.

- Heritage Quest: http://www.heritagequest.com
  Books and electronic resources for sale, educational articles, online censuses, genealogical software.

you should also branch out to those from other locales. For example, an article in a California publication on research methodology might give you some ideas on how to further your Ohio research. It might even contain an article on an Ohio research library.

WORK WITH A SEASONED RESEARCHER

At a genealogical society meeting you may strike up a friendship with another researcher who offers to mentor you or give advice occasionally. If you attend meetings where everyone has a few minutes to talk about their research, don't hesitate to use *your* minutes. See if the society has special interest groups or branches, such as those for computer genealogy or Germany, Sweden, or other countries. The suggestions you receive from fellow members may direct you to the information you seek.

Professional genealogists can assist you one-on-one in a research repository or by mail. You can have a joint project, with each of you doing some work. In some cases you may need some tutoring so you will know the sensible next steps to take. Or you might not be able to get back to Buffalo to check for obituaries that may hold the clues you need to continue your research; the professional may be your key to obtaining these. Additional suggestions regarding professional researchers are in chapter sixteen.

Oral History

Don't Become Overwhelmed

Review this chapter to refresh your memory about sources of help. Your family history is important and needs to be gathered before it is too late. **Too many people say, "If only I had talked to my grandaunt before she died; everyone says she was a treasure trove of stories about our family."** Do the learning and research a step at a time. Don't forget to include medical history details. Continue learning, and stay up-to-date on new records, microfilms, techniques, and indexes. You can do only a little family history, or you can become fully immersed in it. Whichever you choose, at least don't miss your chance to gather details from living relatives.

PART TWO

Access to the
Library Collection

THREE

FamilySearch Internet Genealogy Service

THE LIBRARY'S WORLDWIDE ELECTRONIC FRONT DOOR

Easy access to Family History Library (FHL) information increased dramatically with the debut of the library's Web site, FamilySearch Internet Genealogy Service, in May 1999. From your home computer, free of charge, you can learn the specifics of the library's collections, access large genealogical databases, share information, and locate research assistance and educational opportunities.

The FamilySearch Internet site <http://www.familysearch.org> was an overnight success. Recording over a billion user hits within months after its launch, the site immediately became one of the largest and most extensively used genealogical sites in the world. It has been a significant challenge for the FHL and other departmental staff to establish and maintain this Internet site. Human resources are stretched thin in any monumental undertaking, and this has been such a task. But the rewards to genealogists worldwide have been significant, and the site continues to grow and improve. An upgrade in September 2000 gave the site enhanced features and a new easy-to-use style.

Language options for FamilySearch Internet include English, Spanish, French, German, Portuguese, Swedish, Finnish, Norwegian, and Danish.

What Can You Do at This Web Site?

FamilySearch Internet enables individuals around the world to take advantage of many of the FHL's research tools from the convenience of their homes. You can learn and prepare in advance, then focus your time at a Family History Center (FHC) or the FHL on the actual microfilmed records. FamilySearch Internet is one simple way to use the FHL Catalog. You can search the library catalog in a variety of ways, including using combinations of keywords. The site helps individual researchers learn more about genealogy, and it provides pathways in the catalog to pertinent records for ancestral areas. The site contains many helpful components such as "Genealogical Word Lists" under the "Research Guidance" link, which provides translations of words and phrases often found in ancestral records that were compiled in another language. The

FAMILYSEARCH INTERNET: USE THIS WEB SITE OFTEN!

http://www.familysearch.org

Updates to FamilySearch Internet

This chapter introduces you to some features of FamilySearch Internet. The site's content and features are rapidly evolving. When you visit this Web site, be sure to look at the "News" tab on the home page. Information there will provide an update on recent additions and enhancements to the site.

"Research Guidance" and "Research Helps" information is enormously helpful, particularly to newer researchers. For Internet researchers, it can point the way to using microfilmed original records. The site also helps researchers link to and collaborate with others who are interested in common families, surnames, topics, or localities.

ARE YOU HESITANT TO USE THIS WEB SITE?

Will Church missionaries show up on your doorstep if you use the FamilySearch Internet site? No. In a press release regarding the Internet site, the Church anticipated this question and answered: "No, missionaries will not be sent unless a user requests this service through a link on the site." Just as in the FHL itself, no attempt is made to provide Latter-day Saints religious information unless a researcher specifically asks for that information. In the more than twenty years we have been researching in the FHL and at FHCs, we have never been proselytized.

Thousands of people each day use this Web site as a quick way to check the vast FamilySearch system of databases, which indexes hundreds of millions of records of ancestral individuals or families. If you've already used this site to do a surname search, you should take another look. Enhancements have made the search capabilities more powerful and flexible. You can now search the databases for a specific event and refine a search to a specific year or time period and to a broad or specific locality. The search results you see on the computer screen are *not* your ancestors' actual records. The database information, like the library catalog, are tools that can point you toward original microfilmed records in the library collection. **While this may change someday, the records themselves are not presently available on the Web site.** But the powerful features that FamilySearch Internet brings to your computer take you one giant step closer to easily identifying and locating those ancestral documents.

The FamilySearch Internet Menus and Options

The home page is clearly laid out. From the control bar at the top of all other site pages, you can select from four tabs: Home, Search, Share, or Library.

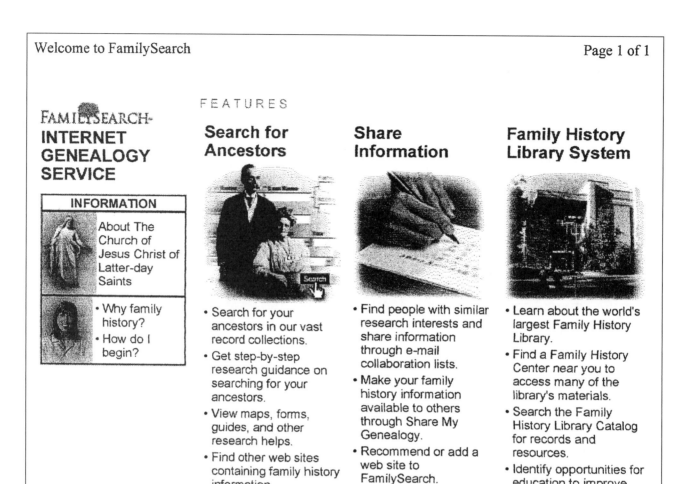

| Welcome to FamilySearch | Page 1 of 1 |

FamilySEARCH·
INTERNET GENEALOGY SERVICE

FEATURES

Search for Ancestors

Share Information

Family History Library System

INFORMATION

About The Church of Jesus Christ of Latter-day Saints

• Why family history?
• How do I begin?

• Search for your ancestors in our vast record collections.
• Get step-by-step research guidance on searching for your ancestors.
• View maps, forms, guides, and other research helps.
• Find other web sites containing family history information.

• Find people with similar research interests and share information through e-mail collaboration lists.
• Make your family history information available to others through Share My Genealogy.
• Recommend or add a web site to FamilySearch.

• Learn about the world's largest Family History Library.
• Find a Family History Center near you to access many of the library's materials.
• Search the Family History Library Catalog for records and resources.
• Identify opportunities for education to improve your research skills.

Figure 3-1
The home page of the FamilySearch Web site. *Reprinted by permission. Copyright © 1999–2000 by Intellectual Reserve, Inc.*

Internet Source

Using those tabs, you can easily navigate among the many specific valuable resources. At the top of each page of the site you can also click on Feedback, Site Map, Glossary, and Help. The site map is an easy way of identifying information categories quickly.

- **Home:** This page has tabs for news, frequently asked questions (FAQs), and ordering/downloading products. An information box includes a link to The Church of Jesus Christ of Latter-day Saints Web site and to answers to some beginners' questions.
- **Search:** Search the online databases or the library catalog, access the online research guides, browse by research category, or search a directory of other helpful Web sites. You can do a search of all the databases available at that time on FamilySearch or on specific individual databases.
- **Share:** To use the Share tab, you must first register as a user, a quick process. You can then collaborate via e-mail with other researchers with common interests and share your genealogical information via the Web site.
- **Library:** Details about the library are well organized. Current information

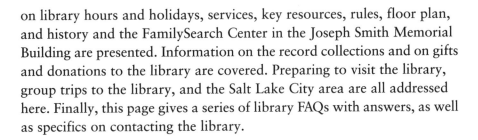

FAMILYSEARCH INTERNET DATABASES

At the time this book went to press, the databases and features of the Family-Search Internet site included

- Ancestral File

- Pedigree Resource File

- Vital Records Indexes: North America, the British Isles, western Europe, and Scandinavia

- International Genealogical Index

Note that the system continues to grow, and announcements of additions are occasionally made at the FamilySearch Internet site. Check the "News" section of the site regularly.

on library hours and holidays, services, key resources, rules, floor plan, and history and the FamilySearch Center in the Joseph Smith Memorial Building are presented. Information on the record collections and on gifts and donations to the library are covered. Preparing to visit the library, group trips to the library, and the Salt Lake City area are all addressed here. Finally, this page gives a series of library FAQs with answers, as well as specifics on contacting the library.

Family History Library Catalog

The FamilySearch Internet site is the only online location where the vast holdings of the FHL are listed. The FHL catalog describes the records available at the FHL in book, periodical, microfilm, microfiche, and electronic formats. It lists many types of records (census, military, courthouse, church, cemetery, business, and much more) and published materials (histories, maps, atlases, indexes, record abstracts, guidebooks, genealogies, and family histories.) Copies of most microfilm and microfiche records can be sent to FHCs for local use. Read chapter five, which is devoted entirely to using the FHL catalog, one of the most important tools available for any family historian.

The Databases

The FamilySearch name originally referred to the system of large databases and the FHL catalog that were available only at the FHL and FHCs. Now that the Web site bears the FamilySearch name also, it can be a little confusing. The library catalog and many, but not all, of the databases available at the FHL and FHCs are now available on FamilySearch Internet. The following listing highlights databases that are currently part of FamilySearch Internet. The information in this chapter merely touches on the research capabilities the Web site offers with these databases. Make use of the site's online help and instruction, as well as the resources in appendix B, to learn more.

Ancestral File

Ancestral File contains generationally linked files of basic vital information on individuals and multiple generations of families. Information has been submitted in computer files or on paper pedigree or ancestor charts for this database. Ancestral File includes names and other vital information (such as date and place of birth, marriage, or death) for over twenty-three million individuals who lived in countries throughout the world. You can view most information and print it in family groups or in pedigree chart formats or download it to your computer. To encourage contact and coordination of research efforts, the file lists the names and address of individuals who contributed the information. Updates and corrections can be made to information in Ancestral File by the original contributor or by others.

Efforts to compile generationally linked information in the Ancestral File computer format were begun by the Church in 1981. The information included in this database has been submitted by Church members and by nonmembers.

Pedigree Resource File

Pedigree Resource File (PRF) is a computer file that contains names; family relationships; and birth, marriage, and death information for millions of people. PRF is compiled from information uploaded by individuals to the FamilySearch Internet site through the "preserve" function of the site. It gives researchers a means of sharing the results of their research and having that information preserved. Contributors are encouraged to include source information and notes and collaborate with other researchers via e-mail or other communication. Unlike Ancestral File, information in PRF cannot later be changed, and it is merged with information submitted by other researchers. It appears as it was originally submitted by an individual. Corrections and additions are made by submitting a new set of pedigree information for a later PRF edition.

PRF is one of the fastest-growing databases on FamilySearch because it reflects the contributions of the ever-increasing number of Internet users visiting the site and sharing their genealogical information. Approximately 1.2 million names are added to the file *each month*, and new editions of PRF are published regularly on the Web site. CD-ROMs of each new release of PRF are also available for sale at the distribution center and online. At present, some additional information on the individual CD-ROMs is not included in the online listings. You can use the Web site as an index and then obtain any CD-ROMs that would contain the full family information in which you are interested.

Vital Records Indexes

In 1999, the library began making available inexpensive CD-ROM Vital Records Indexes to several regions of the world. Gradually, many of those index series are also being added to FamilySearch Internet. These are partial indexes to the records that exist for these areas and time periods. But because they are

Pedigree Chart

FamilySearch™ Ancestral File v4.19

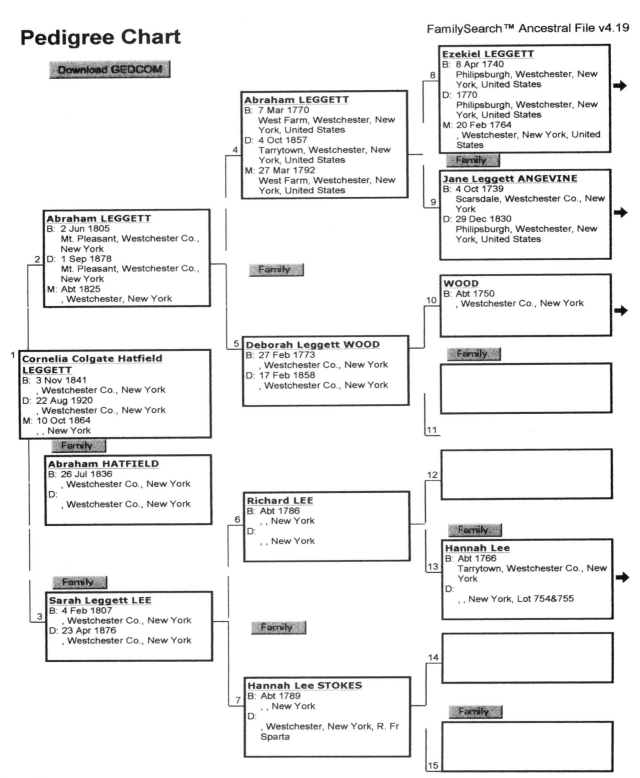

Download GEDCOM

Ezekiel LEGGETT
B: 8 Apr 1740
Philipsburgh, Westchester, New York, United States
D: 1770
Philipsburgh, Westchester, New York, United States
M: 20 Feb 1764
, Westchester, New York, United States
8

Abraham LEGGETT
B: 7 Mar 1770
West Farm, Westchester, New York, United States
D: 4 Oct 1857
Tarrytown, Westchester, New York, United States
M: 27 Mar 1792
West Farm, Westchester, New York, United States
4

Family

Jane Leggett ANGEVINE
B: 4 Oct 1739
Scarsdale, Westchester Co., New York
D: 29 Dec 1830
Philipsburgh, Westchester, New York, United States
9

Abraham LEGGETT
B: 2 Jun 1805
Mt. Pleasant, Westchester Co., New York
D: 1 Sep 1878
Mt. Pleasant, Westchester Co., New York
M: Abt 1825
, Westchester, New York
2

Family

WOOD
B: Abt 1750
, Westchester Co., New York
10

Deborah Leggett WOOD
B: 27 Feb 1773
, Westchester Co., New York
D: 17 Feb 1858
, Westchester Co., New York
5

Family

11

Cornelia Colgate Hatfield LEGGETT
B: 3 Nov 1841
, Westchester Co., New York
D: 22 Aug 1920
, Westchester Co., New York
M: 10 Oct 1864
, , New York
1

Family

12

Abraham HATFIELD
B: 26 Jul 1836
, Westchester Co., New York
D:
, Westchester Co., New York

Richard LEE
B: Abt 1786
, , New York
D:
, , New York
6

Family

Hannah Lee
B: Abt 1766
Tarrytown, Westchester Co., New York
D:
, , New York, Lot 754&755
13

Family

Sarah Leggett LEE
B: 4 Feb 1807
, Westchester Co., New York
D: 23 Apr 1876
, Westchester Co., New York
3

14

Family

Hannah Lee STOKES
B: Abt 1789
, , New York
D:
, Westchester, New York, R. Fr Sparta
7

Family

15

Figure 3-2

A page from Ancestral File. *Reprinted by permission. Copyright © 1999–2000 by Intellectual Reserve, Inc.*

Individual Record

FamilySearch™ Ancestral File v4.19

Abraham HATFIELD (AFN: 13JX-1B0)
Sex: M

Event(s):
Birth: 26 Jul 1836
, Westchester Co., New York
Death:
, Westchester Co., New York

Parents:
Father: Abraham HATFIELD (AFN: 13JX-18K)
Mother: Eliza Hatfield WAKEMAN (AFN: 13JX-1FL)

Marriage(s):
Spouse: Cornelia Colgate Hatfield LEGGETT (AFN: 13JW-R6S)
Marriage: 10 Oct 1864
, , New York

Submitter(s):

About Ancestral File:
Ancestral File is a collection of genealogical information taken from Pedigree Charts and Family Group Records submitted to the Family History Department since 1978. The information has not been verified against any official records. Since the information in Ancestral File is contributed, it is the responsibility of those who use the file to verify its accuracy.

Please Note:
Names and address of submitters to Ancestral File and those who have a research interest are provided to help in the coordination of research. The use of this information for any other purpose, including commercial use, is strictly prohibited.

Figure 3-2A
Individual record from Ancestral File. *Reprinted by permission. Copyright © 1999–2000 by Intellectual Reserve, Inc.*

such large indexes, it is a quick first source to check. In some cases these may help a researcher zero in on an ancestral family or locality. Indexes from this series presently available on the Internet include

- **Vital Records Index—Western Europe:** Records of more than 10 million births and christenings and 2.5 million marriages from selected localities in six regions of western Europe are indexed in this series. The regional

Family Group Record

Humphrey WARREN Sr. / Eleanor SMOOT
E:\PRF\CD14\PRF14

6 Jan 2001

				LDS ORDINANCE DATA B = Baptised SS = Sealed-to-Spouse E = Endowed SP = Sealed-to-Parent		
Husband's Name Humphrey WARREN Sr.					Date	Temple
Born	1632	Place ,,London,England		B		
Chr.						
Mar.				E		
Died	1671	Place ,Charles Co.,Maryland,America		SS		
Bur.				SP		
Father Edward WARREN		Mother Anne DAVENPORT		Parent Link Biological		
Husband's other wives						
Wife's Name Eleanor SMOOT					Date	Temple
Born				B		
Chr.				E		
Died				SS		
Bur.				SP		
Father Thomas SMOOT		Mother		Parent Link Biological		
Wife's other husbands						
Children					Date	Temple
1.Sex Name M Thomas WARREN						
Born	abt 1655	Place Westminster,London,,England		B		
Chr.				E		
Mar.				SS		
Died	1710	Place Frailty,Port Tobacco Hun,Charles Co.,Maryland		SP		
Bur.				Parent Link Biological		
Spouse Mary BARTON		There are other marriage(s)				

Figure 3-3

Pedigree Resource File search result. *Reprinted by permission. Copyright © 1999–2000 by Intellectual Reserve, Inc.*

divisions, made up of multiple countries with a common cultural, historical, or geographical past, were established to make locating and searching the records easier.

- **Vital Records Index—North America:** More than 4.6 million names which were transcribed from church and vital records as part of the Record Extraction Program are included in this index. Birth, christening, and marriage records from 1631 to 1888 in the United States and Canada are included. It concentrates on some states and provinces more heavily and represents only a small percentage of those events during those time periods.

- **Vital Records Index—British Isles:** Birth, christening, and marriage records from England, Wales, Scotland, and Ireland are included. These records are from as early as 1538 and as late as 1888. Not all counties in all four countries are represented. Some parish registers for centuries are indexed here, while it may include only a thirty- or forty-year span of records for other parish registers.

- **Vital Records Index—Scandinavia:** This series was about to be added to FamilySearch Internet as this book went to print.

International Genealogical Index

The International Genealogical Index (IGI) is one of the largest genealogical databases in the world, containing more than 760 million names from around the world. For many of those names, the date of a specific event—often a birth,

---

You searched for: James Johnson, North America
Exact Spelling: Off

[refine search]
Prepare selected records for download

Results: International Genealogical Index/North America
(200+ matches)

Select records to download - (50 maximum)

☐ **1.** JAMES JOHNSON - International Genealogical Index
Gender: M Birth: Aug 1875 Sandy, Jackson, West Virginia

☐ **2.** Jas. JOHNSON - International Genealogical Index
Gender: M Census: 1840 Buncombe, North Carolina

☐ **3.** Jas. J. JOHNSON - International Genealogical Index
Gender: M Census: 1845 Iredell, North Carolina

☐ **4.** James A. JOHNSON - International Genealogical Index
Gender: M Census: 1844 Campbell, Kentucky

☐ **5.** James JOHNSON - International Genealogical Index
Gender: M Birth: 10 Jan 1863 Bayonne, Hudson, New Jersey

☐ **6.** James JOHNSON - International Genealogical Index
Gender: M Census: 1828 Montgomery, Tennessee

☐ **7.** James W. JOHNSON - International Genealogical Index
Gender: M Census: 1858 Livingston, Kentucky

☐ **8.** James JOHNSON - International Genealogical Index
Gender: M Birth: Abt. 1872 Of, Laurel, Kentucky

☐ **9.** James Turner JOHNSON - International Genealogical Index
Gender: M Birth: 2 Jan 1829 Warren Co., Georgia

☐ **10.** James JOHNSON - International Genealogical Index
Gender: M Birth: 1824 Grundy, Tennessee

☐ **11.** James W. JOHNSON - International Genealogical Index
Gender: M Birth: 1843 Of, Hancock, Tennessee

☐ **12.** James Washington JOHNSON - International Genealogical Index
Gender: M Birth: 16 Mar 1845 Hancock, Tennessee

☐ **13.** James JOHNSON - International Genealogical Index
Gender: M Birth: 1859 Of Lvngst, Kentucky

☐ **14.** Jamie B. JOHNSON - International Genealogical Index
Gender: M Birth: 1876 Of, , Tennessee

Figure 3-4
IGI entries include a "Batch Number," which can lead you back to the specific microfilmed original records or submission forms from which the IGI data was extracted. Check the Family History Library publication *Finding an IGI Source* for specific tips on how to follow that record path. *Reprinted by permission. Copyright © 1999–2000 by Intellectual Reserve, Inc.*

baptism, marriage, or death—is listed. The IGI information has been compiled in two ways: the Name Extraction Program and Church member submissions.

Much of the IGI information was extracted from vital records or church records covering roughly 1500 to 1885. Thousands of volunteers have been part of the Name Extraction Program, extracting data from parish records and vital records of many countries. Those areas most extensively covered were the United States, the British Isles, and the Scandinavian countries. In the last couple

---

Individual Record Page 1 of 1

IGI Record

Select record to download - (50 maximum)

☐ James A. JOHNSON
Sex: M

Event(s):
Census: 1844
       Campbell, Kentucky

Parents:
Father: A. W. JOHNSON
Mother:

Source Information:

Batch number:	Dates	Source Call No.	Type	Printout Call No.	Type
7009918	-	0538487	Film	NONE	
Sheet: 94					

Return to search results Prepare selected records for download

Figure 3-4A
IGI Individual Record. *Reprinted by permission. Copyright © 1999–2000 by Intellectual Reserve, Inc.*

of years, much information has been added from dozens of other countries.

Much of the IGI information was contributed by members of The Church of Jesus Christ of Latter-day Saints who submitted an individual entry form or a family group sheet. **These entries may or may not provide any information identifying the submitter or the sources used in compiling the information.** A library publication that is most helpful in identifying sources for IGI extractions is the Resource Guide titled *IGI (International Genealogical Index): Finding a Source.*

Warning

The extent of the records indexed in the IGI makes it a useful tool for pinpointing possible ancestral areas of origin, and sometimes even specific church parishes, particularly if the surname is not a very common one. That can help you narrow a search effort to specific areas in order to locate or rule out the ancestral family in those areas. Because so many births, christenings, and marriages are indexed, it is often a way of linking generations. For example, if you can find a baptismal entry for an ancestor's brother or sister, that may be the clue to identifying your ancestor's parents.

Under the library's basic privacy policy regarding living persons, the Internet version of the IGI does not display *anything* on living people, including names. (The compact disc version available at the FHL and FHCs does show the name

Warning

> **WARNING!**
>
> Electronic databases like IGI, Ancestral File, and Pedigree Resource File can provide quick, easy access to information on millions of ancestors worldwide. But the information contained in these files is of uneven quality. Some is the result of painstaking, well-documented research; some is not. It may be difficult to distinguish which is which without verifying the data using actual records. Do not assume a listing in these files is proof of any event or relationship. Indexes and databases are valuable if used as *clues* and *finding aids* to point you to original records and further research.

Notes

THE INTERNATIONAL GENEALOGICAL INDEX GROWS

In 1999 the FamilySearch Web site made its debut, and the IGI online database grew to 320 million names. As of the end of the year 2000, this online database included more than 760 million names.

only of living persons if they are Church members.) Church ordinance data does not appear on the Internet version of the IGI or the Ancestral File.

Other FamilySearch Internet Features
U.S. Social Security Death Index
A searchable database of deaths reported to the U.S. Social Security Administration, mostly after 1961. Other versions of the data from the Social Security Administration are available commercially in CD-ROM format and on other Internet sites.

Lots of Help!
Throughout FamilySearch Internet, prompts and one-click shortcuts take you directly to additional information and assistance. Try the following shortcuts to see how much information and help is at your fingertips
- Research Guidance
- Research Helps
- Glossary
- Collaboration Lists (more than 125,000 groups of researchers sharing and helping via e-mail)
- Site Map

There is even help that goes well beyond what's on FamilySearch Internet. Using the "Web Sites" feature on the Search page, you can link to thousands of other Internet sites. Hundreds of volunteers have evaluated Internet sites to identify those that might be relevant to names you submit in "Search for Ancestors" selections. The search uses the names and any dates that you submit to try to identify sites that might have interest or value to your ancestral search. At the end of the year 2000, FamilySearch Internet was searching more than thirty-five thousand family history Web pages for matches on this type of search.

Personal Ancestral File Software
A powerful computer genealogy software program, you can download Personal Ancestral File from FamilySearch Internet to your computer. **There is no cost to**

FAMILYSEARCH DATABASES *NOT* ON THE INTERNET SITE

For various reasons, some electronic databases that are available at the FHL and at FHCs are not accessible on the FamilySearch Internet site. Don't overlook these as important research tools. A regular trip to your local FHC will keep you current with these. Databases not presently available on the library's Web site include

Scottish Church Records: A database index to the Old Parochial Registers of Scotland and a few nonconformist records. Under the library's agreement with the Scottish government, which has the database on its Web site (with a fee for access), this database cannot be included on the FamilySearch Internet site. However, the information is available in the computers at the FHL and at FHCs.

U.S. Military Index: A database listing individuals in the U.S. military service who died or were declared dead from 1950 to 1975 in Southeast Asia (Korean or Vietnam Wars). This also can be used at the FHL and FHCs.

1880 U.S. Census: Released in May 2001, both the transcribed federal census images and the national index to this census are available in CD-ROM from the FHL for under $50.

1881 British Census: The result of thousands of volunteers' work over many years to compile an index critical to research for British Isles ancestral families. It includes twenty-nine million names from England, Wales, and Scotland.

you for the program, which is designed to record, manage, and share genealogical information using a personal computer. Like other genealogical software, it is a simple method of organizing family history information and printing charts and forms with family data. It can also be a powerful research tool, and it has many special features designed to make the ongoing use of FamilySearch databases such as Ancestral File easier and more effective.

PAF was a pioneering program developed and distributed by The Church of Jesus Christ of Latter-day Saints to help develop a universal base for sharing computerized family history. Several updated versions have been issued over time, and it is still in wide use by the general genealogical public. A Macintosh version is available, but recent enhancements have been made only to the Windows-based program. Version 4.04 added features, including the ability to select the language for the program to use: English, Spanish, German, French, or Portuguese. Version 5.0 is now available. PAF is compatible with all other major genealogical software packages, so data can readily be shared or exchanged with other family members or researchers.

For More Information

These are among the numerous articles and books provide specific tips on making the most of the powerful capabilities of FamilySearch Internet.

- Rhonda McClure's *The Complete Idiot's Guide to Online Genealogy*,

which includes an excellent chapter that gives an overview of the FHL and FamilySearch Internet resources.

- Barbara Renick's series in the *NGS-CIG Digest* portion of the bimonthly *NGS Newsmagazine* during the year 2000 included the two-part article "Fruitful Searching at the FamilySearch Internet Web Site" in the January/February and the March/April issues and "Not the Same Old FHLC" in the September/October issue. Another article by Renick, "Where Do I Look Next? Research Guidance at FamilySearch Internet," appeared in the November/December 2000 issue.

- *Using FamilySearch Internet Genealogy Site*, a 113-minute videotape introduction to the Web site, produced by The Studio of Hurricane, Utah. This is an independent production, not a Family History Library– or Church-produced product, but it has been praised by reviewers. At about fifteen dollars, it is an inexpensive visual walk through the site. Go to <http://www.123genealogy.com/store/video/051535.htm> for more information and ordering details.

- *Contributing Information to Ancestral File*, Family History Library publication #34029, updated 4/98.

- *Correcting Information in Ancestral File*, Family History Library publication #34030, updated 4/98.

- *Using Ancestral File*, Family History Library publication #34113, updated 6/98.

- *Finding an IGI Source*, Family History Library publication #31024, updated 1/00.

- *Parish and Vital Records List*, Family History Library publication #33702, updated 8/97.

- Fawne Stratford-Deval's "English & Welsh Roots: The LDS FamilySearch Web Site: Using the Batch Numbers," an online article appearing at *The Global Gazette* Web site, <http://globalgazette.net/gazfd/gazfd36.htm> 17 September 1999, volume III, no. 17.

Be sure to check major genealogical periodicals for other recent articles on the topic. Several periodicals are listed in chapter four. Look for recent books on Internet genealogy and the FamilySearch Web site. Like for any computer or Internet topic, FamilySearch literature quickly becomes outdated as the Web site continues to evolve and expand.

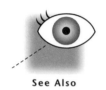

See Also

For information on how to obtain FHL publications, see chapter four.

FOUR

Other Sources for Family History Library Information

B eyond the FamilySearch Internet site an abundance of other material can help you learn about the Family History Library (FHL) resources and how to use them from near your home or in Salt Lake City. Family History Centers (see chapter six) are excellent places to learn more about the library resources.

Here we list a variety of sources, including books, magazines, Web sites, and audiotapes, all examples of the helpful information available about the library. Take advantage of the experience and suggestions of other researchers in this material as you prepare to use the library collections. You will find useful tips and details on sources, geographic areas, topics, and research tools that will be of specific use to you in your research. However, some of the most straightforward, concise, useful information about the library, its collections, and accessing and using them is the material that the library has published.

FAMILY HISTORY LIBRARY PUBLICATIONS

In addition to helping patrons in the FHL, the library staff has the tremendous task of keeping information updated and correct in both the library's publications and on FamilySearch Internet. Library staff, with others in the Family and Church History Department, have done an admirable job. **The library has published more than 150 how-to publications and forms designed to help anyone use the collections and services.** The publications cover a wide variety of topics and geographic areas and range in size from one page to more than sixty. In addition, a rapidly growing collection of CD-ROM publications, called resource files, is available. Examples of many are included below. Most of these publications are not repeated in appendix B.

Printed Source

FHL General Information Pamphlets

Many of the pamphlets are of general interest and may be useful to people using FamilySearch Internet, a FHC, or the library.

- *Library Services and Resources: Family History Library and Family History Centers:* Updated annually, it is the best available brief explanation of the collections and services available from the FHL and FHCs.

Figure 4-1
A sampling of Family History Library publications. *Reprinted by permission. Copyright © 1999–2000 by Intellectual Reserve, Inc.*

- *A Guide to Research:* (This twenty-two-page beginning guide explains initial steps and the research cycle. It includes basic blank forms: pedigree chart, family group record, and research log.)
- Family History Center address lists are updated periodically. Separate lists cover various regions of the world.
- *United States and Canada Research Checklist:* Use this one-page checklist of basic resources to check for any family in any locality. The reverse side has a very useful map of the United States and Canada and shows capitals and other key cities.
- Other forms available include worksheets for the U.S., British, Canadian, and Irish censuses; family group records; pedigree charts; and research logs.

FHL Research Outlines by Geographic Area

The library's Research Outlines provide an excellent introduction to research in a specific geographic area. An outline has been compiled for researching in each of the U.S. states and Canadian provinces. Outlines that deal with research in specific countries are also available.

The available country-level outlines include

- for North America: United States, Canada, Mexico
- for the British Isles: England, Ireland, Scotland, Wales

Printed Source

AVAILABILITY OF FHL PUBLICATIONS

Many library publications and forms are available at the library and at some FHCs. Most of the same information is available online at the FamilySearch Internet site (in "Research Helps" on the Search page) and may be ordered or downloaded and printed from that site. The publications may also be ordered from the Church's Salt Lake Distribution Center by phone (801) 240-2504 or by fax (801) 240-1584. The Family History Materials List (publication #34083) lists the publications, prices, and most current updates. This list is updated at least once a year. You can request a faxed copy of this list by phone (800) 537-5971 or fax (800) 240-3685. You can order the publications by fax at that fax number. Many of the publications are free; most are no more than one dollar (U.S.). The resource files on CD-ROM are priced at cost, and thus are inexpensive. Orders can be charged to MasterCard, Visa, or American Express.

Many of the library's publications have been collected in the reference areas on the appropriate floor of the FHL. A few are bound as books, but most are in three-ring binders. In some cases they may be combined with other reference material on the topic or locality.

- for the Pacific: Australia, Philippines
- for Europe: Germany, France, Italy, Netherlands
- for Scandinavia: Norway, Sweden, Denmark, Finland
- for Central and South America: Brazil, Latin America

FHL Resource Guides and Research Outlines by Topic

The library has also published several extensive Research Outlines on significant topics, as well as other brief Resource Guides to specific collections in the library. These are some examples:

- *Tracing Your Immigrant Ancestor* Research Outline
- *U.S. Military Records* Research Outline
- *The Ireland Householders Index* Resource Guide
- *PERiodical Source Index on Microfiche (PERSI)* Resource Guide
- *Hamburg Passenger Lists, 1850–1934* Resource Guide
- *Using the Family History Library Catalog* Resource Guide

FHL Language Helps

- Word lists help acquaint researchers with foreign words and terms commonly found in genealogical records for areas where that language was used. They include the terms and their English equivalents. Word lists are available for many languages, including German, Spanish, Norwegian, Swedish, Italian, French, Latin, Afrikaans, Czech, Danish, Dutch, Finnish, Hungarian, Icelandic, Polish, and Portuguese.

RECORD SELECTION TABLE: ILLINOIS

This table can help you decide which records to search. It is most helpful for post-1850 research.

1. In column 1, select a research goal.
2. In column 2, find the types of records most likely to have the information you need.
3. In column 3, find additional record types that may be useful.
4. Look in the section of this outline that corresponds to the record type you chose. It explains what the records might tell you, how to search them, and how to find the records in the Family History Library Catalog™ using the Locality Search. Some records are not at the library.
5. If you do not find the desired information, see the Records Selection Table in the *United States Research Outline* (30972) for more suggestions.

Note: Records of previous research (Genealogy, Biography, History, Periodicals, and Societies) are useful for most goals, but are not listed unless they are especially helpful.

1. If you need	2. Look first in	3. Then search
Adoptions	Court Records, Vital Records	Probate Records, Census
Age	Census, Cemeteries, Obituaries	Vital Records, Military Records, Naturalization and Citizenship
Birth date	Vital Records, Obituaries, Cemeteries	Church Records, Military Records, Biography
Birthplace	Vital Records, Church Records, Obituaries	Census, Military Records, Funeral Homes
Boundaries and origins (places)	Maps, Gazetteers	History, Societies
Children	Census, Probate Records, Obituaries, Genealogy	Vital Records, Church Records, Land and Property
City or parish of foreign birth	Vital Records, Obituaries, Biography	Naturalization and Citizenship, Church Records, Funeral Homes
Country of foreign birth	Census, Naturalization and Citizenship, Vital Records	Obituaries, Military Records, Minorities
Death information	Vital Records, Cemeteries, Obituaries, Newspapers	Probate Records, Funeral Homes, Church Records
Divorce	Divorce Records, Vital Records, Court Records	Newspapers, Census
Emigration information	Emigration and Immigration, Naturalization and Citizenship, Census, Maps	Obituaries, Biography, Minorities, Land and Property, Court Records
Ethnic background	Native Races, Minorities, Emigration and Immigration	Naturalization and Citizenship, Church Records, Census, Periodicals
Historical background	History, Periodicals, Gazetteers, Native Races	Maps, Land and Property, Church Records
Immigration date	Emigration and Immigration, Naturalization and Citizenship, Census, Societies	Court Records, Biography, Obituaries, Periodicals
Living relatives	Obituaries, Probate Records, Census	Funeral Homes, Land and Property, Biography
Maiden name	Vital Records, Obituaries, Probate Records	Church Records, Funeral Homes, Bible Records
Marriage information	Vital Records, Obituaries, Census, Genealogy	Church Records, Probate Records, Military Records

Figure 4-2

Record Selection Tables are being added to U.S. Research Outlines as they are updated. Each is specifically adapted to the resources available for that particular state. *Reprinted by permission. Copyright © 1999–2000 by Intellectual Reserve, Inc.*

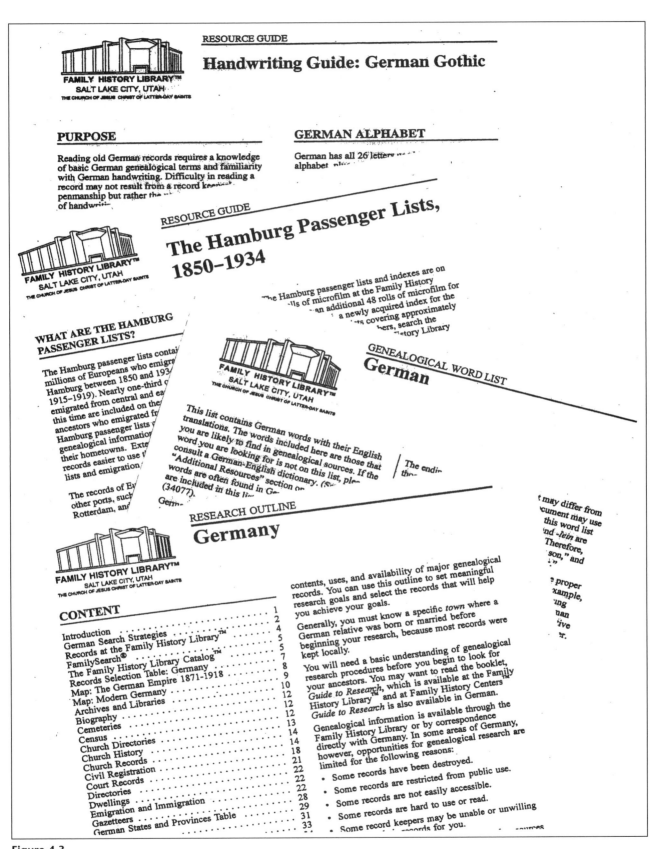

RESOURCE GUIDE

Handwriting Guide: German Gothic

FAMILY HISTORY LIBRARY™
SALT LAKE CITY, UTAH
THE CHURCH OF JESUS CHRIST OF LATTER-DAY SAINTS

PURPOSE

Reading old German records requires a knowledge of basic German genealogical terms and familiarity with German handwriting. Difficulty in reading a record may not result from a record ke... penmanship but rather th... of handw...

GERMAN ALPHABET

German has all 26 letters ...
alphabet ...

RESOURCE GUIDE

The Hamburg Passenger Lists, 1850–1934

FAMILY HISTORY LIBRARY™
SALT LAKE CITY, UTAH
THE CHURCH OF JESUS CHRIST OF LATTER-DAY SAINTS

...e Hamburg passenger lists and indexes are on
...lls of microfilm at the Family History
...an additional 48 rolls of microfilm for
a newly acquired index for the
...ts covering approximately
...hers, search the
...story Library

WHAT ARE THE HAMBURG PASSENGER LISTS?

The Hamburg passenger lists contai...
millions of Europeans who emigra...
Hamburg between 1850 and 193...
1915–1919). Nearly one-third o...
emigrated from central and ea...
this time are included on the...
ancestors who emigrated fr...
Hamburg passenger lists ...
genealogical information...
their hometowns. Exte...
records easier to use t...
lists and emigration...

The records of E...
other ports, such...
Rotterdam, an...
Gern...

FAMILY HISTORY LIBRARY™
SALT LAKE CITY, UTAH
THE CHURCH OF JESUS CHRIST OF LATTER-DAY SAINTS

This list contains German words with their English translations. The words included here are those that you are likely to find in genealogical sources. If the word you are looking for is not on this list, ple... consult a German-English dictionary. (S... "Additional Resources" section on... words are often found in G... are included in this li... (34077).

GENEALOGICAL WORD LIST

German

The endin...
th...

...t may differ from
...cument may use
this word list
...nd -lein are
Therefore,
...son," and
...,"

...proper
...xample,
...ing
...nan
...ive
...r.

RESEARCH OUTLINE

Germany

FAMILY HISTORY LIBRARY™
SALT LAKE CITY, UTAH
THE CHURCH OF JESUS CHRIST OF LATTER-DAY SAINTS

contents, uses, and availability of major genealogical records. You can use this outline to set meaningful research goals and select the records that will help you achieve your goals.

Generally, you must know a specific *town* where a German relative was born or married before beginning your research, because most records were kept locally.

You will need a basic understanding of genealogical research procedures before you begin to look for your ancestors. You may want to read the booklet, *Guide to Research*, which is available at the Family History Library™ and at Family History Centers™ *Guide to Research* is also available in German.

Genealogical information is available through the Family History Library or by correspondence directly with Germany. In some areas of Germany, however, opportunities for genealogical research are limited for the following reasons:

*   Some records have been destroyed.
*   Some records are restricted from public use.
*   Some records are not easily accessible.
*   Some records are hard to use or read.
*   Some record keepers may be unable or unwilling ...cords for you. ...sources

CONTENT

Figure 4-3
Examples of FHL Publications useful for German research. *Reprinted by permission. Copyright © 1999–2000 by Intellectual Reserve, Inc.*

- Letter-writing guides have been developed for about half of the languages listed on page 37. The guides provide English phrases with their equivalents in the appropriate language to aid communication with those who may not understand English.
- Also available is *Handwriting Guide: German Gothic* to help read the Gothic script used in many handwritten records.

OTHER SOURCES OF INFORMATION
Periodicals

General genealogical periodicals as well as society newsletters and journals often have news or articles about the library, the FHCs, and their resources. Some are listed elsewhere in this book. Examples of those that often include such information are

- *UGA News:* The Utah Genealogical Association's newsletter is a good source for updates on significant additions made to the library collections. The *UGA News* is a benefit of membership in UGA. (Contact: UGA at P.O. Box 1144, Salt Lake City, UT 84110. Its Web site is <http://www.info uga.org>.)
- *Avotaynu: The International Review of Jewish Genealogy:* This publication's staff orchestrates an incredible amount of information useful to anyone with Eastern European ancestry. This is the best source for information on access to original records, to what is being filmed, and to what has been filmed for that region of the world. Specific FHL resources are frequently discussed. (Write to *Avotaynu*, P.O. Box 900, Teaneck, NJ 07666. The Web site is http://www.avotaynu.com.)
- *Family Tree Magazine* is a bimonthly subscription and newsstand magazine. Capsules of past articles, subscription information, and much more genealogical information is available at the *Family Tree Magazine* Web site http://www.familytreemagazine.com. This publication ranks with the best of the major newsstand genealogical periodicals for the scope and quality of both its content and presentation. (Subscribe at the Web site, by phone at (888) 403-9002, or by mail to *Family Tree Magazine*, P.O. Box 3279, Harlan, IA 51593.)
- *Ancestry* and *Genealogical Computing* are also high-quality bimonthly magazines, which periodically feature articles on the library's resources. (They are published by MyFamily.com, Inc., 360 West 4800 North, Provo, UT 84604. The Web site is <http://www.ancestry.com>.)
- *Forum:* The periodical of the Federation of Genealogical Societies, *Forum* sometimes features articles on collections or changes at the library. Examples listed in appendix C include a series of articles by Dean Hunter on the British collection and a series by Elizabeth Nichols on the IGI. (Write to FGS, P.O. Box 200940, Austin, TX 78720-0940. Their Web site is <http://www.fgs.org>.)
- *NGS Newsmagazine:* Published by the National Genealogical Society

(NGS), with input from the NGS Computer Interest Group, this publication sometimes includes information or updates on the library collection or FamilySearch Internet. (Contact NGS at 4527 Seventeenth Street N, Arlington, VA 22207-2399. The Web site is <http://www.ngsgenealogy .org>.)

Specific Articles and Books

- Cerny, Johni, and Wendy Elliott, eds. *The Library: A Guide to the LDS Family History Library*. Salt Lake City: Ancestry, 1988. (While the library has had many changes and additions in the years since this detailed guide was published, it still holds a wealth of information. An updated edition is planned. The published volume is out of print, but it is available in many libraries and included as part of the *Ancestry Reference Library* CD-ROM.)
- Schaefer, Christina Kassabian. "Your Key to the Vault." *Family Tree Magazine* 1, no. 2 (April 2000): 60–64. (This is an excellent article on accessing FHL collections through local FHCs.)
- Meyerink, Kory L. "An Insider's Guide to the Family History Library." *Ancestry* 18, no. 4 (July/August 2000): 20–23.
- Milner, Paul, and Linda Jonas. *A Genealogist's Guide to Discovering Your English Ancestors*. Cincinnati: Betterway Books, 2000. (This excellent guide for English research explains in detail many of the basic English records available through the FHL.)
- Parker, J. Carlyle. *Going to Salt Lake City to Do Family History Research*. 3d ed. Turlock, Calif.: Marietta Publishing Co., 1996.
- Warren, Paula Stuart, and James W. Warren. "Genealogy City: Salt Lake City." *Family Tree Magazine* 1, no. 4 (August 2000): 44–49.

Audiotapes

The Federation of Genealogical Societies and the National Genealogical Society each host an annual national genealogical conference. The collections of the FHL are a frequent focus of conference lectures, and hundreds of other lecture topics of value to researchers are presented. Audiotapes from most lectures at FGS and NGS conferences are available for purchase from Repeat Performance. (See contact details in the "Miscellaneous" section of appendix B.) **Their Web site, <http://www.audiotapes.com>, has an extensive catalog and sample audio clips.** Audiotapes of sessions presented at major genealogical conferences include

Internet Source

- Bryson, Randy W. *Finding Information in FamilySearch Internet Genealogy Service*. Lecture Session T-69 at the National Genealogical Society 2000 Conference in Providence, Rhode Island.
- Burroughs, Tony. *Using the Resources of the Family History Library for African-American Research*. Lecture S-172 at the Federation of Genealogical Societies 2000 Conference in Salt Lake City.
- Hunter, Dean J. *The Pot of Gold at the End of the Rainbow: Irish Holdings of the Family History Library*. Lecture Session T-62 at the Federation of Genealogical Societies 2000 Conference in Salt Lake City.

- Metcalfe, Wayne. *Record Preservation in an Uncertain World*. Lecture Session T-91 at the National Genealogical Society 2000 Conference in Providence, Rhode Island.
- Parker, Jimmy B. *Native American Research in the Family History Library*. Lecture Session T-69 at the Federation of Genealogical Societies 2000 Conference in Salt Lake City.
- Turley, Richard E., Jr. *The Family History Library: Its Past, Present, and Future in Identifying and Linking the World Family*. Lecture Session T-42 at the Federation of Genealogical Societies 2000 Conference in Salt Lake City.

Conference Syllabuses

Each attendee at FGS and NGS national conferences receives a conference syllabus, a book that combines the four-page handout material supplied for each lecture by most of the speakers. Often the speakers whose topics related to the FHL have provided valuable reference information in their syllabus material. Many syllabuses from past conferences are in some genealogical and public library collections. Past years' syllabuses may be available for purchase from FGS or NGS. See "Libraries and Genealogical Societies" in appendix B for contact information for these two organizations.

Electronic Newsletters and Mailing Lists

- *Ancestry Daily News:* a free electronic newsletter delivered daily via E-mail. Published by Ancestry.com. In December 2000, this newsletter reached 1.1 million subscribers each weekday. You can sign up for a free subscription at the Ancestry Web site at <http://www.ancestry.com/DailyNews>.
- *Eastman's Online Genealogy Newsletter:* Another free electronic newsletter, usually published once a week, Eastman's newsletter is one of the best and most current sources for what's going on in the rapidly evolving world of electronic genealogy. You can subscribe at <http://www.rootsforum .com/newsletter.htm>.
- FAMILYSEARCH mailing list: This electronic mailing list is designed to assist anyone with questions regarding the use of the Internet for researching family history. Its scope is not limited to FamilySearch Internet. For information on how to subscribe to this and several other Rootsweb mailing lists, visit <http:// www.rootsweb.com/~jfuller/gen_mail_computing.html>.
- *Family Tree Magazine Update:* a weekly e-mail newsletter with genealogical news, tips, links, worthwhile Web sites, and information on articles in *Family Tree Magazine*. Excerpts from some of the magazine's articles and from Betterway genealogy books also appear. For a free subscription go to <http://www.familytreemagazine.com>.

Internet Source

Web Sites

The FamilySearch Internet site is by far the most useful and informative Web site regarding the library and FHCs. Cyndi's List is well known and used by genealogists and Web surfers alike. However, **a number of other Internet sites**

contain useful information. The comments and experience of other researchers can be particularly valuable. Keep in mind that some of these sites are not updated regularly and comments from individual researchers reflect their opinions and preferences. A few sites are listed below. Many provide links to other sites.

- **Cyndi's List** <http://www.cyndislist.com>: Recognized as the premier site for identifying and linking to genealogical Web sites, Cyndi Howells's many years of developing this site pay off daily for thousands of genealogists. Go to the category "LDS & Family History Centers," where you will find hundreds of links to sites in fourteen categories.

- Tips on Making Your Salt Lake City Research Trip a Big Success <http://www.rootsweb.com/~genepool/slc.htm>: This site includes links to other Web sites, some city and library information, and lots of practical advice submitted by researchers who have been to Salt Lake City.

- Salt Lake City, Here I Come! <http://www.aros.net/~drwaff/slc2.htm>: suggestions from researchers who have made a trip to the FHL in Salt Lake City.

- Utah Valley PAF Users Group: The Salt Lake Family History Library <http://www.genealogy.org/~uvpafug/fhlslc.html>: A fairly extensive introduction to the library and its collection. At the time this book went to press, the site had not been updated in more than two years, but much of the information is well organized and still valuable.

- The Salt Lake City Family History Library <http://www.aros.net/~drwaff/slcfhl.htm>: This site has a few brief comments about the library and several worthwhile links to other pertinent Web sites. Note that this is not an official FHL Web site.

IN SUMMARY

This chapter presents just a sampling of the material that is available. Use the Web sites and recent issues of periodicals and newsletters for updates and to identify additional resources. As the pace of change accelerates, they are most useful in helping you stay current with the additions to and changes in the library's collections, equipment, and procedures.

FIVE

The Family History Library Catalog

YOUR KEY TO ENTERING THE LIBRARY'S COLLECTIONS

The vast collections of the library can seem overwhelming. The Family History Library catalog opens the door to those collections and provides a pathway to material that can be of use to you in researching your family history. Learning to use the catalog effectively is the key to unlocking that door to your ancestral records.

Quotes

VOICES OF EXPERIENCE

"Catalogers can do a lot to help library patrons, but there's a lot patrons can do to help themselves. They can't let the catalog intimidate them. If you don't know what something means, study it. Ask questions. Find a book and look it up. Otherwise you'll never find those ancestors."

—Irene Johnson, Family History Library cataloger

What Does the Catalog Include?

The FHL collections—including microfilm, microfiche, books, periodicals, and electronic resources—are described in the catalog. It includes all materials that have been added to the library collections, regardless of where they are housed. Therefore, materials in the library, the Joseph Smith Memorial Building, or off-site storage are listed in the catalog. The Chinese catalog has been automated, and the Japanese and Korean holdings catalogs are in the conversion process.

Where Is the Catalog Available?

The catalog is available on the Internet at <http://www.familysearch.org>, at Family History Centers worldwide, in the FHL, on a single CD-ROM you can purchase, and in various formats at many other libraries and historical societies.

Technique

FHL Catalog Subject Headings

The collections are cataloged primarily by locality, surname, and subject. These headings are used for all levels of localities: national, local, and everything in between. Many of these categories also have subcategories under which material is organized. Explore the categories carefully and imaginatively. You may find passenger lists under "Emigration and Immigration," wills under "Court Records" or "Probate Records," and divorce records under "Vital Records" or "Court Records." You may find unexpected detail about people under "Dwellings" and apprenticeships under "Occupations." The headings currently used by the FHL catalogers are:

Almanacs	Language and languages
Archives and libraries	Maps
Bible records	Medical records
Bibliography	Migration, Internal
Biography	Military history
Business records and commerce	Military records
Cemeteries	Minorities
Census	Names, Geographical
Census—Indexes	Names, Personal
Church directories	Names, Personal—Indexes
Church history	Native races
Church records	Naturalization and citizenship
Colonization	Newspapers
Correctional institutions	Obituaries
Court records	Occupations
Description and Travel	Officials and employees
Directories—Bibliography	Orphans and orphanages
Dwellings	Periodicals
Emigration and immigration	Politics and government
Encyclopedias and dictionaries	Poorhouses, poor law, etc.
Ethnic newspapers	Population
Ethnic relations	Postal and shipping guides
Ethnology	Probate records
Folklore	Public records
Funeral homes	Schools
Gazetteers	Social life and customs
Genealogy	Societies
Genealogy—Societies	Statistics
Historical geography	Taxation
History	Vital records
Jewish history	Vital records—Newspapers
Land and property	Voting registers

Evolution of Various Catalog Formats

Over time, the library has changed its catalog formats to make access faster and easier. Years ago, the library moved from a card catalog system to computerized printouts that were filmed on microfiche. This was a relatively efficient way to distribute periodic catalog updates to FHCs worldwide. The FHCs were started in the 1960s to provide local access to much of the filmed collections.

As computer technology advanced, the electronic FamilySearch system, including the library catalog, began to circulate to the FHCs on a set of compact discs. At that time computer terminals were added in the library for the compact disc catalog version.

Place:	England, Essex
Topics:	England, Essex - Archives and libraries England, Essex - Archives and libraries - Inventories, registers, catalogs England, Essex - Biography England, Essex - Biography - Dictionaries England, Essex - Business records and commerce England, Essex - Cemeteries England, Essex - Census - 1851 England, Essex - Census - 1851 - Indexes England, Essex - Census - 1881 - Indexes England, Essex - Census - Indexes England, Essex - Church directories England, Essex - Church history England, Essex - Church history - Medieval period, 1066-1485 - Sources England, Essex - Church records England, Essex - Church records - Bibliography England, Essex - Church records - Indexes England, Essex - Church records - Inventories, registers, catalogs England, Essex - Civil registration England, Essex - Court records England, Essex - Court records - Inventories, registers, catalogs **Numbers 1-20 of 78 matching topics for this place** [View next set of matching topics] Get topics from number: [ ] Get records

Figure 5-1
Catalog entry for Essex County, England from the catalog on the Internet.
Reprinted by permission. Copyright © 1999–2000 by Intellectual Reserve, Inc.

In October 1998, the library converted its cataloging system to a commercial library cataloguing system using Windows-based software. This change paved the way to provide Internet access to the catalog, as well as putting the data in the Windows format that would make it compatible with the majority of personal computer systems in use today.

Dramatic changes in catalog access have recently taken place. The mid-1999 introduction of the library's Web site at <http://www.familysearch.org> provided easy access to the library catalog for millions of Internet users. In mid-2000, the catalog on a single CD-ROM was released for purchase by individuals for the incredible price of only six dollars (U.S.). Shortly after that, the Internet interface was significantly enhanced to improve ease of access.

The rapid evolution of this catalog has created some equipment headaches. Moving the library from microfiche readers to compact disc computers to a Windows-based system with Internet access has been a large, ongoing project. Taking over 3,400 FHCs down that same technology path has been an expensive and much longer process. Accordingly, you may find FHCs in your area that still use the compact disc system or even the microfiche catalog.

Reminder

CATALOG REMINDERS

When using any of these widely available catalog formats, it is important to remember that

- They are only current as of the date they were produced or last updated.

- The technology, and the schedule for updating information, will continue to evolve and change rapidly.

- You need to check for material at various levels of localities. (For example, Canadian research could include the national, provincial, county, and local levels.)

- Some catalog entries have extensive notations that help describe the collection or book and help you use it. Many entries have little or no explanatory detail.

- The Internet version of the catalog is not necessarily the most current information available.

- Many different people have cataloged this material over the decades. Don't assume things. Check all the entries in all the categories for your ancestral localities.

- The new CD-ROM and online catalogs give us flexibility we never had before in searching the catalog. Take another look at areas you've already researched using these tools.

The Catalog Versions

The various formats have different strengths. The CD-ROM version can be fast, easy to use, and flexible, particularly with keyword combination searching capability. Using the microfiche catalog, however, you can easily identify records by sublocality for a county or state in which you are researching. So **it is wise to use both computer and microfiche versions of the catalog to help identify more resources.**

Tip

Computer, Internet, and CD-ROM catalogs

Various versions of the computerized FHL Catalog are available in the FHL, at FHCs, in other repositories, and on the Internet; the CD-ROM catalog is available for individual purchase. The different versions are steadily coming closer to being standardized, and it is likely that all computer terminals in the library eventually will include all the computerized versions of the catalog.

The new Windows-based catalog provides much more powerful search capabilities than the old library computer catalog did. Searches can be conducted by a variety of keys:
- location
- surname
- author
- title
- film/fiche number
- call number (for printed books, periodicals, and maps)
- keyword
- subject

"Help" is always an option on the computer screen. The FHL catalog on computer is easy to learn and use. On-screen prompts and options make it easy for researchers to move one step at a time to the information they seek in the catalog.

Microfiche Catalog

The microfiche version is available at the FHL, FHCs, and some other research facilities. It is no longer available for individual purchase. At present, future limited editions of the fiche catalog are planned. The fiche catalog is printed in four separate series:
- location
- surname
- author/title
- subject (A limited index that does *not* include nearly all the material available by subject using the computerized catalog versions.)

The fiche catalog is an alternate when the computers at a FHC are in use or when computers are down at the FHL. This catalog version may be available in other research facilities that do not have the computer catalog. The author/title portion is a quick way to check for a book when you know the author or title.

If you are researching a specific county or comparable jurisdiction, using the fiche you can quickly scan all of the towns, villages, townships, and cities in a county for material of interest. On the microfiche, the material will be listed in this sequence:
- state-level information, alphabetical by subject entry
- county-level information, alphabetical by subject entry

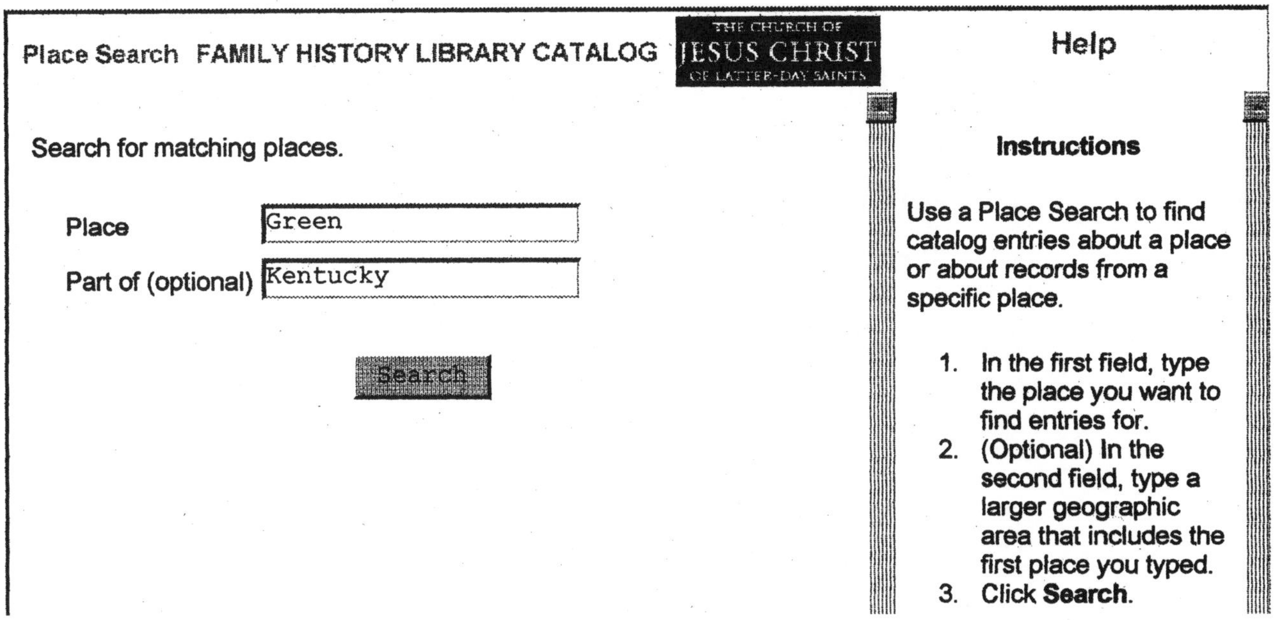

Place Search   FAMILY HISTORY LIBRARY CATALOG   THE CHURCH OF JESUS CHRIST OF LATTER-DAY SAINTS

Help

Search for matching places.

Place   `Green`

Part of (optional)   `Kentucky`

[Search]

Instructions

Use a Place Search to find catalog entries about a place or about records from a specific place.

1. In the first field, type the place you want to find entries for.
2. (Optional) In the second field, type a larger geographic area that includes the first place you typed.
3. Click **Search**.

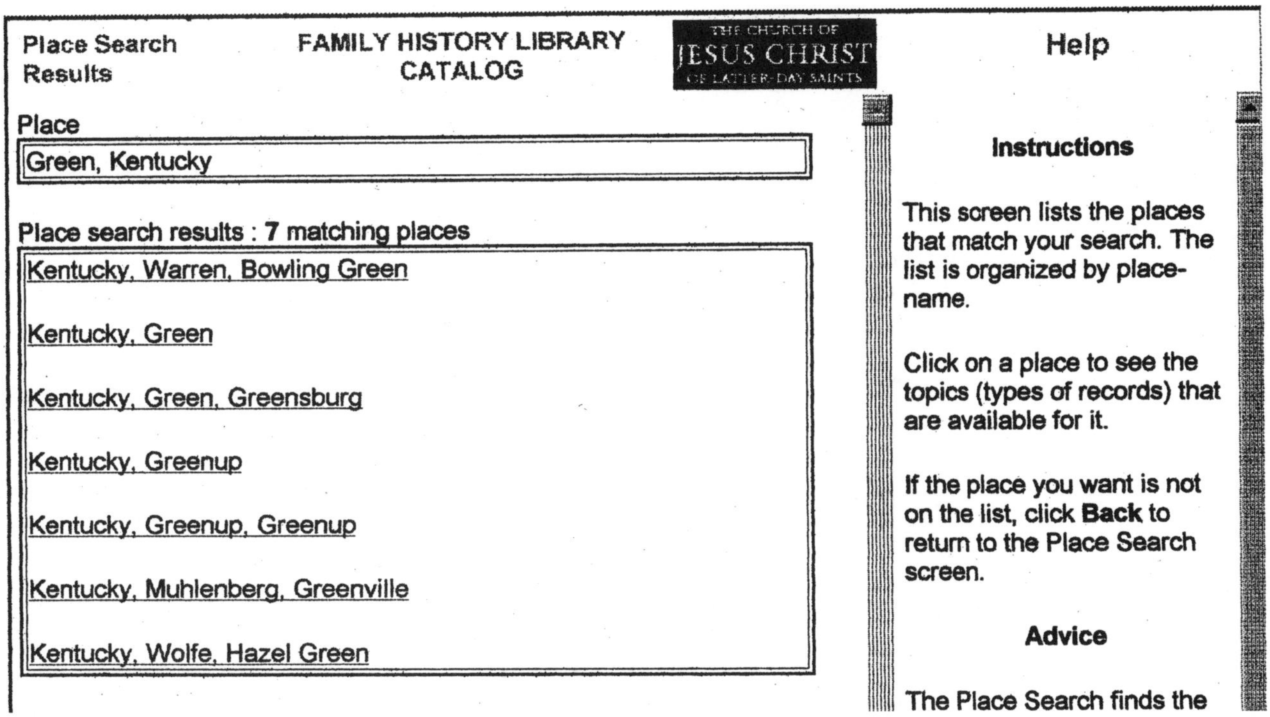

Place Search Results   FAMILY HISTORY LIBRARY CATALOG   THE CHURCH OF JESUS CHRIST OF LATTER-DAY SAINTS

Help

Place

`Green, Kentucky`

Place search results : **7 matching places**

Kentucky, Warren, Bowling Green

Kentucky, Green

Kentucky, Green, Greensburg

Kentucky, Greenup

Kentucky, Greenup, Greenup

Kentucky, Muhlenberg, Greenville

Kentucky, Wolfe, Hazel Green

Instructions

This screen lists the places that match your search. The list is organized by place-name.

Click on a place to see the topics (types of records) that are available for it.

If the place you want is not on the list, click **Back** to return to the Place Search screen.

Advice

The Place Search finds the

Figure 5-2A & 5-2B
A locality search for "Green County, Kentucky" is done *without* the word "County." The result shows localities to select from, including Green.

Reprinted by permission. Copyright © 1999–2000 by Intellectual Reserve, Inc.

View Related Places

Place	Kentucky, Green
Notes	1792, created from Lincoln and Nelson counties.
Topics	Kentucky, Green - Biography Kentucky, Green - Cemeteries Kentucky, Green - Census Kentucky, Green - Census - 1850 - Indexes Kentucky, Green - Census - 1850-1860 Kentucky, Green - Census - 1870 Kentucky, Green - Church records Kentucky, Green - Court records Kentucky, Green - Genealogy Kentucky, Green - Guardianship Kentucky, Green - History Kentucky, Green - History - Periodicals Kentucky, Green - Land and property Kentucky, Green - Military records Kentucky, Green - Military records - Revolution, 1775-1783 Kentucky, Green - Officials and employees Kentucky, Green - Probate records Kentucky, Green - Schools Kentucky, Green - Slavery and bondage Kentucky, Green - Taxation Kentucky, Green - Vital records

Figure 5-3
When "Green" is selected, these are the first in the series of subjects from which to select.
Reprinted by permission. Copyright © 1999–2000 by Intellectual Reserve, Inc.

- local-level information (town, village, township, city), alphabetical by the name of the locality and then by the catalog subject.

  For example, when researching Dalton in Wayne County, Ohio, you would check for newspapers under

  Ohio—Newspapers
  Ohio, Wayne—Newspapers
  Ohio, Wayne, Dalton—Newspapers

Why Bother With Localities *Near* the Place My Family Lived?

It is important to check all the localities in the county where your ancestors lived, and possibly localities in the nearby counties as well. The church your ancestor attended, the cemetery where some family members were buried, or the newspaper that carried their obituaries may be in a neighboring village or township or county. The cemetery transcriptions for an adjoining county may

Topic	Kentucky, Green - Land and property
Titles	<u>Commissioners deeds, 1837-1911</u> Green County (Kentucky). Clerk of the County Court
	<u>Deeds, 1793-1952</u> Green County (Kentucky). Clerk of the County Court
	<u>Green County processioner's reports, 1796-1830</u> Simmons, Barbara Durham
	<u>Green County, Kentucky land entries, 1796-1834</u> Smith, Randolph N
	<u>Green County, Kentucky survey desposities, 1783-1828</u> Daughters of the American Revolution (Illinois)
	<u>Green County, Kentucky, abstracts of deed books</u> Wright, Barbara
	<u>Land depositions, 1795-1828</u> Green County (Kentucky). Clerk of the County Court
	<u>Land entry books, 1780-1898, 1903, 1918</u> Green County (Kentucky). Clerk of the County Court
	<u>Mineral lease books, 1892-1919</u> Green County (Kentucky). Clerk of the County Court
	<u>Record book, 1803-1822</u> Kentucky. Circuit Court (Green County)
	<u>Survey books, 1793-1906</u> Green County (Kentucky). Surveyor

Figure 5-4
"Land and Property" is selected next, and this series of book and film titles appears on screen.
Reprinted by permission. Copyright © 1999–2000 by Intellectual Reserve, Inc.

include a couple of cemeteries in your ancestors' county—maybe even the cemetery you were looking for. That book of transcriptions may be listed in the library catalog only under the adjoining county.

Sources for Help With the FHL Catalog

- **Online:** The Internet provides worldwide accesss to the FamilySearch Web site, <http://www.familysearch.org>. The catalog is available on that site, which provides excellent step-by-step help for learning and using the catalog. On-screen prompts and additional help screens make it easy. Check other Internet sources listed in chapter four of this book.
- **CD-ROM:** For just six dollars, anyone can purchase the complete FHL catalog on one CD-ROM for use on a personal computer using Windows. Order it online at the FamilySearch Web site or by mail, phone, or fax from the Distribution Center. (See address in "Family History Library Publications" at appendix B.)

Title	Land entry books, 1780-1898, 1903, 1918
Authors	Green County (Kentucky). Clerk of the County Court (Main Author)

Notes	Microfilm of original records at the Green County courthouse.
	Includes indexes except for the last volume.
	Many of the early entries are land warrants.

Subjects	Kentucky, Green - Land and property

Format	Manuscript (On Film)
Language	English
Publication	Morgantown, Ky. : E & K Microfilming, 1990
Physical	1 microfilm reel ; 16 mm.

Figure 5-5
One entry from the titles that were available under the category "Land and Property" for Green County, Kentucky.
Reprinted by permission. Copyright © 1999–2000 by Intellectual Reserve, Inc.

Research Tip

SEARCHING BY CALL OR FILM NUMBER

If you have the call number for an item in the library collection, you can easily check the catalog to get the title, author, and details of the item. The catalog contains two shortcuts: Film/Fiche Search, and Call Number Search.

Film/Fiche Search allows you to key in the microfilm or microfiche number and then displays the titles, authors, and item summary for the material on the film or fiche. Call Number Search allows you to enter the call number that appears on books.

Check the online or CD-ROM catalog to see how these simple tools work. The "Help" screen alongside the entry screen provides direction on how to enter a call number correctly.

- **Family History Centers:** There may be a FHC within easy traveling distance of your home. The catalog may be used there and is often available in both computer and microfiche formats. This is a good place to practice

Title:	Computer printout of Strathdon, Aberdn., Scot

Note	Location Film
Births and Christenings, A thru Z 1667-1712 1731-1857 (2 microfiches)	FHL BRITISH Fiche 6902866
Marriages, A thru Z, 1672-1710 1731-1820 1824-1857 (1 microfiche)	FHL BRITISH Fiche 6902867

Numbers 1-2 of 2 film notes

Figure 5-6

A catalog printout showing the microfiche numbers for Births, Christenings, and Marriages for Strathdon, Aberdeenshire, Scotland. The location number shows that it is physically located on the British floor in the Family History Library.

Reprinted by permission. Copyright © 1999–2000 by Intellectual Reserve, Inc.

using the catalog, and the volunteers who staff the FHC may be able to help with some of your questions. See chapter six for more information on finding and using FHCs.

- **Family History Library:** You can learn by using the computers in the library itself. The on-screen prompts and help makes it easy to learn. If Salt Lake City is far from where you live, however, you may want to learn to use the catalog at a local FHC, online, or with the CD-ROM catalog before coming to the FHL.

- **Joseph Smith Memorial Building in Salt Lake City:** Located just across Temple Square from the FHL, the FamilySearch Center here provides an unhurried atmosphere, on-screen tutorials, and volunteers close by to help you learn or use the FamilySearch system, including the FHL catalog. The computers at this facility tend to be less crowded than those at the FHL. See chapter twelve for details on the Joseph Smith Memorial Building facilities.

- **Other Research Facilities:** Many libraries, historical societies, and genealogical societies have the FHL catalog on CD-ROM or microfiche or provide Internet access to the FamilySearch Web site. Staff or volunteers in these facilities are sometimes familiar with the catalog and may be able to provide pointers.

There are no film notes available for this title.

Title	The descendants of Edmund and Jane (Webb) Price compiled by M. Frederick Amos, Gerald Keith, and Myrtle Perry. Appendix 1
Stmnt.Resp.	compiled by M. Frederick Amos, Ronald Keith, and Myrtle Perry
Authors	Amos, M. Frederick (Malcolm Frederick), 1926-. (Main Author) Keith, Ronald (Added Author) Perry, Myrtle K. (Myrtle Geneva Keith), 1915-. (Added Author)

Notes	Consists of additions and corrections to the original work. Includes Hovey, Price, O'Donnell, Alward, Moores, Perry, and related families.

Subjects	Price Hovey O'Donnell Alward Moores Perry

Copies	
Call Number	**Location**
929.271 P931a supp.	JSMB FAMHIST Book

Format	Books/Monographs
Publication	[Canada? : s.n., 1999]
Physical	262 p.

Subject Class	929.271 P931
References	(Supplement to) The descendants of Edmund and Jane (Webb) Price

Figure 5-7

Family histories and genealogies may be available on film or on the book shelves. They may be catalogued under a dozen surnames or more, though the title may indicate only one family name.

Reprinted by permission. Copyright © 1999–2000 by Intellectual Reserve, Inc.

Place Details

Place:	Germany
Notes:	German place names in this catalog are listed as they are spelled in the following gazetteer: Meyers Orts- und Verkehrs-Lexikon des Deutschen Reichs / E. Uetrecht. 1912-1913. Call number 943 Microfilm numbers 496640-496641. E5mo
Topics:	Germany - Public records - Handbooks, manuals, etc. Germany - Public records - Inventories, registers, catalogs Germany - Religion and religious life Germany - Religion and religious life - Bibliography Germany - Religion and religious life - Periodicals - Inventories, registers, catalogs Germany - Obituaries - Indexes - Periodicals Germany - Occupations Germany - Occupations - Dictionaries Germany - Occupations - Indexes Germany - Officials and employees Germany - Officials and employees - Genealogy - Sources Germany - Pensions Germany - Periodicals Germany - Periodicals - Bibliography Germany - Politics and government Germany - Politics and government - Bibliography Germany - Population Germany - Population - History Germany - Postal and shipping guides Germany - Public records Numbers 220-239 of 253 matching topics for this place [View previous set of matching topics] [View next set of matching topics] Get topics from number: [_____] [Get records]

Figure 5-8
Computers are not perfect! Notice in this listing for Germany that the topics are not in alphabetical order. Computerized tools let us work quickly, but don't go so quickly that you miss something that's in front of you.

Reprinted by permission. Copyright © 1999–2000 by Intellectual Reserve, Inc.

SIX

Family History Centers

ACCESS FHL RECORDS FROM WHERE YOU LIVE

The collection of the Family History Library and the general interest in research-ing family history both grew at astonishing rates in the last half of the twentieth century. Beginning in 1964, a network of local branches of the FHL was begun. The intention was to make resources from the FHL more readily available to researchers elsewhere. Today there are over 3,400 branches, called Family His-tory Centers, in seventy-five countries. In recent years, about two hundred new centers have been added annually.

WHERE ARE THE FAMILY HISTORY CENTERS?

You will find FHCs in large metropolitan areas and in small communities. Most of them are housed in local church meeting houses of The Church of Jesus Christ of Latter-day Saints. **There are several ways to find the FHC closest to you:**

Notes

- Check the FamilySearch Web site at <http://www.familysearch.org>, or call Family History Support at (800) 346-6044.
- Look in your local white pages under "Church of Jesus Christ of Latter-day Saints," and call a nearby Church to ask if they have an FHC. If not, they can normally advise you of nearby locations.
- Check genealogical guidebooks or genealogical society periodicals related to your specific ancestral locality. Some include addresses of FHCs.
- The FHL publishes regional listings that include many of the FHCs. Chap-ter four tells how to order such materials.

Some public and private libraries and historical societies also have made arrangements with the FHL to function as FHCs. These include such major U.S. genealogical research facilities as the New England Historic Genealogical Society in Boston; the Dallas Public Library in Texas; and the Allen County Public Library in Fort Wayne, Indiana.

RELIGION AT THE FHC

Some genealogists are reluctant to go to a FHC, worrying that they will be proselytized. Just as at the library in Salt Lake City, however, FHC staff and volunteers are there to help find ancestors, not to push religion. They will talk to you about their religion if you specifically ask for that information. Relax, and make use of the resources that the FHC offers to people of all faiths. It's also interesting to note that many patrons and volunteers at FHCs are not members of The Church of Jesus Christ of Latter-day Saints.

WHAT DO FAMILY HISTORY CENTERS MAKE AVAILABLE?

The FHCs vary widely in size. But they all serve basically the same function: to provide local access to the FamilySearch databases, the library catalog, and most of the library's microfilm and microfiche material. Most FHCs have the catalog on microfiche or FamilySearch on CD-ROM, and more are adding online access. That provides you with local access to the various FamilySearch databases and the catalog for the full FHL collection.

Using the FHL Catalog, you can identify microfilm and microfiche that might be of value to your research. The FHC can then borrow the film or fiche for you to use at the FHC. The charge for this service currently averages between three and four dollars (U.S.), and higher in some countries, per roll of microfilm. This covers the cost of duplicating the microfilm and mailing it. Most of the film is borrowed from the Salt Lake City facility for a limited time period, usually thirty days, and the fee may be paid again at most FHCs to renew the film. Microfiche costs considerably less and remains at the FHC.

While you can borrow most film and fiche in the library collection this way, some you cannot. That may be true for some film or fiche the library purchased rather than filmed. Other items are not circulated, usually due to restrictions the original record holder placed. The published books and periodicals in the library collection do not circulate to FHCs either. Many of those books have been filmed by the library, however, and can be loaned to the FHCs in that format. The FHL Catalog indicates when a microform does not circulate to an FHC. There may be some special finding aids or indexes at the FHC that you will not find in Salt Lake City. Many special finding aids at the FHL are not in microform and thus not available to FHCs. Others that you find in Salt Lake City are available to borrow on microform at your FHC.

Most FHCs have one or more computers (for access to the catalog and the rest of FamilySearch) and microfilm and microfiche readers, and many have reader-printers so you can make copies from the microfilm. Check to see if you need an advance reservation to use the computers. Copy costs vary at the FHCs.

Many FHCs also have at least a small collection of reference books and other materials, other FHL databases on CD-ROM, and some microform materials on permanent loan. Often the permanent items are those frequently requested in the locality of that FHC, and sometimes the permanent loan is requested and paid for by local societies or researchers. If an area has a heavy interest in a particular set of indexes or records for Poland, Germany, or Ireland, for example, those films may become part of the permanent collection at the FHC due to the efforts of local genealogists. There may be some surprises, too: One of the FHCs in Minnesota has some Arkansas federal census microfilms. Some FHCs don't have room to house many permanent microfilms.

The FHCs have a collection of important general reference books on microfiche. Some have a CD-ROM collection of databases, indexes, and record abstracts from various sources.

The FHCs may have some FHL publications and forms for sale, and they may have FHL CD-ROMs (for example, the FHL catalog) for sale.

Notes

GROWING FAMILY HISTORY CENTERS

Some FHCs have grown to become major research repositories in their own right. For example the Los Angeles, California, Family History Center is known for its large British Isles collection. The Utah Valley Regional FHC in Provo, Utah, has an extremely diverse permanent collection. Others sponsor classes and all-day seminars. Some work closely with area genealogical societies. Others house collections of materials compiled by area genealogists. Some are even developing their own Web sites with information on the local FHC, its holdings, and some genealogy basics.

Step By Step

HOW DO I USE RECORDS AT AN FHC?

- Find the location of the FHC in your area (see page 56).
- Call the FHC to learn the hours it is open to researchers. (Most FHCs are staffed only by volunteers and open part-time; some larger ones are open many days each week.) Ask if reservations are needed to use any of the equipment.
- Visit the FHC during open hours. Give yourself time to become oriented to the facility, the resources, the equipment, and the procedures.
- Use the FHL catalog at the FHC, online, or on CD-ROM to determine what you want to order.
- Order a roll or two of microfilm. Inquire as to how long it will take to arrive and how you will find out when the film reaches the FHC.
- When the film or fiche arrives, search it for the people or information you are seeking. Carefully document the source of the information, including the FHL film number, and make copies of pertinent information.

THE STEP-BY-STEP PROCESS

When ordering records through a FHC, you may perform a multistep process. If, for example, you wish to find microfilmed deed records from 1820 to 1850 for your Green County, Kentucky, ancestors, you would

- Check the FHL catalog (online, on CD-ROM, or at the FHC) to see what deed indexes exist for those years and that locality. Several series of indexes may cover the same time period. These are found under the topic "land" for this county.

- At the FHC order and pay for the pertinent microfilm rolls of index volumes.

- Wait for the film to be duplicated and sent to your FHC.

- Go to the FHC when the film arrives, and use the microfilm reader there to search that film for all the names connected to your family. Those indexes will point you to specific volumes and pages of Green County deed books.

- Check the FHL catalog again to determine the film numbers for the microfilm of the actual deed records you need to search, based on the index entries, and order those films.

- Wait for the film to be duplicated and sent to your FHC.

- Go to the FHC when the film arrives, and search the filmed deed books for the deeds connected to your ancestors. Copy those of interest if a film copier is available. Otherwise, handwrite the complete information. Document the source of the information.

You can accomplish a tremendous amount of research this way through local FHCs. But you can also see the appeal of a research trip to Salt Lake City. There, the delay between viewing the filmed index and the filmed deeds is only the time it takes you to walk a few steps to the microfilm cabinets. Working through an FHC, several weeks may pass between ordering and receiving the indexes, then several more between ordering and receiving the filmed deeds.

This is just an example; it does not always apply. Some groups of records are contained on just one or two rolls of film that include an index so there is no wait for additional film. Many records are not indexed fully or at all. That's when you start to understand what real research is all about: time—it takes lots of time!

OVERWHELMED?

The first visit to any library can be daunting. To become comfortable at your local FHC, visit it several times and observe the other researchers. What are they doing there? Where do they go for lunch? Do they sit and talk about genealogy? Are there roving volunteers offering help? Where do you order

For More Info

For more information on Family History Centers, read Christina Schaefer's "Your Key to the Vault" in the April 2000 issue of *Family Tree Magazine* (volume 1, number 2) on pages 60–64. This excellent article on the FHCs was written by a former FHC director.

films? Ask about rules and guidelines for this FHC. Is there a catalog for the permanent collection there? Are there books and finding aids on open shelves? If so, browse a bit. After a few visits you will be like one of the regulars.

DO MANY GENEALOGISTS REALLY USE FHCs?

Do they ever! Currently, more than 100,000 rolls of microfilm are circulated each month between Salt Lake City and the FHCs. That's a lot of people all over the world taking advantage of this local access to the world's largest genealogical collection.

Two other important resources at your FHC are the volunteers and the other researchers. Worldwide more than 25,000 people volunteer at the FHCs. Don't just come and go without talking to people. You may find a distant cousin or someone with expertise in your ancestor's area in Sweden.

HOW IMPORTANT ARE FHCs TO GENEALOGY?

For folks who never travel to Salt Lake City, the FHC offers access to many records of the world. Those 100,000 rolls of film ordered each month are evidence of the value of FHCs. The FHCs are so important that the Federation of Genealogical Societies has begun to host at its annual conferences a series of sessions presented by FHC staff and volunteers. The Utah Genealogical Association offers support sessions at its annual seminar. Online assistance and published guides for staff running an FHC are becoming more numerous.

FHCs are an important resource, located much closer to home for most of us than the library itself. Make the most of them, and use tips provided in chapter seven on preparing for a trip to the FHL.

SEVEN

Going to Salt Lake City

PREPARATION MAKES A DIFFERENCE

No matter how often you've been to the Family History Library, there is definitely excitement in planning a trip to use the world's largest genealogical collection. The reality, however, is that no genie waits at the library door to lay the records of your ancestors at your feet. A successful and enjoyable research trip usually results from investing time and energy to plan and prepare before the trip and to research during the trip.

Over the years, the single most frequent comment we've heard from first-time visitors to the library is, "I wish I had spent more time preparing and organizing before I came here." Even if your busy schedule doesn't allow for all the preparation this book suggests, you can still have a successful research experience. **Effective preparation just makes it more likely you will locate the records you seek successfully and with minimum frustration.**

This chapter will outline five steps to prepare for your Salt Lake City trip:
1. Organize what you already know.
2. Determine what you need to find out.
3. Learn where to find that information.
4. Practice, practice, practice—what you can do *before* your trip.
5. Make arrangements and final checklists.

Timesaver

STEP 1: ORGANIZE WHAT YOU ALREADY KNOW
What Do You Know?

Start with what you have compiled on your family history. Think about the research you have done so far. In what condition are your notes, files, and charts? If a friend called with a free airline ticket for Salt Lake City—leaving tomorrow—you might be willing to go, but would you really be ready? Most airlines will not let you bring along a whole file cabinet of papers!

The FHL has collected, preserved, and made accessible many of the records of the world. You are doing the same thing, on a smaller scale, with the records of your family. Just as the library collections are organized and cataloged, you need to organize your data in a summary that is portable and readily accessible

Step By Step

as you do research. Review the material you have, organize it, and summarize the significant information. Condense your material to a manageable size.

Take advantage of the organizing tips included in this chapter. They are simple things that you can do either with pen and paper or a computer. Either way, these will help you prepare effectively and then research effectively.

Family Group Sheets

Collect family group sheets and pedigree charts in a three-ring binder. This is one effective way of condensing the basic facts about families you will research at the FHL. Review the information and records you have accumulated so far, and update your family group sheets to reflect that information. Be sure you have noted the source of each detail. Make additional notes on the back of the charts to save room. For further space saving, photocopy two charts side by side and reduce to fit on 8½″×11″ paper.

If you use a genealogical software program, update the information there. Even if you will bring a laptop computer on your trip, you may want to print out those charts to take along. This will allow you to continue your research if you have computer problems on the trip.

When you travel to Salt Lake City, bring along family group sheets even for the families you don't plan to research. If the research plan you outlined doesn't work out well, you'll be prepared to work on families.

Surname Quick Reference Cards

Make an alphabetical list of all the surnames you are researching and include the Soundex codes. (See chapter eight for more on Soundex.) Write the list on an index card; or key it into a word processing, spreadsheet, or database program so changes and additions will be easy to make. Use this quick reference when you are searching indexes or using Soundex indexes. The list can keep you from missing important clues. You might find it useful to expand the surname list to include other helpful information, such as time periods and localities as shown on the top of page 63.

Name	Soundex	Name	Soundex	Name	Soundex
Cheek	C200	Hanley	H540	Slaker	S426
Daoust	D230	Hatfield	H314	Stuart	S363
Dow	D000	Johnson	J525	Warren	W650
Fee	F000	Rowan	R500	Woodward	W363
Green	G650	Ryan	R500		

Locality Quick Reference Cards

Make similar cards or sheets alphabetizing the localities for which you are doing research. Include both general (state, province) and specific (county, town, district, parish, village, township) localities. This can be useful when material is

Name	Soundex	Time	Localities and Notes
Hanley	H540	1840s	Family in Hamilton, Ontario
		1857	Michael in Winona Co., Minn.
Hatfield	H314	1861–65	Abraham in Civil War from Indiana
		1908	Abraham died in Johnson Co., Ark.
Slaker	S426	1853	Wm. Rudolph to Wisconsin. The name in Germany may be Schleicher (a butcher)
Stuart	S363	1819	James born in Strathdon, Aberdeenshire, Scotland
		1852	To Wisconsin
Warren	W650	1790	William in Green Co., Ky.
		1830	Son Hardin to Greene Co., Ind.
		1842	William died in Ky.
		1842	Hardin Jr. in Johnson Co., Ark.

cataloged or indexed by locality, and it can help you quickly recall a specific place name. Add information as your research uncovers new ancestral places.

Time Lines

A time line or chronology is a reference tool that can be helpful when you are trying to track a family or an individual and don't recall dates and locations. It can also help you keep track of families where many people had the

LOCALITY LIST—WARREN FAMILY RESEARCH			
Locality	**Time Period**	**Surnames**	**Notes**
Arkansas	1830–present	Cheek, Hatfield, Warren	
Clarksville, Ark.	1840–present	"	Johnson County Seat—courthouse, library
Green Co., Ky	1787–present	Warren	Hardin to Greene Co., Ind., in 1820s
Greene Co., Ind.	1820–1838	Warren	Hardin to Ark. ca. 1838
Indiana	1815–1878	Hatfield	Crawford, DuBois Cos.
	1820–1838	Warren	Greene Co.
Johnson Co., Ark.	1830-present	Warren	
	1878–1930	Hatfield	Ozone area
Newton Co., Ark.	1840–	Cheek	
Ozone, Ark.	1830-present	Warren, Hatfield	Johnson Co.

Time Line for Griffin Family	
1750	John T. Griffin born in Virginia
1790	John T. Griffin and family move to Green Co.
1795	Green Co. splits, forming Smith and Johnson Counties
1810	Sally Griffin on the Green Co. census; John appears to be missing
1850	John T. Griffin Jr. and family are in Johnson County, Ind.
1865	Alvin J. Griffin dies in Scott County, Iowa, as a result of war injuries
1870	Alvin's widow, Annabelle, remarries Samuel McGuire in Scott Co.
1880	Can't find Annabelle and Samuel McGuire in Scott County census

same first names. List the years and localities for important events within each ancestral line. Note also changes to a county boundary or name. Add notations concerning records that you need to locate. For example, for U.S. ancestors, any year ending in zero after 1790 is a federal census year. For those years, your time lines should include the census information or a notation to search for census data. The chart above is a sample time line for the fictitious Griffin family.

Make Lists Using Genealogical Software

If you use a genealogical software program, you probably can easily generate name lists and time lines. It is important to take a complete listing of names with you. Inevitably, you will stumble across information on families or localities other than the ones you intended to work on. Even if you didn't bring along detailed research notes on those families, at least you will have the basic information. Even if you don't bring your computer to Salt Lake City, bring disks with all your genealogical data. You may need to access some of that information. You should be able to rent or borrow computer or printer time, but no one else will have your collection of family history data.

Family Summary Notebooks

For each family branch you intend to research in Salt Lake City, prepare a file folder of information, such as family group sheets, copies of records and research, maps, and notes. Add to it as you prepare for your trip and your research plan evolves. Many researchers indicate that organizing their material in family notebooks works well when they take research trips to Salt Lake City. You may want to combine the sets of information into one or two working three-ring binders for your trip.

STEP 2: DETERMINE WHAT YOU NEED TO RESEARCH

Where are the gaps on your charts? What information do you presently rely on that came from secondary sources, such as published books, rather than original records? If your early research was anything like ours, you'll have some painful discoveries when you review that material. You may find some incomplete material: for example, copies of book pages without the book's title or author.

You may come across records that you forgot you had. They are wonderful to rediscover, unless you've spent the last six months researching information you already had found and tucked away.

Review the Basics of Genealogical Research

Read chapter two for a quick review of the basics of family history research. Guidebooks suggested there will help you zero in on facts and sources upon which you need to focus your additional research.

Develop a Research Plan

As you review the family history information you have and determine what you need to learn, start to map out a research plan for your Salt Lake City trip. Ask yourself what types of records would fill in some of the blanks on your charts and flesh out the lives of these individuals. Begin to list research steps you need to take on specific family lines, individuals, and localities to help solve the problems. You may need to do a number of quick lookups. **Begin a list of things that you should be able to accomplish quickly.** You'll need those as breaks from a frustrating or slow-moving, extensive research problem.

Tip

You may want to focus on one or two of those extensive research problems for your Salt Lake City trip. The FHL is the one place where you have access to extensive records and reference materials for many areas. It's the place to solve those research problems that require a complete review and evaluation of the records of the area. You may have a long list of research goals for your family branches, but you'll be most effective if you narrow your focus.

Localities Outside the United States

If you are tracing immigrants to the United States back to the old country, do your best to identify in the ancestral country the *exact* location the immigrant came from. Remember that the port from which people departed was often not the locality that was home. Don't jump to the foreign research too soon. Be sure you have thoroughly researched all the U.S. sources first for the extended family. Sometimes a census record for the immigrant's cousins' family indicates that more family members came to America. You never know which U.S. obituary or church record for a niece or brother of the immigrant will state the exact locality in the old country where that family lived.

If no place of origin is readily identified, you will need to find it to give yourself a decent chance of making headway in the foreign records. Check obituaries, death certificates, naturalizations, census records, biography files and indexes, family histories and family files, military records, county histories, tombstone inscriptions, and church records for your immigrant ancestors. Then do the same for their siblings, children, nieces and nephews, cousins, or neighbors who appear to have come with them. In short, scour the country to which an ancestor came before you head to the homeland.

STEP 3: LEARN WHERE TO FIND THE INFORMATION YOU NEED
Look for Resources Close to Home

Libraries, historical societies, genealogical societies, colleges, bookstores, and FHCs in your home area may hold much that will help. Internet resources continue to grow daily. Making use of nearby resources can help you prepare for your Salt Lake City trip. You may also find some of the information you are missing before the trip. Try to accomplish some of your research goals close to home so your Salt Lake City time will be spent doing things you can't do effectively elsewhere.

Learn About the FHL and Its Resources

Most of us can do plenty with a week in Salt Lake City, but to make the most of it, focus your sights on what is most important to your research. The FHL's collection is massive, but it certainly does not have all records from everywhere. Not all records for any area have survived, and only some of those surviving records have been filmed. To help you develop a research trip plan that will work, you need to learn about the FHL resources and how to use them.

Chapters three, four and five introduced you to sources of information about the library. Chapters eight, nine and ten outline the kinds of records in the collection. Before your trip, review the resources discussed there. Many FHL publications (and information at FamilySearch Internet) can be of tremendous help. They primarily discuss the sources available at the library, but many also provide practical hints and helps, making it easier for you to access and use these records. The country and state Research Outlines can be especially useful in helping you determine what resources in the library may be of use.

Talk to people who have been to the FHL. You'll find them at genealogical society meetings and classes and at research repositories. You'll run into other people who want to go to Salt Lake City, and sometimes you can learn from them as well. **They may have ideas you hadn't thought about, and you can benefit from their ideas and plans.**

Idea Generator

Chapter four included a number of articles, audiotapes, books, and Web sites that can help you prepare for a trip to Salt Lake City and accomplish some of your research in advance. You can also learn from genealogists who have experience with the records of the geographic areas where your ancestors lived. You may have personal contact with such researchers through genealogical societies. Others may have shared their expertise in journal articles, guidebooks, or seminar and conference lectures. Look for that specific expertise in genealogical and historical society library collections, or order lecture tapes of pertinent topics from national conferences. Use these resources to prepare for your Salt Lake City trip and to determine specific resources to use once you are there.

Family History Centers

There is only one Family History Library, but it has more than 3,400 branches worldwide—the Family History Centers—where you can learn about the library's collection. Chapter six gives information about locating and using Family History Centers. Find those in your area, and visit them to learn more about the library and its collections and to prepare for your trip to Salt Lake City.

The FHL Catalog

You should become acquainted with the library catalog before your trip to Salt Lake City. You can access it online at the library's Web site <http://www.family search.org>. You can also purchase it on a CD-ROM; at only six dollars (U.S.), that CD-ROM is one of the best research investments you can make. Chapter five provides some direction on this powerful tool. (If you take a laptop computer on your trip, plan to take your CD-ROM of the catalog or buy one there. You can use it right at the film reader.)

If you've used the FHL Catalog in the past to see what was available for your locality, don't be surprised to find that new material has been added. Perhaps a book of record abstracts was published that includes a county you are researching. The transcriptions of cemetery stones in a neighboring community may have been microfilmed. A newly accessible statewide or federal index may include entries of value to you. Go back to the catalog on a regular basis to check for new and updated entries. Enhanced search capabilities make it possible to look more creatively for sources of interest.

Use the FHL Catalog to study what microfilm, microfiche, books, and periodicals pertaining to your research localities are available. Print out the listings of resources available for the county, local, state, and federal records you may want to use. That will help you logically plan what to look for before your trip and set priorities for your research at the FHL. You will need less time to search the catalog in Salt Lake City and have more time to research actual records.

Languages

If your research agenda for the FHL involves work in records written in a language you don't read, a bit of preparation can further your work. Use the word lists available from the FHL and on the FamilySearch Internet site. Another way to get ahead in your research is to take a class in that language.

STEP 4: PRACTICE, PRACTICE, PRACTICE: WORK IN ADVANCE ON YOUR GOALS

You may accomplish some of your research goals without ever leaving home. By using repositories in your area before heading to Salt Lake City, you'll add to your list of things to do there.

Practice Close to Home

Practice the research skills you will need to use at the library, and make some progress on your family research in the process. Do that when you visit the FHCs and other research facilities in your home area. Larger public libraries,

Reminder

PRACTICE THESE

- It's important to be able to ask questions when you really need to, so that's something you may need to practice. Don't be shy about it or worried about looking like you don't know what you're doing. The really good genealogists ask lots of questions!

- While you're at it, practice showing your appreciation. No matter where you research, a friendly smile and thank-you increase your chances of receiving help, and make you and other genealogists welcome there the next time.

- Finally, practice some patience with yourself. Give yourself the latitude to learn and grow and make a few mistakes. When you go to a local library or archives or courthouse for the first time, give yourself time to learn the facility, its procedures, and the records. Use those first visits to local facilities to practice being new in a repository. It will help you adjust more quickly when you make your first trip to Salt Lake City and the Family History Library.

---

college and university libraries, and any genealogical or historical collections may be valuable practice grounds. Look there for other films, books, maps, and periodicals pertaining to the counties, states, provinces, countries and research topics in which you are interested.

Use Reference Guides

There are many guides to research in specific localities or types of records. Check your area repositories for these and other basic genealogical reference material. In the process, you might find some surprises—information on your family or clues to other possible sources of information about them. With each local research visit, try to add a little to what you know about your ancestors and how to research their lives.

Maps—A Basic Locality Resource

Do you have maps of the localities whose records you plan to research? Reference books, atlases, and map collections available at public, college, or historical libraries in your home area may be useful sources. Start to develop your personal ancestral map collection by making photocopies of those maps or pertinent sections of them. **Gathering and using the maps in your preparation will provide you with a valuable research tool.** Maps will help you understand the geographic realities of areas where your ancestors lived, and identify nearby places that might be of significance.

Research Tip

Use Indexes

Use any indexes to material that you may find in repositories near your home or online. At your local FHC, order microfilmed indexes to records you hope to use in Salt Lake City. Ordering and viewing two dozen rolls of film that hold

---

ORDERING FILMS STORED OFF-SITE

At one time, a number of films from all floors were removed to off-site storage due to space constraints. These films have been moved back into the collection in the main library building. United States and Canada microfilms that were housed in the overflow area on floor B1 have been moved to the second floor with the balance of the U.S. and Canada microfilms.

Some films, however, still will not be found in the library. The catalog may not always indicate this, but the library is attempting to identify all these in the catalog. These are generally films that are not frequently used, as well as some newer acquisitions. Contact the FHL in advance to see about ordering films so that they will be in the library during your trip. The FamilySearch Internet site has a section that gives contact information for ordering films in advance. Check this site for any updates to this ordering information. We suggest ordering these films two to four weeks in advance. Order in advance by e-mail (fhl@ldschurch .org) or by fax (for United States and Canada microfilms, (801) 240-1924; for international microfilms, (801) 240-1929; for British microfilms, (801) 240-1928).

If, while you are in the FHL working, you find that films you need are not physically in the building, you can order these at the library attendant window and generally receive them within twenty-four hours on regular working days. If you are from out of town, be sure to let the attendant know this. Ask how long the needed films will take to arrive at the library. The FHL has limits on the number of films ordered per day per individual researcher and an overall limit of orders that it can process.

---

the deeds for your ancestral county can be time-consuming and expensive. But the deed index may be on just two or three rolls of microfilm. Order the index, and use it to list all the deeds you need to research in Salt Lake City. Then check the FHL Catalog and list the film numbers for the rolls of film containing those specific deeds. In Salt Lake City, you can go right to the specific rolls of records. Anything you can accomplish before the trip frees up valuable research time in Salt Lake City for things you can't easily do anywhere else.

Practice Developing and Using a Research Plan

Plan your day's research in advance. Bring along the reference information, and the supplies and equipment you need. At the end of the day, evaluate what happened. Did your lists of family surnames and localities work effectively for you, or do you need to add more details to make them truly useful? What records did you not know how to use? What other supplies and equipment would be helpful? Are there blank forms or form originals that you should bring along? Develop your Salt Lake City goals and a packing list based on these experiences.

Practice Using a Variety of Equipment

Most of the collection at the FHL is on microfilm or microfiche, so it helps if you go there prepared to use film and fiche readers. If you haven't had much experience with the readers, practice using them near your home to become comfortable with this important tool. There's nothing overwhelming or particularly difficult about using film or fiche readers. Like any other equipment, they simply take a little getting used to.

You will likely find a variety of equipment at libraries, colleges, archives, and FHCs. Use them! Become familiar with the various types. Your local Family History Center is one place where you may be able to get some help learning the equipment and some practice using it.

If you do not have Internet access at home, an FHC or a local public library might be an excellent place to become familiar with FamilySearch Internet.

Do you have a laptop computer that you plan to use in Salt Lake City? Practice taking it to local research repositories and using it during your research. Learn what ways you find most efficient to use the capabilities and reference information in your computer.

Develop Research Trip Checklists and Refine Your Salt Lake City Goals

Based on your local research trips, make adjustments to your research plan and the organization of your materials. All you learn from these local excursions will help you plan for Salt Lake City. Learn about yourself while you research. How long can you sit at a microfilm reader? What are the time limits for your arms, back, eyes, and brain? Use that information as you plan your trip. Some people come to Salt Lake City and literally spend fourteen hours a day at a microfilm reader. (Some go home ill.) Many of us simply can't do that for days on end. **We need to plan our research time with regular breaks: short walks, research in the books (to get away from the film readers), even a short nap at the hotel after lunch.**

Important

STEP 5: MAKE ARRANGEMENTS AND FINAL CHECKLISTS

Start Making Travel Plans

Whether your Salt Lake City trip is a spur-of-the-moment opportunity or a trip carefully planned well in advance, you must arrange a few basics. Transportation and accommodations need to be scheduled. The FHL in Salt Lake is ideal for visitors to reach. The airport is less than ten minutes away. Amtrak uses the Santa Fe depot, just seven blocks from the library. The bus depot is on the same block as the library. If you are driving, the City Center exit from Interstate 15 is just a few blocks from the library. Parking is available right behind the library and in many parking ramps in the blocks surrounding the library.

Tip

**THINGS TO THINK ABOUT WHEN YOU PLAN
A SALT LAKE CITY TRIP**

- Make travel arrangements. If you're visiting with others, plans will have to be coordinated.

- Consider visiting with a group. See chapter fifteen for suggestions.

- Make hotel arrangements. See chapter eighteen for information on accommodations.

- Obtain local information. The Salt Lake Convention & Visitors Bureau is a good source. Review the information in chapters seventeen, nineteen, and twenty.

- Make specific trip plans and prepare a written itinerary.

- Start on a packing list.

Trip "To Do" Box

Label a box "Family History Library trip." Each time you think of something you will need to do while you're there, write it down and toss it in the box. One day during lunch, pull out your ancestor charts and family group sheets and jot down things to do in Salt Lake City based on the gaps on the charts or information you wish you had about a certain ancestor or family. Periodically incorporate these accumulated notes into your research plan and to do lists. This will help you prioritize work to do before your trip, as well as plan and schedule time in Salt Lake City.

Tip

Plan What to Take

Everyone's travel packing list is a bit unique. Some of our suggestions will apply to many people. You will see a wide range of clothes in the library, everything from dressy to very casual. One of the most useful things you can wear is clothing with pockets, or, alternatively, a fanny pack. Most people simply bring clothing and shoes in which they will be comfortable for the long hours of research. Plan to dress in layers. The temperature in the library can vary by day and season, and the same is true of the city. Salt Lake City is a high desert area. Summers are warm, and winter often means snow. Fall and spring are beautiful.

Stationery Items to Pack

Bring your own small stapler or some paper clips. These come in handy to keep your copies together. A highlighter is useful for marking important entries on your personal copies. A magnifying glass will help you read some films. You might find it useful to bring a clipboard or sturdy notebook to write on. Be sure to put your name on the notebook, clipboard, stapler, and other items, as well as on your briefcase, backpack, or shoulder bag. Some other items to

Idea Generator

IDEAS FOR WHAT TO TAKE TO SALT LAKE CITY

- a magnifying glass, for hard-to-read film images and photocopies

- a carry-on bag, with wheels and a handle, so you won't have to lug a briefcase with thirty pounds of paper in it

- return address labels, to identify file folders, papers, and other items

- a cable lock, to attach your laptop computer to your workstation

- empty file folders, labels, notebooks, and sheet protectors

- originals of forms that you use in your research, to copy there

- an empty foldable bag, to bring home the copies you make

- an umbrella

- medications, prescriptions, extra eyeglasses (in your carry-on)

- address/phone book or list

---

consider bringing are rubber bands, pens (include a red one), pencils, three-hole punch (there are flat styles), a small notepad, blank family group sheets, and ancestor charts. Bring along this guidebook and any others you may need to consult while on your trip.

Plan Your Time

Begin to set your priorities and plan your time for a Salt Lake City trip. An example of a simple time schedule is included in chapter thirteen, "Working in the Library." A blank form is included in appendix C. As you list your research goals and plans, start to block out time on that planning calendar. Think realistically of what you can do in a day and for several consecutive days. Plan plenty of breaks and varied work to keep yourself alert and focused. Be flexible, and leave yourself options about what you do with your time and money during your trip.

Plan Your Budget

You do not have to go broke making a research trip to the Family History Library. Meals, lodging and transportation to the city are the significant expenses. There is a full range of lodging options from inexpensive to deluxe close to the library. Beyond that, you can keep your expenses minimal, although you will also have lots of options close by for shopping, cultural events, genealogical books, and professional assistance. One area you should plan to invest money in is photocopies at the library. The other expenses of your trip are all intended to get you there so you can find and copy those records, so be sure to do that.

PART THREE

The Records in the Family History Library

EIGHT

Major U.S. Collections

T his chapter covers materials that are national or regional in scope. It focuses on some of the general U.S. collections found at the Family History Library (FHL). We hope the discussions entice you to search for these in the FHL Catalog and check for others that may pertain to your own research.

To learn more about each type of record discussed in this chapter, check general genealogical guidebooks, consult guidebooks written on the specific subject, attend a class or lecture on a particular topic, or purchase an audiotape of a lecture given on the topic. The FHL has Research Outlines or other helpful information sheets on many of the localities and subjects covered in this chapter; it has as well the general *United States* Research Outline. The reference areas on the first and second floors have binders of these Research Outlines for your use in the library. Many guidebooks on specific topics and geographic areas are listed in appendix B.

BROADEN YOUR SEARCH

The category of U.S. records may hold many research sources for you. We frequently check for our town, parish, or county in the FHL Catalog. General country-level resources are important. If you check under "United States" and then under the categories "biography" or "genealogy" you will find large collections of material gathered by individual genealogists. These frequently cover people in many states and may not always be cataloged for all localities the collection covers. These collections are valuable for research but do require extra time, as many are not indexed or categorized. When checking for any special occupation, an ethnic group, or a business, don't forget to check the basic sources such as census records, directories, biographies, and general histories, among others. These are abundant at the FHL. Often researchers get so involved in the particular subject they neglect other sources that might yield additional details. The subjects covered in this chapter are overviews of some major U.S. collections or research groups that are well represented in the FHL collection.

You may find that a set of records covers a region such as the original colonies or the southern states. This may include many record types as well as historical background information.

LOCATING ITEMS IN THE FHL CATALOG

Finding the most specific descriptions under "United States" requires a bit of patience and creativity. Today we are fortunate to have catalog access via keyword in addition to locality. Of course, you can type in the phrase "United States" for a locality and then sit and wait for the computer catalog to bring up a long list of topical entries, each with many records behind it. With the keyword capability you can narrow this search by topic and related keywords.

For example, using keywords in the 2000 edition of the FHL Catalog on CD-ROM

- United States AND Military would yield 2,924 entries,
- United States AND Military AND Pension would yield 263 entries,
- United States AND Military AND Pension Index would yield 141 entries,
- United States AND Military AND Pension Index* would yield 150 entries. Using the truncated keyword includes the words *index*, *indexes*, and *indexed* in the search.

All of these search results include the set of records sought: "Old War Index to Pension Files 1815–1926" on seven rolls of microfilm. You might relish the thought of scanning 2,924 entries to find this one, but most people don't. If you do have time, this can be a good education and introduction to the catalog, though. Searches through the titles for large collections often produce some pleasant surprises. If you know the title (or most of it) of what you are searching for, you can shorten the search time.

For example, type in the keywords "United States Index Pension Old War." This results in six possibilities, including the seven rolls of film as well as Virgil White's *Index to Old Wars Pension Files, 1815–1926*.

Do a keyword search using

- "United States Old War Index" results in only one match, and it is not the same set of records
- "United States Old War Pension Index" results in no matching titles
- "Old War Index Pension Files" results in the "Old War Index to Pension Files 1815–1926" on seven rolls of microfilm.

The lesson is that you need to be creative with any library catalog to find all possible entries for any type of record you seek. Don't give up too quickly!

FINDING AIDS

The FHL has produced many finding aids to help researchers learn the background of a record and zero in on the specific rolls of film needed. Those for the United States are located on the main and second floors in special reference areas. The counters and tables have signs designating the category of finding aids in each section. The sections are rearranged from time to time, and the finding aid binders are sometimes moved. Finding aids for the most-used categories of records—cemetery, church, city directories, immigration, Latter-day Saints, military, naturalization, passenger lists, states censuses and vital records—may disappear for a while. The finding aid you need may be in use or may have been returned to the wrong place. If you browse for a bit the missing book or binder usually turns up.

One finding aid is the *Register of U.S. Lineage Societies*, compiled by Jayare Roberts. Described and listed in this register are records of lineage societies available in the FHL, along with information on some societies whose records are not available in the library. Some societies which are no longer in existence are covered. The information provided about each society includes its official title, its membership requirements, its headquarters address, and references to the book call numbers or microfilm numbers of records available at the FHL. Among the records listed as available at the FHL are applications, biographical sketches, chapter registers, index books, names of descendants, pedigrees of members, and rolls of ancestors.

Other finding aids are discussed throughout this and other chapters.

African-American Records

The FHL has many items specific to African-American research, including some Freedmen's Bureau records (Bureau of Refugees, Freedmen, and Abandoned Lands), plantation records, military records, slave census schedules, histories, and more. The FHL also has National Archives microfilms of records for African-American research. Some finding aid binders list many books and records at the FHL related to African-American research. "Minorities" is an important subject category to check in the FHL Catalog. The library publication *African American Guide to Records* is available in the library or from the Distribution Center.

Bible Records

Some Bible records may be located by looking up a smaller geographic location or surname, but many are larger compilations. Some are regional in nature. The FHL Catalog has thirty-seven collections or publications relating to Bible records covering a wide area of the United States. Unless the collection description specifically mentions a state, you will not find it cataloged under the name of an ancestral state. The National Society, Daughters of the American Revolution has collected family Bible records for decades. Many published volumes and microfilmed volumes of these are at the FHL.

Biography, Genealogy, and History

The FHL has voluminous material under these subject entries, and much of it is national or regional in nature. Some items are biographical compendiums that cover time periods rather than specific states or cities. As discussed earlier in this chapter, the wonderful collections under "United States—Genealogy" may hold some manuscripts you don't yet know about. National and regional histories may help you focus your research on a specific place or time period by providing you with some historical background related to an ancestral era.

Census Schedules and Indexes

The library has a virtually complete collection of federal-level population census schedules and indexes in both printed and microform formats. These cover extant censuses from 1790 to 1920. The 1930 census will be added in 2002. We believe the FHL has the most complete collection of printed census indexes anywhere. Additionally, with online access at the ever expanding FHL computer workstations, patrons can check online digitized censuses and indexes to these. Other census indexes which have been compiled by a variety of people and organizations can also be accessed online.

Technique

SOUNDEX CODES

To save time, generate Soundex codes for and list alphabetically all your surnames before you arrive in Salt Lake City. If you are unsure of how the system works, check one of the basic guidebooks listed in chapter two or appendix B. You might find it beneficial to make several copies of the Soundex code section to place in your notebook or other reference materials you bring to the FHL. We find that having this reference tool handy saves valuable research time. The library has published lists of precoded surnames. With the ever-growing number of online indexes and censuses, the need for Soundex will decrease. However, you may still need to consult these indexes. The Soundex code is used in the indexing of U.S. census records, passenger lists, and naturalization records.

Soundex code = initial letter of surname + three digits based on subsequent consonants (per the chart below)

1–b, p, f, v	4–l
2–c, s, k, g, j, q, x, z	5–m, n
3–d, t	6–r

Note: Disregard vowels and *y*, *w*, and *h*. Code pairs of the same letter as one digit. If necessary, use zeros to complete the three digits. An example listing a series of names that have been Soundex-coded appears on page 62.

At times you may want to do a full county search using a microfilmed census and will need to view more complete pages than you can get on the computer screen. If you are not sure about which reel of film you need, finding aids will help determine that. These exist for many census years and are guides to what county is on which reel of microfilm. An example is Leonard Smith's *United States Census Key 1850, 1860, 1870*. For these federal census years, this book lists for each state.

- which microfilms include which counties
- which microfilms include which townships, cities, and towns
- where applicable, which microfilms include which enumeration districts and wards in large cities (Both the National Archives microfilm number and the FHL microfilm number are provided.)

In 2001, a special electronic version census index was added. The FHL, in conjunction with the University of Minnesota, indexed the 1880 U.S. population census schedule. Thousands of people actually extracted the information, according to Richard Turley, managing director of the Family and Church History Department of The Church of Jesus Christ of Latter-day Saints. The index has some wonderful search features. If you know the place, you can zero in on that area. If you don't know the place, you can search the overall index, which includes all members of a household. The index will show the name, place of residence, film FHL call number, page number of the full entry, and relationship to the head of the household. Further, it includes the sex, marital status, race, age, birthplace, occupation, and country or state of the person's parents' birth. You can also zero in on neighbors in this index. Other features allow you to search using some of the known details rather than a full name and some using special locality search features.

Church Records

The FHL has several collections of church records, many histories, and many inventories of church records found at the national level. These are especially important when records of a specific denomination from across the country or a large region are gathered together at an archive. Early American church records are often cataloged under the United States or by region; however, since an individual church has a specific location, you will usually find these when searching under a county or local geographic designation. The wider histories of a specific denomination may help you to determine likely places of origin or migration. They may also identify other repositories that may be helpful.

City Directories

City directories, often published annually, list residents' names and addresses year after year. Initially these were head of household listings. In the twentieth century, wives' names were added. Adult children living in a household were listed for many locations. Generally, a person's occupation is given and possibly the employer's name. The FHL has directories for many cities and towns all across the United States. The topic category is "Directories" in the catalog. The collection, while extensive, does not include every directory ever published. Most of the library's directory collection is in microform. In the general reference area on the second floor, researchers will find a bound volume and a binder with listings and call numbers for many, but not all, of the directories the library holds. The FHL has microform copies of city directories for fifty-three major U.S. cities. The finding aid *City Directories 1902–1930s* allows quick access to these. It provides a detailed description of each directory, along with the micro-form number.

Another finding aid is *City Directories in Book Form*, which is the collection register of U.S. and Canadian city directories in book form in the FHL. It has, besides the section on Canadian directories, one section each for U.S. general and regional directories, then entries by state. The guide provides the FHL call number (and microfilm number if it has also been filmed) and its location, either in the open stacks or in high-density storage. Sometimes when a book call number is listed, you will find that the book is no longer on the open shelf, and you will need to check the FHL catalog to find a microfilm number.

Daughters of the American Revolution (DAR)

Since the early twentieth century, the Genealogical Records Committee (GRC) of the National Society, Daughters of the American Revolution has actively gathered genealogical information. It has produced more than 14,000 volumes that cover transcriptions, indexes, and abstracts of Bible, cemetery, church, military, probate, vital, and other records. Those that were at the DAR Library in Washington, DC, as of the early 1970s were filmed by the FHL. The micro-films total more than 2,700 in number. These volumes are important, as often they contain abstracts or compilations of records or tombstones that are no longer extant. Some of the subjects under which you might find these cataloged at the FHL are Bible records, cemeteries, church records, genealogy, probate, and vital records.

Due to the newer keyword search capability of the FHL catalog, if you type in the county or town name and related record category, such as cemetery or

Case Study

USING GRC'S PUBLICATIONS

An example of the usefulness of these DAR GRC publications is in one of the author's own family research. Volume four of the Minnesota GRC publications contains Winona County, Minnesota, cemetery information. A copy of this volume is at the Minnesota Historical Society, and in it Paula's great-grandfather is listed. The more modern cemetery transcriptions done by area genealogists do not list this information. This is also a case, however, where the FHL Catalog presents a research problem. Once at the FHL Paula wanted to verify the entry on this page for Michael Hanley to use in checking some other records. Checking under Winona County in the FHL Catalog, Paula did not find any reference to the cemeteries in that volume. Checking under the state name and the category of cemeteries, Paula did find the GRC publications related to Minnesota, but no reference to Winona County. Fortunately, Paula remembered the number of the volume in which his entry appeared. This shows the importance of using state-wide collections even if there is no specific reference in the FHL Catalog to your specific locality or surname. You never know what you might find with a bit of browsing!

birth records, you will get the DAR collection entries which pertain to that locality. However, this is only true if the original catalog entry contained the name of that locality in the description or title.

Since some of the records consulted for GRC publications were in private hands and their location today may be unknown, the GRC records are valuable. There are several finding aids for portions of the GRC publications at the FHL and at other libraries on microfilm. These are listed in appendix B. It is important to use these guides and the FHL Catalog and to browse the films for your state. **You may also find more details in the DAR catalog online at <http://www.dar .org/library/onlinlib.html>** and the catalogs from major libraries where DAR publications are housed in each state.

Internet Source

Family Histories and Surname Periodicals

The FHL has an extensive collection of published family histories spanning many geographic localities and nationalities. Those with a U.S. connection are numerous. Many of these detail multiple generations of a family, others have only names and dates, and a growing number of these include more background information on people and the places where they lived. More people are now including source documentation when writing their family histories. You may also find a catalog entry for a surname periodical related to one of your ancestral lines.

The books and periodicals in print form that focus on U.S. families or surnames are housed in the Joseph Smith Memorial Building on the fourth floor. About 70 percent of these have also been microfilmed and are available on the second floor of the FHL if they have a U.S. connection. A significant number of the books and periodicals that have been microfilmed or microfiched are no longer available in printed format.

Military Records

The collection of U.S. federal-level military records at the FHL is particularly strong, as are the finding aids for those records. Several volumes of U.S. military records finding aids are on the second floor in the reference area. The four volumes of the *Register of Federal United States Military Records* steer you to the library call numbers for pertinent microfilmed records and indexes. These cover records from the Revolutionary War into the twentieth century. Of course, you may also look for these records in the FHL Catalog. These volumes and the binder describing World War I draft registrations and the film call numbers are great time-savers.

- Volume 1 covers U.S. military activities from 1775 to 1860
- Volume 2 covers the Civil War
- Volume 3 covers 1866 through World War II
- Volume 4 covers mostly new military records acquired by the FHL since the publication of the first three volumes

These volumes point the researcher to many types of military records found in the FHL, including service and pension records, bounty land applications, enlistment registers, prisoner of war records, material related to officers, draft records, personnel records, state-level records, burial records, veterans' homes records, quartermaster records, Loyalists, correspondence, returns and veterans records. These volumes also help researchers locate a multitude of indexes to many of these records. The records are grouped for presentation in the books in a variety of ways: on the national level, by specific war, by state, and by branch of service.

The library has published an extensive sixty-page Research Outline on U.S. military records that is very useful. It includes summaries of types of military records and has specific examples of them. Some of the military records available at the FHL for specific wars are

- Revolutionary War service, pension, and bounty land records
- Civil War service record indexes (Union soldiers)
- Civil War pension indexes (Union soldiers)
- Confederate service records
- War of 1812 pension and service record indexes
- World War I draft registrations

The binder titled *World War I Draft* is a marvelous finding aid to the World War I Selective Service System draft registration cards, 1917–1918, which have been microfilmed and are available in the FHL. The information is arranged alphabetically by state. Under each state the counties are listed alphabetically, followed by the alphabetic or surname range included on each microfilm. In the case of counties and large cities with multiple draft boards, the draft boards are listed numerically, followed by the alphabetic or surname range included on each microfilm. With this finding aid, a task that used to be time-consuming and often frustrating—looking up the correct microfilm number for a needed draft card—now takes a few seconds!

National Archives and Records Administration (NARA) Publications

You may have checked the various National Archives publications either in print form or online at <http://www.nara.gov> and found many sources you want to check at the FHL. These are generally microfilm publications. You should have noted the National Archives assigned numbers—such as "M505" or "T414"—and titles for the material.

Internet Source

If you use the FamilySearch edition of the catalog and enter the author as "United States Government" or check the locality section of the catalog under "United States," you will find hundreds of entries. With the advent of the catalog versions where keyword searches are feasible, you can cut down on the resulting entries if you add other search terms. Many reference tools on the main and second floors have catalog printouts or other compilations that will allow you to quickly find the FHL call number for some National Archives material, such as passenger or military records. If you are looking for other, less common, NARA records, as well as the passenger or military records, you can use the microfiche edition of the FHL catalog. Use the Author/Title section and check under "United States." The National Archives publications are listed alphabetically and numerically. See the example on page 83 of such a catalog entry.

There is National Archives material at the FHL that you might not find in many other places. The Regional Records Services Facilities (branches of the National Archives, which is located in Washington, DC) hold many records which have been locally microfilmed and not listed in the main National Archives microfilm catalogs. Some of these have been filmed by the FHL. Generally the only two places you will find lists of the microfilms and the actual microfilms are in the FHL and at the appropriate regional facility.

Native American Records

The FHL has an excellent collection of Native American records and finding aids. What makes this collection so strong is the wealth of records that are in the FHL in addition to the well-known National Archives microfilms of Native American records. The library has many American Indian records that were filmed at the National Archives regional facilities. Many of these records were filmed by the FHL and do not appear in the main catalog of Native American microfilms of the National Archives. Included are birth and death records, school records, probate records, censuses, and more. Additionally, the FHL has films of some church and missionary records, records of agents and others involved with American Indians, and other manuscript sources. The collection also includes the Eastern Cherokee or Guion Miller Roll, the Dawes Rolls, and many other Cherokee and Five Civilized Tribes records. Check for these in the catalog under the state and county of interest. Some may also appear only under the locality "United States." The library has many published directories and histories of tribes. Check the general reference areas on the first and second floors for a myriad of binders and bound volumes of Native American finding aids. Many of the records are cataloged under the main subject category "Native Races," with several subdivisions under that. Check under the specific topics, such as probate, for additional entries not always additionally cataloged under the "Native Races" category.

Naturalization Records

Most federal-level naturalization records found at the regional facilities of the National Archives are on film at the FHL. These include a variety of indexes, some of which cover naturalizations in several states. To find the federal-level naturalization records, check under the state name and the category "naturalization and citizenship." Another way to make sure you have found all possibilities is to use a keyword search for the location of the regional archives where the records were filmed, such as Kansas City. There are also films for a variety of naturalization records from other governmental levels, including many cities, counties, and states. Even with all of this, there are still many naturalization records from these levels that are not at the FHL.

```
          RN:0161074
    ++++++++++++++++++++++++++++++++++++++++++++++++++++++++++++++++++++++++
    National Archives microfilm publications ; M1299
                                                          +----------------+
    United States.  Immigration and Naturalization Service.   |US/CAN     |
        Index to New England naturalization petitions, 1791-1906. --   |FILM AREA |
        Washington, D.C. : National Archives, 1983. -- 117 reels ; 35  +----------------+
        mm. -- (National Archives microfilm publications ; M1299)

        Microfilm of original records in the National Archives,
        Washington, D.C.
        An index to naturalization documents in courts in Connecticut, Maine,        National Archives
        Massachusetts, New Hampshire, Rhode Island and Vermont, from                 Microfilm Number
        1791 to 1906.
        Index cards are organized by state and then by name of petitioner,
        arranged according to the Soundex system.  Index gives name
        and location of the court that granted the naturalization,
        date of naturalization, and volume and page (or certificate)
        number of the naturalization record.

        Connecticut  A000 (Isaac) - A536 (Zacharis) ------------------ 1429671
        Connecticut  A540 (Antonio) - B346 (William) ----------------- 1429672
        Connecticut  B350 (Albert) - B565 (Solomon) ----------------- 1429673
        Connecticut  B600 (Abel) - B646 (Vincenzo) ------------------ 1429674
        Connecticut  B650 (Abraham) - C165 (Vincenzo) -------------- 1429675    Family History Library
        Connecticut  C166 (Angelo) - C452 (Zygmont) --------------- 1429676     Microfilm Numbers
        Connecticut  C453 (Alexander) - C616 (William) ----------- 1429677
        Connecticut  C620 (Abraham) - D126 (John) ---------------- 1429678
        Connecticut  D130 Absalom) - D451 (Virgilio) ------------- 1429679
        Connecticut  D452 (Adam) - E146 (Martin) ---------------- 1429680

        Connecticut  E15( (Andrew) - F400 (Wladyslaw) -------------- 1429681
        Connecticut  F410 (Adam) - F640 (William) ----------------- 1429682
        Connecticut  F641 (Alfred) - G424 (Martin) --------------- 1429683
        Connecticut  G425 (Abraham) - G620 (Zaharia) ------------- 1429684
        Connecticut  G621 (Abraham) - H230 (Wolf) --------------- 1429685
        Connecticut  H232 (Andrew) - H463 (Walter) ------------- 1429686
        Connecticut  H533 (Philip) - J212 (Wolfe) ------------- 1429687
        Connecticut  J213 (Allan) - K216 (Youkle) ------------- 1429688
        Connecticut  K220 (Adam) - K456 (Willias) ------------ 1429689
        Connecticut  K460 (Agnes) - K651 (William) ---------- 1429690
        Connecticut  K652 (Abe) - L366 (Otto) -------------- 1429691
        Connecticut  L400 (Adam) - M165 (Leonidas) -------- 1429692
        Connecticut  M200 (Abram) - M252 (Zuzanna) ------- 1429693
        Connecticut  M253 (Abraham) - M425 (Willias) ---- 1429694
        Connecticut  M426 (Andreas) - M520 (Wicenta) --- 1429695
        Connecticut  M521 (Albert) - M635 (Wilhelm) --- 1429696
        Connecticut  M636 (Adamo) - N654 (Giuseppe) -- 1429697
        Connecticut  N655 (Alof) - P200 (Zigemond) -- 1429698
        Connecticut  P210 (Alfred) - P622 (Yadwiga) - 1429699
        Connecticut  P623 (Adam) - R216 (William) -- 1429700
        Connecticut  R215 (Andrew) - R500 (William) - 1429701
        Connecticut  R600 (Frederick) - S266 (Joseph) - 1429702
        Connecticut  S300- (Fageraas) - S415 (William) - 1429703
        Connecticut  S416 (Aaron) - S531 (William) -- 1429704
        Connecticut  S532 (Aaron) - T463 (Luigi) --- 1429705
        Connecticut  T500 (Albin) - V542 (Ursula) -- 1429706
        Connecticut  V453 (Adolfe) - W424 (Wladisaw) - 1429707
        Connecticut  W426 (Abram) - Z660 (John) --- 1429708
        (W425 is not available at this time)
        Rhode Island  A100 Alphonse) - C166 (Francesco) ---------- 1429709
        Rhode Island  C200 (Alexander) - D515 (William) --------- 1429710
        Rhode Island  D516 (Alexander) - G652 (Thomas) --------- 1429711
        Rhode Island  G653 (Albert) - L122 (Ernest) ----------- 1429712
        Rhode Island  L123 (Carl) - M352 (Gregor) ------------ 1429713
        Rhode Island  M355 (Hezekiah) - P563 (Santino) ------ 1429714
        Rhode Island  P600 (Alfred) - S536 (William) -------- 1429715
        Rhode Island  S540 (Andrew) - Z653 (Gaprial) ------- 1429716
        Maine, Massachusetts, New Hampshire, and --------- 1429717
        Vermont Index - A535 (William G.)
        Maine, Massachusetts, New Hampshire, and --------- 1429718
        Vermont  A536 (A.) - B226 (Pietro)
        Maine, Massachusetts, New Hampshire, and --------- 1429719
        Vermont  B230 (A.T.) - B356 (William)
        Maine, Massachusetts, New Hampshire, and --------- 1429720
        Vermont  B360 (Abraham) - B460 (Xavier)
        Maine, Massachusetts, New Hampshire, and --------- 1429721
        Vermont  B461 (Agapit) - B616 (Xavier Leroy)
        Maine, Massachusetts, New Hampshire, and --------- 1429722
        Vermont  B620 (A. Bernard) - B626 (Zotique)
        Maine, Massachusetts, New Hampshire, and --------- 1429723
        Vermont  B630 (A.M.) - B650 (Woolf)
        Maine, Massachusetts, New Hampshire, and --------- 1429724
        Vermont  B651 (A.I.) - C161 (Micheli)
        Maine, Massachusetts, New Hampshire, and --------- 1429725
        Vermont  C162 (Angelo) - C300 (Zephirin)
        Maine, Massachusetts, New Hampshire, and --------- 1429726
        Vermont  C310 (Alonso) - C451 (William)
        Maine, Massachusetts, New Hampshire, and --------- 1429727
        Vermont  C452 (A.J.) - C500 (Woolf)
```

Figure 8-1

An example of a Author/Title entry from the FHL Catalog on microfiche showing a National Archives Microfilm Number and the FHL call numbers for the series of films. *Reprinted by permission. Copyright © 1999–2000 by Intellectual Reserve, Inc.*

Passenger Arrival Records

The FHL has an extensive collection of passenger arrival records for immigrants and visitors to the United States. These are found in the catalog under "United States—Emigration and Immigration." There are many printed volumes and indexes, but the vast majority of the collection is on microfilm. The second-floor reference area holds large binders of finding aids to help you locate the proper index and passenger list for the correct port of entry. The finding aids such as *U.S. Passenger [Lists] 1820–[1950s]* bring together all of the microfilm numbers for the passenger arrival lists available at the FHL for the ports of Baltimore, Boston, Galveston, New Orleans, and Philadelphia and the smaller Atlantic Coast, and Gulf Coast, Canadian, Southern and West Coast ports. There is a similar binder for New York City arrivals for 1820 through 1943.

A separate category is the St. Albans District Manifest Records. These records cover the movement of aliens crossing the border from Canada into the United States from 1895 to 1954. The records cover ports of entry across the northern border, but all the records were eventually housed at the port of entry at St. Albans, Vermont. The actual records are called manifests. As with many records, the amount of detail about individuals increased over the years. The early records include full name, last place of residence, whether literate, if the person had been in the United States before, whether the person had been supported by charity or imprisoned. Later records include place of birth (many are specific) and a physical description. There are several types of indexes. All of the records and indexes total almost one thousand rolls of microfilm. To locate these in the FHL Catalog you can check under keywords such as *passenger arrival Canada, St. Albans,* and others. Using the FHL's passenger arrival record finding aids, however, shortens the search process.

WHAT ELSE?

We could go on forever describing the wonderful U.S. collections, but our space is limited. **Do some topical and keyword searches to learn more about the library's holdings of books and microforms related to U.S. records at the national level.** Don't forget to check under "United States" for keywords such as *cemetery, passport applications, probate, plat maps, land, minorities, Methodist history, War of 1812, colonial, slavery, Indians, prisons and prisoners, muster rolls, Bureau of Land Management,* and *taxation.*

Tip

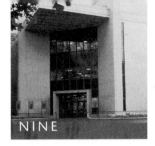

NINE

Resources for U.S. Localities

Quotes

C hapter five lists many of the subject categories for the Family History Library Catalog. Those subjects are important entry points for this chapter. It is vital to check under the name of the state where your ancestors lived as well as the county and the town or city.

COVERAGE OF RECORDS

Checking the FHL Catalog shows that for one of your ancestral states there has been considerable filming at both the state and county levels. The next state you check has very few catalog entries under the state name and even fewer for your county. As things are filmed for the library collection, several factors come into play. The person or government with control over the records may not have allowed filming. The lack of filming may simply be due to limited time. While we genealogists wish to have everything at our fingertips, it takes time to microfilm the millions of records in thousands of localities. For many years FHL filming was concentrated in states where a significant population of Church members resided or where their ancestors migrated from.

IS IT ALL THERE FOR YOUR AREA?

When you find an entry for probate records for a specific U.S. county in the catalog, how do you know if the entire record has been microfilmed? One way is to check at the courthouse or in guidebooks on doing research in that locality. Another way is to check whether during the Works Projects Administration (WPA) era in the late 1930s a survey was done of the records in a specific courthouse and related county government buildings. These were called "Inventory of the County Archives" or "Historic Records Survey." Approximately 85 to 90 percent of county courthouses were surveyed. These surveys tell you what types of records were kept and what books, files, and indexes covering what years were still in existence in the late 1930s. Unfortunately, only about 20 percent of the surveys were published. Few published ones exist for surveys at the town level in New England.

VOICES OF EXPERIENCES

Several unrelated series of documents can be filmed on the same roll of microfilm. Although I had run into that earlier at my local Family History Center, when that situation came up at the FHL in Salt Lake City, I forgot all about that and was instead convinced that I had made some sort of numbering error in that endless sea of microfilm numbers.

—*Lynn Betlock*

Many of these published surveys are at the FHL, and there are some published surveys for state-level vital records offices. The unpublished surveys still exist in manuscript form for many states. Several guidebooks will tell you what was published and where the surveys that were done but not published are located.

Cemeteries

Cemetery records come in a variety of formats. They may be on microfilm, microfiche, or in book form. The records may be the actual cemetery records, transcriptions of tombstones, or records from a church record book. Some will be indexed or in alphabetical order, but many will require extensive search time to scan through page after page of burial listings. With the keyword search you can search by cemetery name. If you don't make a positive connection, remember to search under the city, county, or state name. A statewide cemetery project may include many counties, and all may not be separately cataloged under the city or county name. A prime example of this is the WPA and DAR compilation of Iowa cemeteries. Many, but not all, counties were compiled, and this is a project listed under the state category. A place search will not turn up an entry by county name, but the keyword search will. Type in the place Buena Vista (County) in Iowa, and the WPA compilation does not appear. Type *Buena Vista* and *cemeteries* in as keywords, and you get several catalog entries, including the one for the set of WPA materials.

Federal Census

The FHL has many special finding aids and individual city or state indexes for some federal census years. One is a guide for searching in cities in the unindexed 1910 federal census, *Street Indexes to Unindexed Cities in the U.S. 1910 Federal Census*, by Emil and Maurine Malmberg. Specifically addressed are Boston, Des Moines, Minneapolis, Queens Borough (New York City), and Salt Lake City. The book is arranged by city, street name, and house number, and it provides the census page number, the enumeration district, and the FHL number for the appropriate census record.

Another helpful aid is G. Eileen Buckway's *U.S. 1910 Federal Census: Unindexed States: A Guide to Finding Census Enumeration Districts for Unindexed Cities, Towns, and Villages*. This is a guide to finding census enumeration districts for the cities, towns, and villages in the states for which there is no microfilm Soundex or Miracode index for the 1910 federal census. There are some book indexes for several of these "unindexed" states; these should be used before following the instructions found in Buckway's book. The information provided in this guide is the name of the city, town, village, township, precinct, military post or election district; the county in which it was located at the time of the 1910 census; the census enumeration district for that locality; and the FHL microfilm number for the appropriate census record.

State Censuses

Not all states took state censuses, but many of those that did produced some wonderful research information. Some states only took head of household censuses, and others asked for extensive information. At the FHL you can check

Printed Source

To learn more about WPA published and unpublished records surveys read Child's *Check List of Historical Records Survey Publications*; Hefner's *The WPA Historical Records Survey: A Guide to the Unpublished Inventories, Indexes, and Transcripts*; and Heisey's *Works Projects Administration: Sources for Genealogists*.

a state census for Florida as late as 1945 or the Iowa state census of 1925. That Iowa census includes the mother's maiden name and the state or country where the marriage of a person's parents took place. The 1894 Michigan state census asked mothers how many children they had given birth to and how many were living.

Check the FHL Catalog under the name of your state for these censuses. It is also important to check under a specific county name to see if the library might have a transcription or index of that county's portion of a state census. Most of the state censuses are unindexed. The library has an in-house guide to its large state census collection. Also check the handy two-volume finding aid *U.S. State and Special Census Register: A Listing of Family History Library Microfilm Numbers*. Be sure to check Ann Lainhart's *State Census Records* for more information on the state censuses, many of which are found at the FHL.

Church Records

No matter what the religious denomination of your ancestor, be sure to check this category for all ancestral localities. The FHL has microfilmed many church records at churches and other locations. These include sacramental records, cemeteries, meeting minutes, biographies, and more. Check at the various locality levels. You never know when your ancestral church records might have been filmed at a state or regional religious archives.

Court Records

Many of the other items discussed in this chapter are court records. These may vary by locality but might include probate, birth, death, marriage, naturalization, and other records. These will not appear in the locality part of the catalog under court records. Under this category at the FHL you may find civil and criminal court records, indexes, calendars, minutes, and more.

City and County Directories

As mentioned in chapter eight, the FHL has city directories for hundreds of cities and towns in the United States. That chapter detailed some finding aids. Also check under your city or town name in the catalog for more possibilities. The FHL also has some county-level directories, including some for farmers.

Guidebooks

The FHL has an extensive collection of guidebooks about doing research in different states. Some of these are in the general reference areas on the main and second floors and are shelved alphabetically. Be sure to check in both areas, as not all are duplicated in each area. Remember to check the catalog under your ancestral states to see if there are additional guides.

State, County, and City Histories

Check under the category "history," and you will find a wealth of information sources. Checking under "Indiana, Greene—History" and "Indiana, Greene—History—Indexes" yields eight histories and five indexes. A warning, though:

The indexes and histories might not all match. The index might be to a history not held at the library, and the history you find might not have an index—in the book or separate. Should you still check these? Definitely. That unindexed county history might contain a mini biographical entry for your great-grandfather complete with names of his parents. You can go directly to the FHL's bookshelves for your state and county and check for the histories there. But you will miss the ones that have been microfilmed and are no longer on the open shelf. You will also miss the histories that are for multiple counties and may be shelved with a different county's books.

Land and Tax Records

The FHL has filmed many land records and indexes at both state and county jurisdictional levels. These may include grantor and grantee indexes, deeds, mortgages, and more. Early land records may be written in paragraph form and contain some wonderful details on spouses and previous places of residence. The library does not have a large collection of tax records, but this is a category worth checking for your ancestral areas. **The FHL also has online access to the Bureau of Land Management Web site, <http://www.glorecords.blm.gov>, and the land indexes there.** These are federal-level records, but the sales were made for land in specific states.

Internet Source

Military Records

Though the federal government has created thousands of military records which are available at the FHL, many others are available at the state and county level. These may include histories of specific battles, units, or groups of soldiers; indexes or rosters of soldiers; military censuses; Spanish-American War pension indexes and some state pension records; and Revolutionary War militia lists. The catalog divides the military records by several categories, including "history" and "records" and by war. For some states, including Iowa and Nebraska, the library has Grand Army of the Republic records. The library has an impressive collection of state Confederate pension records. James C. Neagles's *U.S. Military Records: A Guide to Federal and State Sources, Colonial America to the Present* is a good source to learn of possible state-level military records, as well as federal-level records. Guidebooks to doing research in a specific state also provide more details on this subject. One finding aid at the library is *Civil War Records: State & Local Sources*, in which two large binders provide the following for each state:

- a bibliography of books about the state's involvement in the Civil War
- catalog entries of state military records at the FHL
- a bibliography of county and city sources
- a list of published regimental histories

All these entries include a FHL call number, microfiche number, or microfilm number.

Naturalization Records

Many state, county, district court, or municipal naturalization records are at the FHL. Check for your geographic location under the subject "Naturalization and Citizenship." It is important to check at all these levels if you don't know the court level at which your ancestor applied for citizenship. Though the library has many of these, the majority are not at the FHL.

Some special state-level records at the FHL are the Kansas, Missouri, and North Dakota alien registration records. During the World War I era, circa 1918, many questionnaires or surveys were taken that listed U.S. residents who were not U.S. citizens. Many concentrated only on people with German heritage. Few of these records have survived, but three examples are at the FHL. Filmed at the National Archives Regional Service Center in Kansas City, these records are in the catalog under the name of the state and the subject "Naturalization and Citizenship." The content varies but may include the person's name, place of residence, former place of residence, place of birth, occupation, and employer. For some women, a maiden name is listed. For Anna Geis, for example, found in the Kansas registration records, her adopted child was listed, as were Anna's siblings, her father, and her mother (with maiden name). Some registrations contain additional material such as extensive affidavits and letters from other people. The number of aliens in these surviving records is not extensive, but the details make them worth checking.

Newspapers

While the FHL does not actively film many newspaper collections, it does have some older newspapers and many related items on microfilm. Checking under such subjects as genealogy, biography, newspaper indexes, and vital records, you may find filmed newspaper clipping files, necrology files, obituary files, newspaper vital records indexes, and general newspaper indexes. These may also appear in book or pamphlet format. The library also has many guides to newspapers that exist in other repositories.

Periodical Source Index (PERSI)

Genealogical periodicals are published by local, county, state, provincial, national, and ethnic genealogical societies. **PERSI is a topical index to thousands of articles published in most U.S. genealogical and some local history periodicals.** It is published by the Allen County Public Library Foundation of Fort Wayne, Indiana. Some of the periodicals are Canadian, and a few cover other countries. These span from the early 1800s to the present. These are mainly published at the county or state level, though some are national. PERSI has more than one million entries, and searches may be done by locality, surname, or research methodology. It is not an index to every surname appearing in the article. If the article title includes a surname, e.g., "Griffin Family Bible Records," that surname would be indexed.

PERSI leads you to the periodical in which the article appeared and gives a special code and the specific issue details. The codes are explained in PERSI. Some of the information may be cemetery transcriptions, probate indexes, mini

Printed Source

family histories, biographies, newspaper indexes, Loyalists in Canada, church record abstracts, school censuses, Polish research tips, how to find and use city directories, and updates on federal and state census indexes.

PERSI is available in the FHL in several formats, including printed volumes, microfiche, CD-ROM and online via <http://www.ancestry.com>. The FHL has an extensive collection of local, county, and state periodical current and back issues, including many of the periodicals listed in PERSI. A finding aid, usually found on the main floor in the general reference area, lists most of the periodicals the library holds, complete with FHL call numbers. The finding aid *PERSI—Codes With Corresponding FHL Call #'s* quickly leads you to the periodical at the library.

Probate Records

Most probate records are created at the county level. The FHL sometimes films case files with indexes, and other times just case files. The filmed index may cover more years than the case files at the FHL, or an existing index may not have been filmed. For many areas the probate-related materials have not been nicely gathered into probate packets, and you may need to view a variety of records, including letters of administration, wills, minutes, dockets, and decrees. All of these may not have been filmed for the same number of years. Remember to check the probate subject under the state name for some probate compilations, especially for the early years of a state's history.

Town Records

Records created at the town level, especially for New England, are numerous at the FHL. Check under your town name in the catalog. These may include birth, death, and marriage records; warnings out; and town meeting minutes. There are many printed versions at the FHL, but we suggest that whenever possible you check the microfilm of the originals to see if additional notations are made or if you decipher a name differently than the author of the printed version did.

Vital Records

You may find that the state-level vital records or indexes for your ancestral area are at the FHL. For example, the FHL has what are known as the pre-1907 birth, death, and marriage records for Wisconsin. For California the library has marriage and death indexes covering many years. For Illinois the library has the statewide marriage index and many of the county-level marriage records. For Alabama, the FHL has more than 500 rolls of death records and indexes from the state department of health. Coroners records are also under the subject "vital records" for many localities. In addition to checking the FHL Catalog under your state and county name, check Kathleen Hinckley's *Locating Lost Family Members & Friends*, which has a chart of the FHL statewide vital records holdings. The FHL has a binder titled *Vital Records* in the second-floor reference area that lists statewide vital records collections at the library.

The FHL also has some vital records from the town or city level. Examples of these are for St. Paul (in Ramsey County) and Minneapolis (in Hennepin County) in Minnesota. The FHL microfilmed the city-level birth and death records and also the county-level ones for Ramsey and Hennepin counties. This is a case where you might miss something valuable if you neglected to check the city as well as the county. You may also find some localities where you have the luxury of several governmental levels of vital records at the FHL for one locality. Chicago is one area where this is true. Depending upon the year, you may find the index under the county and the record under the city. Even when you find an entry in the index, you may still be confused by the multiple reference numbers on the certificates and not find the one you seek. A finding aid binder devoted to Chicago vital records can help you find the record you seek.

The FHL also has delayed birth records for many counties across the United States. These are listed under the category "vital records" in the catalog. For some of these, the supporting documents that were filed were also filmed.

EXAMPLES OF RECORDS

This next section details some specific state and county collections at the FHL. Our hope is that these may apply to your ancestry or spur you to check the FHL catalog for similar items in your ancestral areas. Most of these references are to microfilms of original records.

- **Arizona: Cochise and Pima Counties**
  Nine rolls of microfilm hold deeds to mines covering 1866–1903 and a deed index to these spanning 1866–1914. Find these under these localities and the category "land and property."
- **California: Lake County**
  Under "vital records" for this county are a coroner's register for 1889–1943 and inquest records covering 1867–1950. The records may also include the court transcript of the coroner's inquest. The records are on six rolls of microfilm.
- **Massachusetts: Town of Pittsfield**
  The Pittsfield town records are at the FHL. The eight microfilm rolls cover births 1761–1888 and town meeting records 1753–1890. These town records are not generally indexed, but indexed or alphabetized versions in other formats for New England towns may help you to zero in on the original entry.
- **Michigan: Jackson County**
  The FHL has marriage records covering 1833–1910 and indexes covering 1867–1964. This is a prime example of an index covering years far beyond the records at the library. These records were filmed in 1973.
- **North Carolina**
  The McCubbins collection on seventy-six rolls of microfilm contains information on many early Piedmont-area North Carolina families collected by an individual named McCubbins. The material covers more than eight thousand surnames in more than 150,000 pieces of material. With a keyword search using "McCubbins Collection" you should hit the jackpot.

This covered many early North Carolina counties and some in Tennessee. There is a rough surname guide on microfilm.

- **Ohio**
  Sixty-four rolls of microfilm comprise the index to Ohio county histories. This is a 450,000-name index compiled by members of the DAR. This is available at the FHL, as are most of the county histories.

- **Oklahoma: Ellis County**
  The FHL filmed school district enumeration reports, 1912–1936. These school censuses vary from year to year, but most contain the students' names and age or grade, parents' or guardians' names, and all school-age children in the family. For this entry, as with many other entries, the FHL catalog also tells when the county was formed and from what previous counties.

- **Oregon**
  Members of the Genealogical Forum of Oregon have compiled a Soundex to the previously unindexed 1910 Oregon federal population census. It was filmed by the FHL.

- **Vermont: City of Rutland**
  This is an example of early church records, covering 1817–1928 for Trinity Episcopal Church. The records include baptisms, records of families, confirmations, marriages, burials, communicants, and some church history. These were not filmed in Rutland, but at the Episcopal Diocesan Center in Burlington, Vermont.

- **Virginia**
  Applications for the relief of needy Confederate women, 1915–1967, is an indexed set of records on twenty-seven rolls of microfilm. It also includes sisters and daughters of Confederate soldiers, sailors, and marines. The soldier's name, the condition of the woman, her birthdate, and her place of residence are given. These are found under the locality "Virginia" and the subject "military records—Civil War, 1861–1865—pensions."

- **Wisconsin: St. Croix County and Others**
  Among the sources cataloged for St. Croix County is a newspaper index that covers Burnett, Pierce, Polk, St. Croix, and Washburn counties. This is a wonderful index to births, deaths, marriages, and other events covering many years. It was filmed in 1980. Researchers using this material might be interested that in the intervening years the staff and volunteers at the Area Research Center at the University of Wisconsin in River Falls, Wisconsin, have made many additions to this index.

TEN

Records of the World

This chapter covers many of the collections that the Family History Library holds for countries other than the United States. An indication of the scope of the holdings is that the FHL has records for more than 150 countries. The records for many of the countries discussed in this chapter are in microform, and some others are in books. There may also be family histories and ethnic genealogical society periodicals related to the country you are researching. Filming and cataloging of records is ongoing in some of these countries, so we suggest you periodically check the catalog to see what records have been added. You may also find some new compiled indexes or abstracts added since the last time you checked the FHL catalog.

SCOPE AND ACCESSIBILITY

This chapter is an overview of the FHL record holdings for the many countries represented in the FHL collection. **You should become familiar with the catalog entries for your ancestral country and its different geographical divisions to determine all the possible records for your research.** For many of these countries, with their boundary changes, political strife, economic problems, and record access difficulties, it is easier to research your ancestry at the FHL rather than in that country. The FHL materials for many of these countries represent more than you may have access to on-site in a country or records that no longer exist in their original format. The bulk of the records at the FHL for these countries cover the eighteenth and nineteenth centuries, but there are some for the twentieth century and others prior to 1700.

The volume of records at the FHL varies from country to country. Be sure to check under a variety of locality jurisdictions including country, province, district, canton, state, duchy, county, parish, village, or other division. For example, you know your ancestral parish in Sweden is Östraby which is in Malmöhus. If you check under "Sweden" or "Malmöhus" in the catalog, you will find many valuable topics and indexes including church records, but you won't find the ancestral parish. Church records are a topic for these localities, but you still don't see your parish name under that topic. You should research

Research Tip

in the items under these other localities in case you find some additional family details, but you still want the actual parish registers for Östraby. Check under "Östraby" in the place category of the catalog search to zero in on the actual parish registers. Now, go back and use the keyword search for "Östraby," and this will yield not only the parish registers but some civil censuses.

At some point in time, your ancestral town or county may have been under the jurisdiction of another county or country. This may be the case for colonies or territories. Fortunately, the FHL has many maps to show this, and often the FHL Catalog points out jurisdictional changes.

GUIDEBOOKS

Appendix B lists guidebooks for specific countries and types of ethnic research. These are important companions to your research. Ethnic genealogical periodicals continue to carry articles about the research techniques and resources for a particular ethnic group. These may contain details on determining the specific geographic locality to help find an item in the catalog. Many explain the historical background, explain boundary changes, and record jurisdictional changes by time period.

For More Info

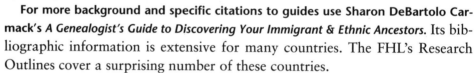

For more background and specific citations to guides use Sharon DeBartolo Carmack's *A Genealogist's Guide to Discovering Your Immigrant & Ethnic Ancestors.* Its bibliographic information is extensive for many countries. The FHL's Research Outlines cover a surprising number of these countries.

For many countries, you will find references and resources similar to those used for U.S. research. This includes biographical compendiums, histories, family histories and records such as military, census, cemetery, church, probate, and vital statistics (birth, death, and marriage). To better understand the boundary, record-keeping, and language changes, it is helpful to read one or more histories of the country and of your specific ancestral area in that country.

LANGUAGES, HANDWRITING, AND NAMES

You will find many records at the FHL in languages that you do not read or speak. The library has word lists to aid in the translation of these records. These are on the FamilySearch Web site, on microfiche, and in the reference areas in the library. You may also purchase word lists near the copy centers on each floor and at the Distribution Center. When working on-site in the library you will find dictionaries in a variety of languages to aid in your translating. The reference counter staff may be able to translate portions of records you have found on microfilm, so you will know if you have located the correct entries.

The records may also be those of a country with a patronymic naming system. This varies some, but an example is that your Scandinavian Anderson family may not always be Anderson from generation to generation. For example, your Johann Anderson may be the son of Anders Carlsson. Thus, the child's (Johann's) name is Anders son. Anders Carlsson is the son of a man named Carl. The women in some Scandinavian records may be Andersdatter, "daughter of Anders."

KEY WORDS

To find and use specific types of Swedish records, you will need to know some key words in Swedish. This section lists key genealogical terms in English and the Swedish words with the same or similar meanings.

For example, in the first column you will find the English word *marriage*. In the second column you will find Swedish words with meanings such as *marry, marriage, wedding, wedlock, unite, legitimate, joined,* and other words used in Swedish records to indicate marriage.

English	Swedish
banns	lysning
birth	födda, födde, född, födelse
burial	begravning
child	barn
christening	döpta, döpte, döpt, döpelse, dop
clerical survey	husförhörslängd
confirmation	konfirmation
death	döda, döde, död, avliden, avsomna
father	far, fader
female	kvinnkjön, kvinna
household examination roll	husförhörslängd, förhör
husband	man, make
index	register
male	mankjön, man
marriage	vigda, vigde, vigd, vigsel, gift, gifte, giftermål, bröllop, brudfolk
military	militär, soldat
mother	mor, moder
moving in	inflyttning
moving out	utflyttning
name, given	förnamn
name, surname	efternamn
parents	föräldrar
parish	socken, församling, kommun
probate	boupptekning
wife	hustru, maka
year	år

GENERAL WORD LIST

This general word list includes words commonly seen in genealogical sources. Numbers, months, and days of the week are listed both here and in separate sections that follow this list.

In this list, optional versions of Swedish words or variable endings are given in parentheses. Parentheses in the English column clarify the definition.

Swedish	English
A	
adel	nobility
adelsman	nobleman
aderton(de)	eighteen (eighteenth)
adlig	noble
adopterad	adopted
adress	address
adressbok	directory
afton	evening
aldrig	never
alla, allt	all
alltid	always
andra	second, others
andtäppa	shortness of breath, asthma
anfall	seizure(s)
angiven	given, stated
ankom	came, arrived
anmärkningar	remarks, annotations
annan	other
antavla	pedigree chart
april	April
arbetare	worker, laborer
arkiv	archive
arrendator	tenant farmer, leaseholder
arton	eighteen
arv	inheritance
arvinge	heir
arvskifte	distribution of an inherited estate
att	that (know *that* he died)
attest	certificate
augusti	August
av	of
avgift	fee
avgång	departure
avgått	moved
avgått med döden	died (departed through death)
avliden	deceased, death
avskedad	discharged, resigned
avsomna	die, death
B	
backe	hill
backstugusittare	one who owned a small cottage, dugout dweller
bagare	baker
bakom	behind
baptist	Baptist
bar	carried
bara	only
bar barnet	carried or held the child (at baptism font)
barn	child(ren)
barnbarn	grandchild(ren)

Figure 10-1

A portion of a word list from the FHL's Swedish genealogical word list.

Reprinted by permission. Copyright © 1999–2000 by Intellectual Reserve, Inc.

TRANSLATION TIP

The reference counter staff may be able to translate portions of some records you have found on microfilm, so you will know if you have located the correct entries. The entries may help you link your ancestor to his or her parents. Simply take both reels of a film to the reference counter, ask for assistance, and place the reels on the reader at the counter so the staff member can read the entry.

Records may be written in the national language of the country for the time period or that of the religious denomination. For example, the German Catholic church records you check may be written in Latin rather than a Germanic language. The same may be true for records in the country to which those ancestors migrated. Swedish church records in Minnesota may be written in Swedish rather than English, the language of the new country.

This is all going to make you wish you had paid attention to that strange language Great-Grandma Tillie spoke. Many genealogists take language classes so they will have some familiarity with the languages used in the records of their ancestral lands.

Are you ready to tackle those foreign-language records? One more obstacle may arise: the handwriting. It may be an older style or a Gothic script or print that requires special study. There may be phrasing or words that were common at the time the records were written but are little understood today. Refer back to the word lists and guidebooks.

SOME AIDS TO READING FOREIGN LANGUAGES AND DECIPHERING HANDWRITING

- Johnson, Arta F. *How to Read German Church Records Without Knowing Much German.*

- Shea, Jonathan D. and William D. Hoffman. *Following the Paper Trail: A Multilingual Translation Guide.* (This covers many languages—German, Swedish, French, Italian, Latin, Portuguese, Romanian, Spanish, Czech, Polish, Russian, Lithuanian with name examples, vocabulary, record examples, and tips.)

- Sperry, Kip. *Reading Early American Handwriting.*

TAPPING THE EXPERIENCE OF OTHERS

The hundreds of ethnic historical and genealogical societies may provide the assistance you need to research your family. For example, if you have never done Norwegian research, join a Norwegian genealogical society or special interest group. Via the meetings, classes, and publications of these organizations you can become familiar with the records, the language, and the methodology for researching in a different country. Do the same thing for your Czech, Irish, Jewish, or other research. The publications, Web site <http://feefhs.org>, and conferences of the Federation of East European Family History Societies are wonderful aids. Ethnic-based organizations often have seminars or workshops which provide specialized guidance from others who have experienced working with the records you are just learning to use.

Don't forget to use the International Genealogical Index and Ancestral File, both discussed earlier in this guide. Many countries have significant ancestral information indexed in these two resources. England, Scotland, and Sweden are prime examples of countries that are well represented in these.

FOREIGN RESOURCES AT THE FHL

Below is a list of many of the countries/areas for which the FHL has microform records and/or books. These are the current or commonly known names of the countries or areas. For some countries the library has been able to microfilm extensively in both church and civil records. In others permission has been granted for only a small segment of records.

Antarctica	Croatia	Italy	Romania
Argentina	Denmark	Korea	Russia
Armenia	England	Latin America	Samoa
Australia	Estonia	Latvia	Scotland
Austria	Ethiopia	Lithuania	Silesia
Bahamas	Finland	Luxembourg	Slovakia
Belarus	France	Mexico	Slovenia
Belgium	Germany	Moldova	South Africa
Brazil	Greece	Netherlands	Spain
Canada	Gruziya	New Zealand	Sri Lanka
Channel	(Georgia)	Norway	Sweden
Islands	Hungary	Philippines	Switzerland
Chile	Iceland	Poland	Ukraine
China	Ireland	Portugal	Venezuela
Congo (Zaire)	Isle of Man	Puerto Rico	Wales

Atlases, Gazetteers, and Maps

The FHL has atlases, gazetteers, and maps from many countries on floors B1 and B2. Canadian maps are on the main floor. Some are flat maps accessible in the map cabinets, others are in book form on reference shelves, and still others have been microfilmed. Use the FHL Catalog to make sure you are not missing any pertinent geographical finding aids. Some of these will clearly delineate boundary changes over many decades or centuries, which will help you determine the correct place name and boundaries for your ancestral era in that country. Many maps are reproduced in binders and

Reminder

LOCATION REMINDER FOR NON-U.S. RECORDS

Main Floor and Second Floor: Canada.

B1 (sublevel or basement 1): International (Scandinavia, Asia, Africa, Latin America, eastern Europe, Germanic areas, and others). The International floor houses the collections for the majority of the countries listed on page 97.

B2 (sublevel or basement 2): British Isles, Australia, New Zealand

---

bound volumes; a number of these have specific parish/county/civil/ecclesiastical borders clearly marked. These are usually found in the general reference areas on each floor.

Census

Researchers accustomed to working with federal censuses for the United States may be disappointed when they check for national-level censuses for other countries. They are not as numerous, and many that were taken have not survived. There are some wonderful exceptions. It is possible to find some censuses for other countries that list religion, wife's or mother's maiden name, and place of birth for each person on the census record. Look in the general finding aids for your country of interest on floors B1 and B2 to see what is listed for census records. Check in the catalog under the subject "census" for all of your area's jurisdictional levels.

Church Records

The church record content and comprehensiveness varies from country to country and often by locality and religious denomination. Some church records at the FHL are only transcripts or extracts. Collections may consist of records such as baptism, marriage, burial, session minutes, dismissals, and transfers, while others may include only written minutes. Don't let your ancestor's religion in one place of residence fool you. A migrating ancestor may have chosen a new religion for a variety of reasons.

Family Histories and Surname Periodicals

As noted in chapter eight, the FHL has an extensive collection of published family histories spanning many geographic localities and nationalities. Those with primarily a foreign connection are not as numerous as those with heavy U.S. emphasis. There may also be a surname periodical for one of your ancestral names. The books and surname periodicals in printed form for all countries are housed in the Joseph Smith Memorial Building on the fourth floor. A significant number of these have also been microfilmed or microfiched, and some may no longer be available in printed format. Those that are available on film or fiche are found on either floor B1 or B2, depending upon the country connection.

Passenger Departure Records

A short list of ports from which passengers departed to another country include Antwerp, Bergen, Bremen, Göteborg, LeHavre, Lisbon, Trondheim, Liverpool, Malmö, and Naples. Passenger departure lists for these ports have not all survived or even been compiled. (You'll probably have better luck with U.S. arrival lists.) Many countries may not have kept specific passenger departure lists, but may have required a type of registration with local authorities for both permanent and transient residents. Some of these are called "police lists" or "registers." The FHL has many departure and registration records. Check under city, port, and country names to find these, or consult the in-house finding aids.

An example of passenger departure records that still exist are the Hamburg Emigration Lists and Indexes covering 1850–1934. These are on film, and the FHL has those films, finding aids, and a Research Outline. Hamburg was a German port but many people from central and eastern Europe departed from this port. The departure lists are more likely to be written by someone who understood the language of the passenger, whereas those compiled in, or on the way to, the new country are more subject to language barriers.

Vital Records

Vital records from many localities in Canada, Germany, Hungary, Poland, Scotland, and other countries are available at the FHL. In some countries these are called "civil registrations," and you may find some records cataloged under either that category or vital records. The content and years of coverage vary widely from one country to the next. Guidebooks about doing research in the records of a specific country may specify the years of coverage.

FOREIGN AND ETHNIC RECORDS

Armenia

The FHL has filmed all Armenian Orthodox church books. Some Armenian church records in Azerbaijan, Georgia, Russia, Ukraine, and Turkey have also been filmed. Some other types of Armenian records have also been filmed covering the years 1795–1811.

Australia

The FHL has many Australian civil, church, cemetery, and probate records. Many of these include extensive indexes. As with other countries, it is important to check at several jurisdictional levels. An example would be to check under Australia, under New South Wales, and under the town of Appin to find all records that might apply to your family in the town of Appin. Under Appin you will find only cemeteries and church records, but under New South Wales you will find guidebooks, cemeteries, census records, church records, civil registration, correctional institutions, court records, genealogies, histories, military records, naturalization records, pensions, probates, vital records, and many more types of records. The library's Research Outline *Australia* is very helpful.

Belarus

Many Jewish, Roman Catholic, and Russian Orthodox church records have been filmed. The FHL has records cataloged under twenty-six topics for Belarus including Revision Lists (taxable persons), biographical and genealogical materials, and a newspaper bibliography.

Canada

The FHL has a wide variety of materials in both microform and book format for Canada. These include Canadian censuses up through 1901 and church, land, probate, and other records. There are not many Canadian census indexes, but the library collects all those it can. The content and breadth of the collection varies greatly from province to province. For example, the collection of Quebec church records for both Roman Catholics and Protestants is excellent. There are many church records for Ontario, but they are not nearly as comprehensive as for Quebec. Researchers with Canadian Loyalist connections will not be disappointed on this subject at the FHL. The collection of Ontario vital records is excellent. The library has a binder of finding aids for these vital records. The overall amount of records available is less for the western provinces, but this is a growing segment.

Croatia

A large collection of Greek Catholic, Jewish, Roman Catholic, and Serbian Orthodox church records in what is now called Croatia is available. The FHL Catalog coverage for Croatia includes more than thirty topics.

Denmark

The FHL collection of Danish census records, parish registers, probate records, and military records is extensive. Your search will also be helped by land records, emigration registers, and some civil registrations. A helpful guidebook is Frank Smith and Finn Thomsen's *Genealogical Guidebook & Atlas of Denmark*. The maps and parish lists are important to your research. With the information listed in Danish parish records it is often possible to track most families from parish to parish as they moved or married someone in another parish. The FHL has several in-house finding aids for Danish research. One is a binder labeled "Copenhagen and Denmark Major Record Collections" that has sections including the Copenhagen Police Census and Danish Chancelry Records; another binder has general information related to Danish research.

England (see also "Great Britain")

The FHL has a particularly strong collection for England. This includes records of civil registration (1837 and forward), censuses (up through 1891 with a name index for all of 1881), churches (particularly Church of England), military, occupations, probate, genealogical collections, quarter sessions, and many others. The catalog has almost five hundred topics for England; this figure does not include all the resources cataloged by town, city, or county name! Paul Milner and Linda Jonas comment in their *Genealogist's Guide to Discovering*

Your English Ancestors that it is easier to trace your English ancestry outside of England than in England. This is only one of many guides that have been published about English research and records.

The library's finding aids for the English collection on floor B2 are extensive. One such aid has maps that clearly show all the parishes in an area with boundaries marked. This enables the researcher to quickly get an idea of alternate parishes to check for ancestral records. This important finding aid is commonly called the "Phillimore's Index"; the full title is *The Phillimore Atlas and Index of Parish Registers*. In this you will find Church of England parishes in England, what parish registers exist, and where you might find them. Many more registers and indexes related to parish and other records are available. Milner and Jonas's guide is a good source for details on these.

One unique finding aid is *Smith's Inventory of Genealogical Sources* compiled by Frank Smith and many volunteers. The English portion is strong. This aid references genealogical data buried in hundreds of items at the FHL. Normally, these references don't appear in the FHL Catalog, as they are not always in the main description of a book or microfilm. This is one of those in-house finding aids that also is on microfiche, so it is available through Family History Centers.

English records and finding aids have been the topic of many lectures at national-level genealogy conferences. Audiotapes of many of these lectures are available, and the syllabus material is found in many major libraries.

The FHL no longer offers the opportunity to order copies of civil registration certificates. Due to the high cost of this service, it has been discontinued. The FHL still has the civil registration indexes on microfilm and microfiche. You need to order the copies via mail or the Internet from the Office for National Statistics. You will find a list of record agents in England available at the FHL. These agents may be able to obtain the certificates for you faster.

Estonia

Many Lutheran and Russian Orthodox church records have been filmed; some are record extracts. A portion of the Lutheran records extends well into the twentieth century. Some court records have been filmed. Guild books for Tallinn, which have records on urban tradesmen and their families, are also available.

Finland

Church, census, probate, school, and land records are just some of the records for Finland at the FHL. Finland took clerical surveys, basically household censuses, which help determine past and subsequent parishes, dates of arrival and moving, and even your ancestor's knowledge of his or her catechism. These surveys were taken annually. Karen Clifford wrote an interesting, helpful, and hopeful article on Finnish research, "The Best Finnish," in the *Genealogical Journal* in 1999. Yes, the title is spelled correctly. You will have to read the article to find out why. The FHL has a finding aid labeled "Finland Misc. Information" which includes sections on archives, parishes, maps, emigration, and vocabulary.

Germany

This is a prime example of a county where the history and boundary changes are important to genealogical research. The FHL has varying amounts of records and years of coverage for geographic areas that have been known as part of Germany. There are civil registrations, church records, family records, military records, passenger departure records, and more. While extensive filming has been done in Germany, not all areas are easily researched due to filming prohibitions or record destruction.

The changes in boundaries as to what constituted Germany used to present more of a problem in the research process. The keyword search capability of the computer catalog makes it easier to find records which may be cataloged under a different country even though the areas were once part of the German Empire. You may find that your German ancestral area is now part of France or Poland and thus may be cataloged as such since the original records are generally housed there. If the catalog description does not reference the various name changes for the locality, you will not be able to easily find the needed records. Gazetteers must be consulted. The catalog uses the spelling of German place names as found in a helpful gazetteer commonly called *Meyers Orts*. The FHL has a guide titled *How to Use the Meyers Gazetteer* that is helpful. Not all German place names are in this gazetteer; others may need to be consulted.

The FHL's Research Outline for Germany is more comprehensive than some others and is a good tool. The FHL finding aids for Germany are helpful, especially for the Hamburg passenger lists discussed earlier in this chapter. Appendix B lists several guidebooks that are quite detailed. *Germanic Genealogy: A Guide to Worldwide Sources and Migration Patterns* discusses other countries with Germanic peoples and their records.

One set of Germanic records at the FHL is *Die Ahnenstammkartei des Deutschen Volkes* on more than 1,200 rolls of film. These are collected family histories of people from Germanic and central European countries. These have been collected in the twentieth century and are mainly in the form of pedigree charts and family group records. A card index of almost three million names is in a rough phonetic order. A separate register has been compiled by Thomas Edlund to these records since the rolls of film were not done in order. The FHL Catalog has an extensive entry describing the records and the idiosyncrasies of them. The catalog entry is found via title or subject search or by place search under "Germany—genealogy" or "Europe—genealogy." Checking under a variety of Germanic localities may yield other compiled genealogical collections.

Great Britain

An every-name index exists for the 1881 census that covers England, Scotland, Wales, Channel Islands, and the Isle of Man. Over thirty million individuals are indexed. This database is on twenty-five compact discs and is divided into regions. Not only does the index on CD search for the name you enter, it searches for common variations. It is more than what we usually find in an index. It is actually a transcription of the entry. Information includes name, age, sex, relationship, marital status, occupation, and where born (parish and county). Another version is on microfiche. For more details on these valuable indexes see Milner and Jonas's *Genealogist's Guide to Discovering Your English Ancestors*, pages 90–99. This census asked for place of birth, and often a very specific place name is listed. When checking for any of the British countries in addition to checking the catalog under the individual country name be sure to check under Great Britain for some additional collections. The general reference area on B2 has extensive finding aids for the British Isles. The Federation of Genealogical Societies' *Forum* has carried a series of articles by Dean Hunter on the growth of the British Collection at the FHL. A list of these articles is in appendix B.

Hungary

Most church records are available, as are many civil registers. The collection also includes censuses, histories, land records, and probate records. As with so many of the countries listed in this chapter, present-day Hungary has very different boundaries than it did in the nineteenth century. For a locality once in Hungary you may have to search today in records cataloged under Slovakia, Romania, and others.

Ireland

You will find numerous helpful Irish records at the FHL. Yes, records were destroyed in a 1922 fire at the Public Record Office in Dublin, Ireland, but not all records were there. According to Dean Hunter, collection development specialist at the FHL, filming has been done at locations in Ireland such as Registry of Deeds, Public Record Office in Dublin (now National Archives), Trinity College Library, General Register Offices in Dublin and Belfast, Public Record Office in Northern Ireland, Linenhall Library, Newry Public Library, Valuation Office, Limerick County Archives, Leitrim County Library, and various Catholic dioceses. The number of films of Irish records has surpassed 15,000, and there are almost 3,500 fiche. The Irish books total almost 4,000. The specific record topics include biographies, censuses, civil registrations of births and deaths (beginning in 1864), civil marriage registrations as early as 1845, tax records, records for many Roman Catholic dioceses, and a few records for Church of Ireland and some other denominations. Other categories include land records, probate records, finding aids, and a variety of materials cataloged under the subject "genealogy." These are just the topics at the country level. Additional topics and specific records are under the county name, such as Kerry, which yields twenty-seven entries including cemetery transcriptions, genealogy collections, newspaper clippings, and histories.

One helpful record is the "Calendars of Grants of Probate and Letters of Administration Made in the Principal Registry and in the Several District Registries 1858–1920." Each volume contains valuable information for each grant of probate: name, address, and occupation of the deceased; the dates of probate and registry; the date and place of death; the name and address of the executor or executrix; and the value of the estate. These were filmed at the Dublin Public Record Office. You can also check under the county name for probate-related records. The FHL has the Griffith's Valuation and related records. A guidebook by James Reilly,

Richard Griffith and His Valuations of Ireland is an important tool for using these. The FHL also has other finding aids related to these taxation records.

Appendix B lists several helpful Irish guidebooks, including one by Dwight Radford and Kyle Betit: *A Genealogist's Guide to Discovering Your Irish Ancestors*. This goes beyond describing many Irish records (many of which are at the FHL) to covering several other countries to which Irish people migrated.

Italy

The majority of the records at the FHL for Italy cover 1809–1865, though for some places the records cover earlier or later nineteenth-century dates. The important jurisdictions for searches are town or parish, province, region, and country. The microfilmed records include civil registrations of birth, death, and marriage; military records, church records, and notarial records. The type of record and years of coverage varies greatly from one place to another.

Jewish

Jewish research may involve many countries of origin. The FHL now has a CD-ROM catalog of all Jewish records on film, microfiche, and in books at the library with searches by categories and locations. Another version is now online at <http://www.jewishgen.org/databases/fhlc/>. Additional Jewish record areas at the FHL include dictionaries, emigration and immigration, encyclopedias, Holocaust, Inquisition, Memorial or Yizkor Books (history and memorial books), military, and names. Extensive finding aid binders for Jewish records appear on all research floors at the FHL.

An overview of some unusual Jewish records at the FHL was in the Spring 2000 issue of *Avotaynu: The International Review of Jewish Genealogy*. This periodical is important for updates on Jewish records in many countries with extensive coverage of records found at the FHL. Most researchers should read current and back issues of *Avotaynu*, as numerous articles in these cover the filming and availability of records pertaining to many ethnic backgrounds.

Lithuania

Old Believer, Orthodox, Lutheran, Reformed, and Greek Catholic church records from the Central Historical Archive have been filmed. The library has also been filming Jewish vital records that are located at the Lithuanian State Archives in Vilnius.

Medieval Section

The library's medieval reference section has been revived. For referral to the staff handling this section check with the British Reference Counter (on floor B2). The staff will be able to share previous research with you, point you to other authoritative resources, and answer basic questions.

Mexico

Mexico is just one of many Hispanic countries for which the FHL holds books and microforms. This includes many civil and church records; some records date well into the twentieth century. Censuses with extensive family information exist for the early nineteenth century for some localities. Your locality may have biographical, census, church, history, genealogical, map, military, probate, and other records. Check under the country, the state, and the town for records. One excellent guidebook for Mexican and other Hispanic research is George Ryskamp's *Finding Your Hispanic Roots*. It covers many records available at the FHL. Check the FHL's Research Outline on Mexico for other information; it was updated in 2000.

Norway

The FHL has census, church, probate, military, emigration, land, and other records for Norway. A unique type of record for Norwegian research is the *bygdebøker*, or rural farm books. The FHL holds many of these, and they include genealogies of farm families. In addition to the patronymic naming system, many families adopted the farm name. Some records for individuals are at the county and parish level. For larger cities and towns, the FHL may hold directories and biographical compilations. As with many countries, the church records may detail your ancestor's arrival and departure from the parish and may even list the U.S. place where your ancestor intended to emigrate.

Poland

Poland is one of those countries that has been there and then it hasn't. If you know the general area where your Polish ancestors were from, you may be able to find some records at the FHL. Poland is also a country whose records may cover what was originally located in another country. Many Catholic church records are filmed, and if your probable parish is not filmed, you may have neighboring parishes to check. A smaller, but still helpful, collection of Germanic related parishes that are Evangelical or Reformed have been filmed. As in many eastern European countries with changing histories and boundaries, the in-house FHL finding aids and Polish genealogical societies and publications are vital in your research process. These will help you to zero in on and understand other Polish-related records that are available at the FHL.

Russia

Many Russian Orthodox records have been filmed from a variety of areas, and some Lutheran records are available. There are almost 150 categories of records in the catalog for the Russian Empire. The catalog connects to almost this number of other localities within Russia for which the FHL has some records.

Scotland

For Scotland the research is a bit easier for some of us, as many of the records are written in English. The collection includes census records covering 1841–1891, civil registration from 1855, Church of Scotland records, probate records, land records, biographies, and genealogies, to name just a few. Scottish church records (as for some other countries) are quite straightforward when reporting on dismissing members or baptizing an illegitimate child.

One of the best Scottish resources is the collection of the Church of Scotland Old Parish Registers. These have been indexed as the OPR Index on microfiche; the index covers the late 1500s through the end of 1854. FamilySearch in the library includes a computerized version. Might these help you? You may find an ancestor in this index (of more than ten million people) which has several search field capabilities.

South Africa

The FHL has microfilmed church registers for various locations in South Africa. As with most countries, to begin your search you will need to know the location where an ancestor resided. These church records include such vital information as births, baptisms, marriages, deaths, and burials. You may also find the names of parents, godparents, and witnesses and transfers in and out of the congregation. Many nationalities settled in South Africa, and others fought various military battles there. Many civil registration records and probate records have been microfilmed, and these are just two of ninety record categories for South Africa at the FHL.

Sweden

Church, military, and probate are just three of the important Swedish record types at the FHL. The clerical survey records in the church records, generally taken every year, offer a picture of the household. All names should be listed, including nonrelatives. You may learn when someone came to and departed from a parish, complete with the new or former parish name. These are interesting records, as they examine your ancestor's religious knowledge. Other parts of the church record include the christenings, marriages, burials, confirmations, and further record of the person's arrival and departure from the parish. Some civil registrations are at the library, as are census, land, and emigration records.

Switzerland

The collection of church registers is extensive. As with Sweden, Switzerland took clerical censuses of families; some are called "household registers." Many collections of compiled family information are at the FHL. For researchers accustomed to checking under the county jurisdiction, the canton geographic designation is a change. The FHL has some notarial records for parts of Switzerland.

Ukraine

Many Russian Orthodox church records have been filmed, as have some for other religions including Greek Catholic.

WHERE IS MY COUNTRY?

At this point, some of you are saying, "They didn't even cover my ancestral country." Check that long list at the beginning of the chapter and remember that the library collection includes more than 150 countries. There simply isn't space to cover them all, or even just those that have extensive records at the FHL, in a general guidebook. Maybe you can write an article or guidebook on research related to your ancestral country.

PART FOUR

Researching On-
Site at the Family
History Library

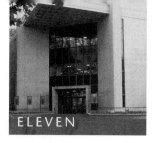

ELEVEN

The Family History Library Building

Figure 11-1
Sketch of Family History Library © *1995 Patrick W. Warren*

W hat is a major tourist attraction in Utah? The Family History Library is. Located on West Temple Street between North and South Temple Streets in downtown Salt Lake City, it is across the street from Temple Square, the number one tourist attraction in Utah. The entrance to the FHL's modern building, opened in 1985, is in the middle of the block. The library has three floors above ground and two below ground; four of these five floors are open to researchers. There is no charge to use the library and its collections.

As you enter the library, you find a large lobby area that has stairways and elevators to all floors. In this lobby are a general information counter, a security

LIBRARY ADDRESS AND CONTACT INFORMATION

Many items such as class schedules, hours, donation information, and more are also available at <http://www.familysearch.org>.

Family History Library
35 North West Temple St.
Salt Lake City, UT 84150-3400

Helpful Telephone Numbers (all area code 801 unless otherwise indicated)
General information: 240-2331 or (800) 453-3860, ext. 2-2331
Fax (general information): 240-5551
Class schedules: 240-1430
Emergency patron contact: (800) 453-3860, ext. 2-3702
Family History Center locations: (800) 346-6044 or (800) 453-3860, ext. 2-1054
Gifts and donations: 240-2337
Group arrangements: 240-1054
Media contact: 240-1054
Publications: 240-1430

Research Questions
FamilySearch: 240-2584
British Isles, Australia, and New Zealand: 240-2367
United States and Canada: 240-2364
International: 240-3433
Research questions fax: 240-1584
Research questions e-mail: fhl@ldschurch.org
TDD: 240-2616

Web site: http://www.familysearch.org

counter, and an exit security desk. A staff person sits at the latter at all times in case someone sets off the exit alarm system, which alerts the staff to the possibility of someone leaving with a book or microform that should remain in the library. The collection materials are security encoded.

All floors except the third floor are open to the public. Each of the public research floors has a reference counter, computer workstations, a copy center, a copy card dispenser, computer catalogs, atlases and maps, worktables, a library attendant's window, rest rooms, lockers, coatracks, and drinking fountains. Three floors have microfilms and microfilm readers. All four research floors have microfiche and microfiche readers. The third floor is the library administrative and cataloging area.

The library, the library grounds, and Temple Square are nonsmoking environments.

LIBRARY HOURS

Monday: 7:30 A.M.–5:00 P.M.
Tuesday–Saturday: 7:30 A.M.–10:00 P.M.
Sunday: Closed

Holiday Closings (Be sure to verify, as these sometimes change from year to year. The library occasionally is closed for more than one day for a holiday and may close early preceding a holiday):

January 1, New Year's Day
July 4, Independence Day
July 24, Pioneer Day (subject to change)
Fourth Thursday of November, Thanksgiving
December 25, Christmas Day

We wrote this chapter as the library was undergoing changes that will impact some locations described. This presented a challenge; a crystal ball might have helped. The subjects are in alphabetical order to make it easier to locate specific topics.

Assistance

Go to the reference counters on each floor to get research guidance. The library attendant windows on each floor are for getting assistance with equipment problems, inquiring about missing library materials, and paying for purchases. The windows are also for requesting restricted microfilms and microfiche. See "Library Attendant Windows" and "Reference Counters" later in this chapter.

Automated Resource Center

CD Source

The CD-ROM collection and online computer access formerly housed in the Automated Resource Center on the main floor of the library have been integrated into a network that is accessible from computer workstations throughout the library. This means access via all computer terminals, not via the individual CD. Those CD-ROMs for which the library could not get networking permission are housed on the appropriate floor for the their subject geographic location.

Bulletin Boards

Each floor has one or more bulletin boards where special notices of genealogical nature are posted. To have a notice posted, stop at the reference counters or the information desk in the main lobby to get the current contact number to obtain permission.

Cafeteria Passes

The Church Office Building, located about two blocks from the library at 50 East North Temple, has a large cafeteria on the lower level. It is accessible

---

GENERAL LIBRARY LOCATOR

Note: Don't be surprised if things move around in the library! The library is growing and adjusting to better serve patrons. Other chapters in this book give more specific details about the records on each floor.

Main Floor: U.S. and Canada floor with a copy center, reference counter, basic reference books, library finding aids, maps, computer workstations, and the snack room.

Second Floor: U.S. and Canada microfilms and microfiche, many microform readers, a copy center, reference counter, frequently consulted reference books, library finding aids, and computer workstations.

Third Floor: Administration and staff offices, cataloging unit, and library donations section.

Basement 1 (B1): International floor with coverage of Germanic, Scandinavian, western and eastern European, Asian, Latin American, and other countries and areas in microfilm and microfiche. Many microform readers, a copy center, reference counter, library finding aids, reference books, maps and computer workstations.

Basement 2 (B2): British Isles, Australia, and New Zealand microfilms and microfiche, many microform readers, copy center, reference counter, library finding aids, reference books, maps, and computer workstations.

---

by stairs and elevators. It features many food choices including hot entrees, hamburgers, sandwiches, frozen yogurt, fruit, prepared salads, and a salad bar. The main entree choices change daily. By 11:45 A.M. each day the cafeteria is usually quite crowded with Church employees. Library patrons may obtain a daily or weekly pass that allows them to purchase meals here. These passes are available at the exit desk in the library's main lobby. For more information about the cafeteria see chapter nineteen of this guide.

Census (United States)

For many years the second floor of the library has housed a separate area of U.S. federal census and Soundex microfilms. Many shelves of printed statewide indexes to these are nearby. As the availability of digitized census images and electronic census indexes increases, there will not be a need for a dedicated U.S. census film area in the library. The library will add more online census sources at individual workstations to use in place of the census microfilms. For those of you who prefer using the censuses on microfilm and checking printed indexes, the films and books will be integrated into the regular book and film collections.

Change Machines

With the introduction of copy cards as a means of paying for photocopies, the need for change machines throughout the library has diminished. You will need to bring U.S. paper money to purchase these cards. The library attendants may be able to break larger bills if it won't deplete their cash on hand. The snack room has a change machine to provide change for the vending machines and telephones. Our suggestion is to bring extra one- and five-dollar (U.S.) bills.

Classes

The library has classrooms where staff members teach free classes on a variety of helpful topics including using the library catalog and databases, researching a specific state or country, and using a particular record type. These classrooms may occasionally be reserved by visiting groups, as discussed in chapter fifteen. Class schedules are posted on each floor near the elevators, and copies are available at the information desk in the main lobby. Shortly before the class is to begin a reminder is given over the public-address system. Current class schedules are available on the library's Web site.

Collection Housing and Identification

Unlike most genealogical libraries, the FHL collection is self-service, with books on open shelves and microfilm and microfiche in patron-accessible cabinets. A small segment of the materials is in storage. Finding the material you need for research is relatively easy once you identify the call number and proper floor from the catalog. The aisles of books are designated by the range of call numbers located in a specific aisle, and the sign lists the countries or U.S. states included in that aisle. Within an aisle, signs mark the beginning of a section for a specific country or U.S. state. Within the countries and states, additional signs designate specific areas or counties.

Each row of microfilm cabinets has a sign indicating the range of film numbers located in that particular aisle. Additionally, labels on each individual drawer of microfilm list the numbers of the first and last boxes of microfilm in that drawer. The microfiche are stored in separate cabinets similarly labeled with the first and last microfiche numbers in each drawer.

Computer Workstations

Numerous computer workstations are available on each floor. The computers, all upgraded, now total 160. Many are adapted to left-hand users. They provide individual access to the library catalog, the FamilySearch databases, and the Internet. Many non-FHL CD-ROMs in the library's collection will be accessible from these computers as the library obtains permissions from publishers. Printers, one for every two computers, take the same copy card you use for film and paper copies. See chapters three and four for more information on the FamilySearch system and other databases. If you need assistance with the computers or printers, library staff are usually in the area to help.

The computer workstation terminals are user friendly, and the instructions on the screen are easy to follow. The workstations have comfortable rolling

Tip

chairs and space for your laptop computer. Don't forget to lock your laptop computer to the workstation with your own cable lock.

Computers: Personal

Having your laptop computer along can be a real time-saver. Your genealogical software programs, databases, and other items are easily searchable. Taking notes on resources you check is easier if you do it as your research progresses. Electrical outlets are available at most readers and computer workstations, but not at all research tables. Patrons can plug in their laptops and dial into their Internet Service Provider and check their e-mail at laptop stations on each floor. A sturdy cable with a lock is a must to lock your computer to the desk where you work. As in any research facility open to the public, unattended computers have occasionally been stolen. **If you have a carrying bag that clearly looks like a computer bag, put it in a locker.** Someone might take the bag, including your valuable files, thinking it has a computer in it.

Tip

Copies and Copy Centers

Copy centers or areas are on each research floor. These house self-service equipment for making copies from books and microforms. The copy centers are along the left side of each research floor as you enter the floor. The library updates the equipment frequently due to ever changing technology, so some of the copiers you became acquainted with on your last trip may have been replaced by your next visit. You will need to learn to use the new machines; library staff are usually in the area to assist with this. After you make a few copies, the process becomes quite familiar. Try to become familiar with the copiers at times when the library is not too crowded.

Researchers at the FHL no longer need coins to make copies. The library uses copy cards. Researchers control their copy card and the amount of money added to the card. Most of the card dispensers take U.S. bills, not coins. (A few paper copiers in the library will still accept coins.) To obtain a card, feed one dollar (or more) into the dispenser. The amount inserted, less sixty cents (the cost of the card) will appear as credit. Usage rules are printed on the back of the card. We suggest bringing one- and five-dollar bills (U.S.) for use in the copy card dispensers. The largest amount of value that can be added to a card is fifty dollars. You can add value to your card at the paper copiers, also. A card dispenser on the main floor can issue receipts.

Money Saver

If your time at the FHL is running short, add only small amounts to your card. If you add twenty dollars and do not use it all, then you need to save the card if you want to use it on your next trip to the FHL. No refunds are given. This same system is used at many libraries worldwide. You must use copy cards on all microform copiers.

Currently, copies from books and paper and computer printouts cost five cents each, and copies from microfilm and microfiche cost twenty-three cents each. The library abides by U.S. copyright laws, and persons making copies are responsible for adherence to these laws. The copyright notice is posted on the various types of copiers. The limit is five copies at a copier if someone else is waiting. The library has a color copier on the main floor, which is staff operated. Color copies cost one dollar each.

Crowds

The library is less crowded early and late in the day, and it is usually busiest from about 9:30 A.M. or 10:00 A.M. until late afternoon (about 4:30 P.M.) and on Saturday afternoons. Summer is generally a busy time, but other times of the year are quickly catching up. Many groups visit the library in the spring and fall months. The Salt Lake Institute of Genealogy brings a large group to the library in early January. The one period of time when the library is usually not crowded is between Thanksgiving and Christmas.

The copy centers are quite busy in the afternoons, especially on Saturday afternoons and evenings as out-of-town visitors make last-minute copies before departing on Sunday. It is almost like a discount store dollar sale or last-minute Christmas Eve shopping!

Elevators and Stairs

All floors of the library are served by three elevators. The buttons inside are clearly marked in descending order for floors 3, 2, M, B1, and B2. "M" refers to the main floor, where patrons enter and exit the library. As the door opens on a floor, the floor designation is posted on the casing surrounding the elevator door and also lights up on the inside elevator control panel.

To the immediate right as you enter the library is a doorway to stairs that serve all levels of the library. In the main lobby on the left is a large open staircase that runs between the main and second floors. Using the stairs is a good way to exercise, but often in the late-afternoon hours of a long research day a genealogist prefers the elevator.

Emergencies

If you are in the library and have an emergency situation or observe one, contact a staff member, who will call for emergency assistance. You may also inform the personnel at the information or security desks in the main-floor lobby. If someone needs to contact a library patron due to an emergency, the number to call is (800) 453-3860, extension 2-3702. The library will make announcements only for emergencies. If your friend is absorbed in reading a microfilm in the library and forgets to meet you for lunch, that is not an emergency!

Hours

See the sidebar on page 110 for the hours of the library. Lines used to begin forming by 7:00 A.M. to await the 7:30 A.M. opening of the doors. A scramble for "favorite" readers would follow. Getting in line early was important then; however, many new microfilm readers and workstations have been added in recent years, and the facilities in the Joseph Smith Memorial Building have opened. These added resources have minimized the 7:30 A.M. frenzy and rush, and finding an open film reader is seldom a problem.

Announcements give you advance notice when it is getting near closing time. As much as we would all like to stay in the library forever, the staff does need a break.

Though the library is open for an abundant number of hours and days each year, it does close on some days. Once in a great while carpeting or other items need to be replaced or refurbished, which might cause some work delays. **Be sure to call to confirm open times before making your hotel and airplane reservations.** One summer several years ago, the library was closed for two days in July during the Days of '47 Pioneer Celebration. We are sure the library staff and volunteers enjoyed this rare long weekend. On the day before that closing, we were amazed to hear several people in the library angrily complain about the library being closed. It was always closed for at least one day at this time. If those people had done their homework before their trip, they would have known about the closure. Calling ahead to the FHL is no different than checking to confirm the hours at a courthouse or historical society before an upcoming research trip. That said, in future years the library may be open during the Days of '47 in July unless the celebration falls on a Sunday.

Hours and holiday closings are also posted on the library's Web site. Utah observes daylight saving time. In the early hours on the first Sunday in April, clocks are set ahead one hour, and on the last Sunday in October, clocks are set back one hour early in the morning.

Important

Identification

Use of restricted microfilm and microfiche collections requires photo identification, such as a driver's license or some other photo I.D. If you are unsure about the type of I.D. you have, call ahead to find out if it is sufficient.

Internet Access

All computer terminal workstations have Internet access, and laptop stations allow you to hook up your laptop to check your own e-mail.

Library Attendant Windows

On each research floor is a Library Attendant Window—the place to pay for anything not paid for via your copy card. Pay here for family group sheets, research outlines, census abstract forms, word translation lists, and other items near these windows. If you have a problem with a reader, printer, copier, or other equipment, ask here for assistance. If your microfilm reader is missing a 16mm (thin) or 35mm (thick) take-up reel, the personnel in this area can supply you with a replacement. If a film is not in the drawer, the library attendant can check its status for you. If the catalog indicates a film is restricted, this is the place to request it. You will be asked to leave a form of photo identification in order to use that microfilm or microfiche. The library attendants are also the wonderful people who reshelve all the books we use. The library attendant windows are open the same hours as the library building.

Library Etiquette and Rules

The library has signs posted in several locations to make you aware of the few simple rules. Be sure to check for informational signs by the readers, by the film cabinets, and in the copy centers. **Here are some rules and guidelines from the library and other researchers:**

Important

- Smoking and caffeine consumption are not permitted in the library or on the grounds.
- No food or beverages are allowed in the library proper. You may not have your water bottle at your reader, no matter how careful you are. Books, film, and readers can be damaged with even the slightest spill.
- Books: The limit is five at a time. When you are finished with a book, return it to the red shelf at the end of the aisle where you found the book. One exception to this return policy is that some centrally located general reference books and finding aids on all floors should be immediately returned to their proper spot on the shelf for use by the next patron.
- Microfilm: The limit is five films per patron at any one time. When you remove a film from the cabinet, be sure to shut the drawer completely so it will not injure the next patron who walks by. Take only one roll of film out of a box at a time so you can be sure to put it back in the correct box. When you are finished with the film, return it to the proper cabinet in the correct film number sequence.
- Microfiche: The limit is five microfiche per patron at any one time. The fiche may be returned to specially marked boxes on the top of the fiche cabinets; however, refiling by the patrons is allowed. On top of the microfiche cabinets are "out" markers for you to place in the spot where you have removed a microfiche. The library catalog, the IGI, Accelerated Indexing Systems (AIS) census index fiche, and some foreign microfiche must be returned to their proper place in the carousel where they were found. To simplify refiling of these, check for a colored dot or dots and find the fiche carousel with the corresponding colored dots.
- Copies: If someone else is waiting to make a film, fiche, or book copy, the limit is five copies at a time. If you need to make more copies, remove your item from the copier and go to the end of the line. One book copier on the main floor has an express line for those needing only one or two copies. If you cannot find the item you wanted to copy, leave the printer or copier to find the correct page or pages, rather than tying up a copier someone else needs to use.
- Readers and computers: If you will be away from a reader or computer for an extended time, take your materials with you so that another patron

may use the equipment. If you are gone for an extended time and no other readers or computers are open, the staff may remove unattended materials. If they remove yours, check at the Library Attendant Window on that floor.

Lighting

In some areas of the library the lighting is a bit dim, which helps in reading microfilms. Try sitting in several different spots to see which area works best for your reading ability.

Lobby Area, Main Floor

At the information desk in the main lobby, friendly volunteers offer general information on the library, the short orientation presentation, and library class information, and they offer a basic "how to begin" brochure. We often hear patrons ask these volunteers about sixteenth-century research, restaurants, historic sites, cultural activities, and more. This is not the main job of the folks at this counter, but they do their best to help; they may refer patrons to the appropriate level of the library or to a tourism office for more ideas. We have heard some good restaurant suggestions from the volunteers at this counter! At the exit desk you can obtain cafeteria passes for the Church Office Building cafeteria. The other desk in the lobby is for security personnel.

Locations of Record Collections and Equipment

Main (First) Floor: United States and Canada Microforms, Books, and General Reference Aids

This area has an expanded section of computer workstations. The copy center has six book copiers. Tables offer room for researchers to sit and check the U.S. and Canadian book collection. The U.S. family histories and surname periodicals in book form formerly located here are now located on the fourth floor of the Joseph Smith Memorial Building, one block east of the library. (See chapter twelve.)

Second Floor: United States and Canada Microforms and General Reference Aids

This floor has hundreds of microfilm readers and many microfiche readers. There are also many computer workstations. Worktable space is limited on this floor. The copy center has several types of microfilm copiers and microfiche copiers. Seats are provided at a few of the microfilm copiers. There is one book copier and two automatic film rewinders. Some overflow microfilms you would expect to find on the second floor have been located on level B1 for several years. The plan is to bring these to the second floor as higher-capacity film cabinets are gradually added.

Basement 1 (B1): International Books, Microforms, and Reference Aids

The major portion of this collection is Germanic and Scandinavian books, maps, and microforms. Other countries represented include, but are not limited to,

Family History Library
MAIN FLOOR

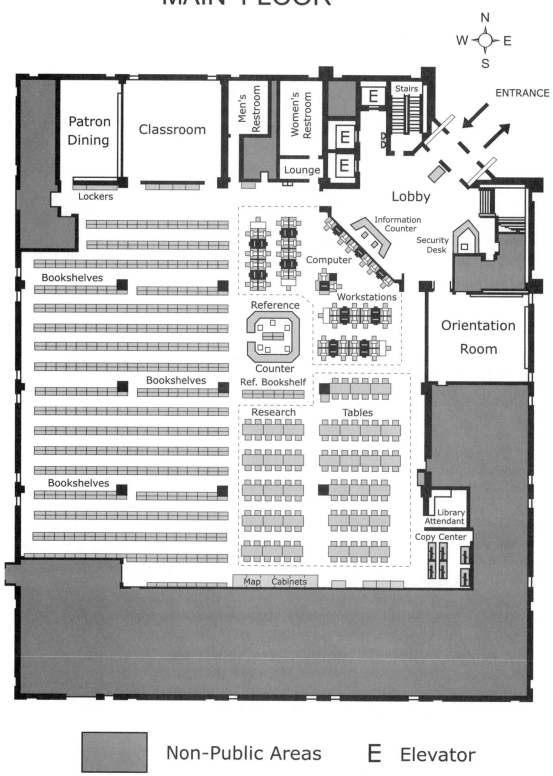

Non-Public Areas   E Elevator

Figure 11-2
Map prepared by Carol Barrett, CRG Digital Design

Family History Library
SECOND FLOOR

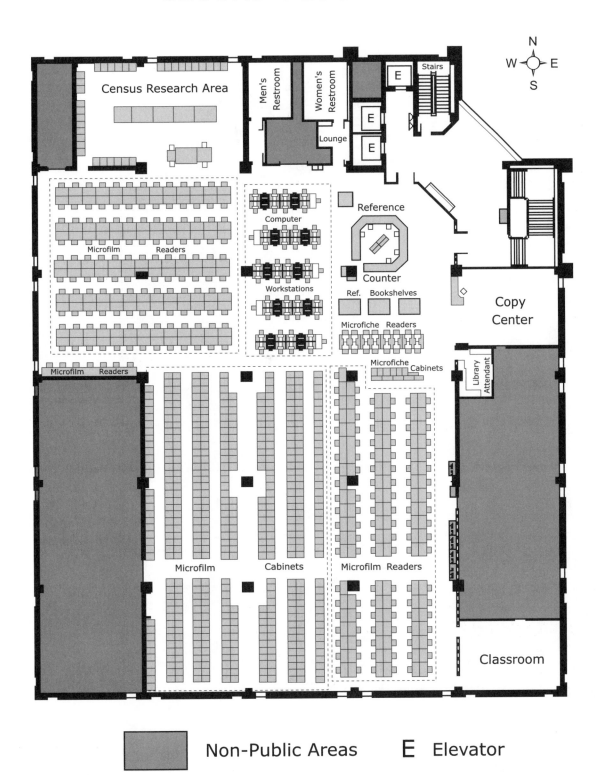

Figure 11-3
Map prepared by Carol Barrett, CRG Digital Design

Family History Library
B1 FLOOR

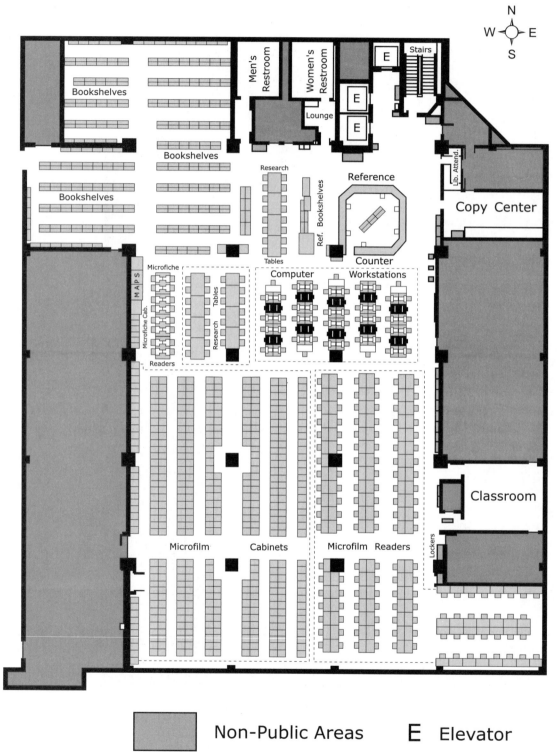

Non-Public Areas   **E** Elevator

Figure 11-4
Map prepared by Carol Barrett, CRG Digital Design

Family History Library
B2 FLOOR

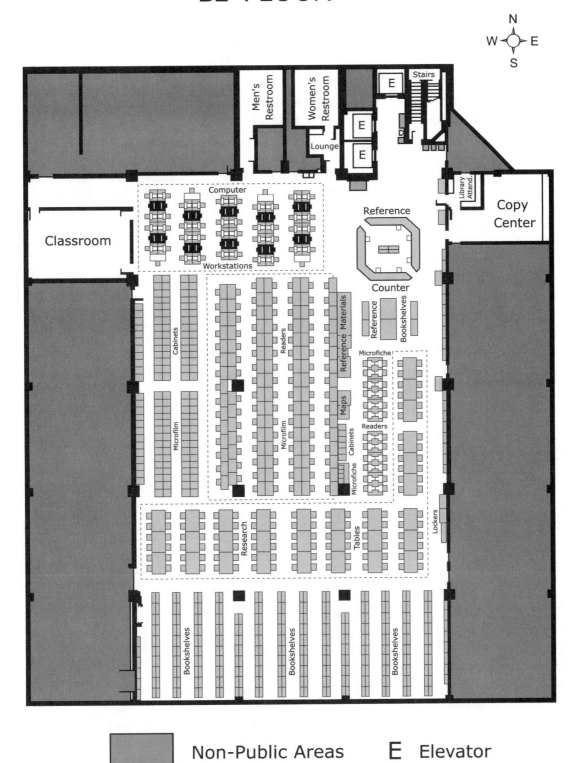

Figure 11-5

Map prepared by Carol Barrett, CRG Digital Design

Croatia, Greece, Italy, Japan, Latin America, Latvia, Poland, Spain, and the Ukraine.

The B1 copy center has several microfilm and microfiche copiers. There is one auto rewinder for microfilm and one book copier. This floor has more than one hundred microfilm readers, several microfiche readers, many computer workstations, and several worktables.

Basement 2 (B2): British Isles, Australia, and New Zealand Books, Maps, Microforms, and General Reference Aids

The B2 copy center has two book copiers, several stand-up microfiche copiers, and several microfilm copiers. There is one automatic film rewinder. This floor has more than a hundred microfilm readers and many microfiche readers. This area has a large section of computer workstations. This floor has considerable table work space. Floor B2 also has a Medieval Section and Special Collections.

Lockers

Lockers are available on each floor. The cost is ten cents each time you open the locker and need to lock it again. Large briefcases may not fit in them. The dimensions of the openings of most of the lockers are $8\frac{3}{4}'' \times 16\frac{1}{2}''$ (22.2cm $\times$ 41.9cm). The lockers are $16\frac{3}{4}''$ (42.6cm) deep. Something a bit wider may fit at an angle, as the inside area is $12''$ (30.5cm) wide. Do not try to leave material in the lockers overnight; security personnel empty them each night.

Lost and Found

If you lose something, first make sure you are looking on the correct floor. Next check for the item at the attendant window on the main floor. Items such as hats, coats, and umbrellas unclaimed after several weeks are taken to the Deseret Industries for distribution to needy people. Staff check notebooks, papers, files, and photocopies to see if a name and address appear. They send a postcard to notify people of the found items. Unclaimed material is discarded after several weeks. If a purse, computer, cell phone, or similar item is found, it is turned over to library security. If a name is found, that person is called over the public-address system to go to the security desk in the main lobby. We hope you will label your files, notebooks, computer, and cell phone now!

Microfilm Readers and Computer Workstations

Hundreds of microfilm readers of varying types and magnification levels are on the second floor and floors B1 and B2. These are all self-service. See "Working in the Library," chapter thirteen, for more details on the readers.

The library has added many computer workstations that contain all versions of the computer catalog. These workstations have room for your laptop computer and provide printing capability for the catalog and databases. These have been added to accommodate the availability of more online and digitally formatted resources and the changing needs of library patrons.

Tip

LABEL YOUR BELONGINGS

Put an address label, other label, or handwritten entry including your home telephone number on each item you bring into the library: your briefcase, computer, coin purse, pencil bag, wallet, computer disks, folders, notebooks. Add the name of the hotel or relative's house where you are staying.

Miscellaneous

- Coatracks are located on each floor.
- A postage stamp vending machine is located near the snack room on the main floor.
- Bulletin boards on each floor near the elevators and rest rooms contain a varied array of informational flyers, meeting notices, and other items.
- A variety of brochures are near the elevators on the main floor.

Orientation

Just off the main lobby is the room where a brief but informative orientation to genealogy and the library are offered throughout the day. It is not a presentation with heavy religious overtones, but if you have questions about the Church, they will be answered. It provides an overview of what items are on each floor of the library, helpful hints on basic genealogical research, and suggestions about where to go for further assistance. A map of the library and an informational brochure on starting the research are handed out to the orientation participants. The orientation session generally lasts for fifteen minutes. There is no tour of the library. As with other services at the library, no fee is charged for the orientation class.

Parking

Parking for library patrons is located behind the library. The patron entrance is on 200 West Street between North and South Temple streets. All-day parking is reasonably priced. You need one-dollar bills to enter the lot. Another patron lot is directly behind the Church Museum, and the entrance is on North Temple Street.

Pencil Sharpeners

Electric pencil sharpeners are located in the copy centers and at the reference counters on each floor.

Personal Safety

Be on the lookout for bags, canes, carts, chairs, children, jackets, and feet in the aisles as you walk through. You can be helpful by keeping any of these as out of the way as you can. No one wants to end up in the hospital with a broken leg when they could be working at the library! Aisles between readers and computer workstations are not wide, and you might check to see if someone is walking down the aisle before you push your chair back. When you stand up to put a new microfilm on your reader, push in your chair rather than leaving it out in the aisle. Try not to gather in groups around a reader. When more than one chair is placed at a reader, it crowds the aisle for others and makes it an obstacle course.

Even in the FHL, it is important to keep an eye on your personal items. The library is open to the public, and any building that draws more than 2,400 people a day will attract a handful who may be there to take advantage of others. Use a cable lock on laptop computers and even your briefcase so it is not vulnerable if mistaken for a computer bag or purse. Put things in a locker if you won't be near them. A hidden pouch, wallet, or fanny pack is a good alternative to carrying a purse, which you might neglect or lose as you move from place to place in the library in pursuit of your ancestors.

Important

Reference Books and Finding Aids

Each of the research floors has an area where useful reference books, finding aids, indexes, maps, atlases, and lists of popular call numbers are found. These are good areas to browse in order to become familiar with these timesaving aids. More comprehensive discussion on these is found in chapters eight through ten.

Reference Counters

Each patron floor has a reference counter with personnel to help address your research questions. Check the overhead signs to make certain you are at the correct side of the counter for the country of your ancestors. These counters also have some special reference aids that are not out in the general collection. The reference counters are open the same hours as the library building. You may find a reference consultant with extensive expertise in your ancestral topic or area, or you may find a volunteer who is also learning. Don't hesitate to ask for help, especially when someone working at the desk might have expertise in your area of need.

Rest Rooms and Drinking Fountains

The rest rooms are in the same spot on each floor. As you enter the main research areas on each floor, the rest rooms are to your right. The women's rest rooms on B1, B2, and the second floor, have small lounge areas with chairs.

In between each set of men's and women's rest rooms are two refrigerated drinking fountains at different heights. Be careful; these sometimes splash the person getting a drink of water.

Security

Library personnel are stationed at the library's main floor exit doors to greet people as they enter and depart. They also make sure visitors do not leave the library with books or microforms. Books, microforms, and other library materials are electronically microcoded to set off the sensors at the door should someone attempt to leave the building with library property. When the sensors buzz, the staff person sitting by the door simply checks the person's briefcase or bag to make sure the person hasn't inadvertently taken library property. As happens often in airports, something else in the person's belongings often sets off the sensors. Occasionally staff members spot-check the bags of everyone leaving the library. Security personnel are on duty all hours the library is open should any problems arise or should someone become ill. The library has additional exit doors marked for emergency exit only. If an emergency occurs or the fire alarm goes off, *exit immediately*; instructions are given over the public-address system. Your personal safety is more important than your computer or briefcase or items in your locker!

Snack Room

Library policy does not allow food or beverages (even water) in the library proper. This keeps crumbs or liquids from damaging the equipment and collections. Even if you are careful, the slightest crumb can draw bugs that can damage the collection. The aroma of your snack might disturb another patron. Take your snack or lunch to the snack room on the main floor of the library. The snack room has vending machines for (caffeine-free) soft drinks, juice, milk, ice cream novelties, candy, pretzels, and light food. It has two microwave ovens. Researchers should not put popcorn in the microwave—this tends to set off the smoke alarms. Your fellow researchers will not be pleased to have to leave the building because of your mistake! Two daily newspapers are posted at eye level on the walls of the snack room for researchers to read while eating.

Special Needs

The library welcomes all researchers. The library entrance has an automatic door. The rest rooms have accessible stalls and sinks, but assistance with the entry door may be needed. Some microfilm readers are designated for wheel-chair access, and some have motorized controls. The plaza area outside the library is flat. The parking lot behind the library has several parking spots designated handicapped with a nearby ramp for access to the library plaza.

The library has one Spectrum, Jr. reader to enlarge printed material for visually impaired users. Contact the library for assistance with hearing impairments and other special needs. Genealogists are a friendly lot; you might ask those around you for brief assistance. Many people need assistance to reach top shelves and drawers for books and microforms. The library staff will also do its best to accommodate your physical needs. The library will also try to accommodate the needs for a non-English-speaking patron. The library has staff members fluent in many languages. The library does appreciate advance notice of special needs, so the proper staff member can be available when needed. The library continually adds lower height reference tables and sections of reference counters.

Telephones and Pagers

Public pay telephones and Salt Lake City area telephone directories are on each floor of the library near the elevators. This area is often noisy, and it may be

Quotes

VOICES OF EXPERIENCE

"We do advise getting out of the building to check downtown restaurants and food courts, and to give your mind and body a break. You will be amazed at how much fresher you are for research-ing. Of course, this means you eat a sensible lunch so that you will stay awake in the afternoon!"

Important

difficult to hear your phone conversation. The library requests that patrons with cell phones use them in this telephone area only and not in the library research areas where they will disturb other patrons. **If you have a pager or mobile phone, it is mandatory to adjust it to vibrate rather than ring or buzz, so other researchers will not be disrupted.**

What You May Bring Into the Library

The library does not presently have any restrictions on what you may bring into it. Many facilities restrict researchers from bringing in briefcases or bags and allow only pencils for writing. This is done for the preservation and security of the collections and applies especially to one-of-a-kind items. Researchers may bring briefcases, purses, bags, and file boxes into the FHL. If you must bring your things in on a wheeled luggage cart, keep the cart out of the aisles so it doesn't present a safety hazard. You may use pens, pencils, or your laptop computer to take notes and document the copies you make. Please be careful not to mark or damage library materials. All materials that you bring into the library are subject to inspection when you leave. Bags normally are searched only if you set off the electronic sensors at the door as you leave the building or if the staff is spot-checking all patron materials as people exit.

World Wide Web

The FHL's FamilySearch system with its many electronic components, is available via the Internet. Check the library's Web site at <http://www.familysearch.org> to see the catalog, research helps, links to other sites, general library information, and various parts of the system—including the International Genealogical Index, the FHL Catalog, the Ancestral File, and more as they become available online. Site improvements and additions occur constantly.

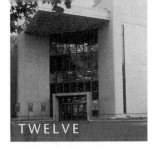

TWELVE

Joseph Smith Memorial Building

ONE BLOCK FROM THE FAMILY HISTORY LIBRARY

The Family History Library's collection has grown beyond its walls. In 1993, a new facility for researchers, the Joseph Smith Memorial Building (JSMB), opened to the public. This building is at 15 East South Temple Street on the opposite side of Temple Square from the library. Formerly the Hotel Utah building, it has been completely and exquisitely renovated. A stop here is a must for anyone visiting the area. It is well worth the short walk from the library (one block, slightly uphill) just to see the stunning chandeliers and lobby, formerly that of a grand old hotel.

Family history research resources are on the first and fourth floors of the JSMB, which are referred to in combination as the FamilySearch Center. Specific portions of the FHL collection are housed here, as are resources geared specifically for genealogical newcomers and those with only a little time to see what the library might have for them.

Parking is available underground, with an entrance on South Temple Street, and in nearby parking ramps. Lockers are available for your belongings. Rest rooms and drinking fountains are on each floor. As with the FHL, there is no fee to use the research resources in this building.

JSMB LOWER LEVEL

The lower level has vending machines and tables for patrons who want to eat. A Distribution Center for genealogical and other materials is located here, too; genealogical forms, Research Outlines, Research Checklists, CD-ROMs, Resource Guides, word lists, and other helpful items are for sale. See chapter four for more information on the many FHL publications.

JSMB FIRST FLOOR

The beautiful lobby entrance to the JSMB is on the south end of the building facing South Temple Street. The north end of the first floor houses part of the FamilySearch Center. This large computer workstation area was intended for

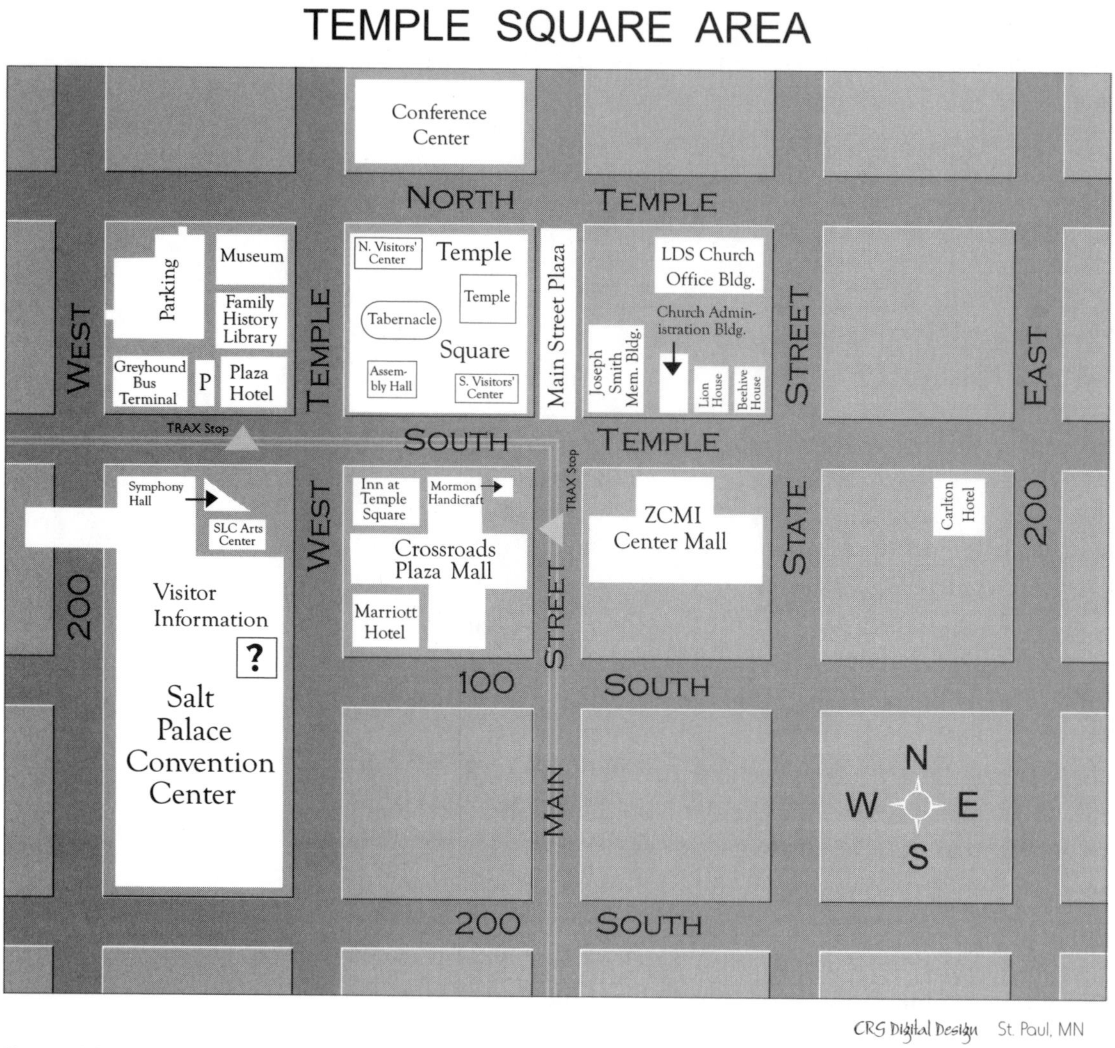

TEMPLE SQUARE AREA

Figure 12-1
Map of Temple Square area including the FHL and JSMB. *Map prepared by Carol Barrett.*

those who are either newcomers to genealogy or the FamilySearch computer system. However, it is a comfortable and generally uncrowded space for any researcher, and experienced Salt Lake City researchers also find it an ideal place to use the library catalog and databases.

WATCH FOR JSMB CHANGES!

Final planning to accommodate visitors to the 2002 Winter Olympics have the possibility of producing substantial changes in the JSMB FamilySearch Center setup. As this book went to press, decisions were being made about shifting resources in the JSMB to other locations. So it is possible that the first-floor FamilySearch Center may be relocated, temporarily or permanently, to another location in the JSMB Building. Watch the FamilySearch Web site for updates.

Computers

More than 130 comfortable individual workstations are on the first-floor FamilySearch Center. A visitor can sit in a padded chair at a library computer and access the complete FamilySearch system of databases. This includes Ancestral File, Social Security Death Index, the IGI, and others, plus the library catalog. Each of the computer stations has plenty of work space and an individual laser printer, and the entire area is a carpeted, peaceful area in which to work.

For beginners, checking family names (including maiden names) in the FamilySearch databases will sometimes produce a connection. If this doesn't, they learn this first lesson that even these huge databases index only a fraction of our ancestors. The FHL Catalog can help point to millions of records not indexed in those databases.

The computers in this area feature an interactive tutorial program to help walk researchers through various ways to use the databases and catalog. Additional assistance is available from the staff and volunteers at the reference desk. These computers also are equipped with Personal Ancestral File, a widely used genealogy software program. Printouts from the computers in the JSMB cost five cents each and are paid for at the reference counter in the FamilySearch area.

At times people must wait to use the computers at the main library, but the JSMB is seldom crowded. This makes it an ideal place to become comfortable with the computer system and spend extended time using the library catalog. It is usually beneficial to plan some time here during your research visit.

THE FAMILYSEARCH CENTER'S ADDRESS AND HOURS

FamilySearch Center
Joseph Smith Memorial Bldg.
15 East South Temple St.
Salt Lake City, UT 84150
Phone: (801) 240-4085
Fax: (801) 240-3718

Classroom/Group Reservations: (801) 240-4673

FamilySearch Center Hours:
Monday through Saturday 9 A.M.–9 P.M.

Closed Sundays, Thanksgiving, Christmas, New Year's Day, first Saturday in April, and first Saturday in October.

These hours differ from the library's hours. Monday evenings, when the library is closed, the JSMB collections offer additional resources, lots of work space, and many underutilized computer stations. The FamilySearch Center is open on some holidays when the library closes.

1920 U.S. Census

At the east end of this area is a complete set of the 1920 U.S. census and Soundex complete with microfilm readers and a copier. Film retrieval is self-service. The 1920 census is also available in the library itself. A duplicate set was placed in the JSMB to allow beginning researchers to easily check this since it is the most recent available U.S. federal census and has a Soundex for all states. (Under federal law, the 1930 U.S. census will become available to the public for research on 1 April 2002. The FHL normally acquires microfilm of a census shortly after its release.) Even visitors with little time and minimal information on their ancestry can usually identify some relatives who were alive in 1920. If those ancestors were living in the United States, visitors have a good chance of finding a record of them by searching this census. The microfilmed Soundex indexes the head of each household on the 1920 census, as well as anyone in the household whose last name was different than that of the head of the household.

Idea Generator

FAMILIARIZE YOURSELF WITH THE JSMB

Plan to spend a little time in the JSMB during your trip to

- use the published family histories on the fourth floor

- check for family newsletters or surname periodicals

- use the 1920 census and Soundex

- take advantage of the abundance of computer workstations

- check the FGR collection for noncomputerized family records

- make use of the JSMB open hours on Monday evening when the library is closed

- view the city from the tenth floor and enjoy a meal

JSMB FOURTH FLOOR

The ornate elevators to the fourth floor bring researchers to another important part of the FHL collection. The entire fourth floor houses more FamilySearch Center resources. When you exit the elevators, the west wing is to your right, and the east wing is to your left. The resources here, especially in the east wing, are seldom heavily used. That makes this another quiet place to make extensive use of a computer workstation or spread out your papers and focus on a research problem.

West Wing
Printed Genealogies and Family Histories
In the spring of 1998, the bound family histories and family/surname periodicals were moved from the library to the JSMB. **More than 70,000 published volumes**

Printed Source

relating to families in the U.S. and other countries occupy twenty-three rows of shelving in this area. Published genealogies and family histories provide valuable clues for your research. Be cautious, however, and do not assume they are complete and accurate. Pay particular attention to whether the sources of information are documented in these volumes. Also valuable for family clues and possible connections to other genealogical researchers are family newsletters and surname periodicals. You will find many of those publications in this area.

Just as in the library itself, the west wing has table space at which to work and read, a reference desk with volunteer staff to answer basic questions, a copy center, lockers, and a few basic reference books and finding aids. Note that many published volumes and periodicals, especially older works, may also be available in microfilm or microfiche format. That film will be available in the library, not in the JSMB. About 70 percent of the printed family histories are also in microform. Check the library catalog entry to see if the entry for a volume indicates it is available in more than one format.

Additional Computers

More than thirty computer stations are available in this fourth floor area. They have the FamilySearch databases, the library catalog, and the Personal Ancestral File software. Several also have access to the FamilySearch Internet site and a number of the resource CD-ROMs published by the Church. By advance reservation, several small meeting spaces and one classroom with about a dozen computer terminals are also available for training.

East Wing

Family Group Sheet Collection

Occupying most of the east side of the fourth floor is the extensive Family Group Records (FGR) collection. Housed in almost twenty thousand binders are family group sheets and pedigree charts which were submitted by Church members and some patrons from 1942 to 1978, and they represent in excess of eight million families. There are two separate sequences of binders, arranged alphabetically by the primary name on the chart. You may make photocopies from them at the copiers in the center of the wing. Near the copy machines are instructions for removing pages from the binders for copying. Four Family-Search computer workstations are in this area also.

For detailed information on this specialized collection, see Elizabeth L. Nichols's article, "Family Group Records Collection and Related Records of the Family History Library" in the *Genealogical Journal* (volume 24, number 1 [winter 1996], pages 11–27). The *Genealogical Journal* is a publication of the Utah Genealogical Association, a state-level genealogical society, and is available in many library collections across the United States.

These Family Group Records are also available on microfilm. Because the FHL collections continue to grow and require facility space, these FGR may not be available in their original form someday. Already, some older FGR are only available on film. The article cited above explains this and tells which of the FGR segments are included in the International Genealogical Index.

JSMB TENTH FLOOR

Two attractions draw researchers up the elevators to the tenth floor of the JSMB: the views and the food. Two observation decks afford beautiful city views. The east side looks out on the Wasatch Mountains, while the west side provides a bird's-eye view of Temple Square.

The tenth floor of this building also has two excellent restaurants, the Roof Restaurant and the Garden Restaurant, which are open to the public. Both overlook Temple Square and the vista beyond. They are often very busy, but worth the wait. See the restaurant section, chapter nineteen, of this guide, for more details. There's nothing like lunch in the Garden Restaurant on a sunny day when the retractable roof is open.

THIRTEEN

Working in the Library

THE FIRST DAY

Make time to become familiar with the Family History Library. The "Give Yourself a Tour" checklist in appendix C provides highlights that will help orient you to the facility. Briefly check out the FamilySearch workstations, copy centers, book areas, and microform readers on each floor. Browse each floor's reference area. The finding aids and other guides will be valuable to you as you research. Note where the rest rooms and drinking fountains are. Look for signs and instructions on each floor. Do a mini tour each time you visit the library to see what changes have been made.

PLAN YOUR DAY

Working in the FHL is like working at many other research repositories. The big difference is that there are so many resources that you can become overwhelmed. That's why it is important to prepare in advance whenever possible and try to schedule the time you will spend in the library.

If you have just started research or are working in the records of a country or state that is new to you, look for the basics. Check the guidebooks, the library's Research Outlines, and the finding aids in the reference area, and ask for suggestions at the reference desk.

Research Tip

Plan the research you hope to do that day, estimate time for carefully reading microforms, and make a rough schedule. Allow yourself time to locate and figure out resources, make copies, and take breaks to stretch your body and brain. How closely you will be able to follow your plan depends entirely on what you find in the records and where that information points you. You may not find anything, and the research you had scheduled two days for will be done in a few hours. Be flexible, but set some daily goals and keep them in mind.

If you are not organized when you arrive in Salt Lake City, permit yourself to spend a couple of sessions of two to three hours in your hotel room. Sort the materials you tossed into your briefcase or carry-on bag. Make your lists of things to do. Update family group sheets and ancestor charts. Then go to the library.

Quotes

VOICES OF EXPERIENCE

Quotes and reminders from researchers in the library:

- "Until I visited the library, it was impossible to realize the resources that are available there right at your fingertips, free of charge."

- "I was overwhelmed at first, but found the library is very well organized, once I understood the system."

- "I find that if I bring along both simple and difficult research tasks I can switch to the simpler ones when I need a lift."

- "If I can't find a book or film where it should be I am tempted to go immediately to the attendant's window. Experience has taught me to double-check the call number in the catalog first in case I wrote down the incorrect number."

- "What do I do when the computer catalogs are not functioning (as all computers act up sometime)? I check for things the old-fashioned way: on the microfiche version of the catalog. Sure, it's not keyword searchable, but it will do in a pinch. When I have my own computer along, I simply check the catalog on my CD-ROM version of the catalog."

- "If a filmed record seems incomplete, it may be that all left-side pages of a volume were filmed and then the right-side pages! Another quirk is some records in the form of index cards were all filmed on the top side and then on the bottom side and are not next to each other on the film. You won't find a lot of these, but they can mystify you for a bit."

- "When you are going to be away from your valuable research materials or computer, put them in a locker. Don't tempt fate."

- "Please pay attention to the limits at the express copier on the main floor."

- "If you get dizzy while reeling the microfilm, slow down, turn off the light, or look away. A different type of reader may help. The higher altitude may impact your dizziness. Check with your physician before your library visit if you have a problem with dizziness."

WORKING IN THE LIBRARY, A TO Z
Animals
Leave your dog, cat, or cockatoo at home. Service assistance animals are welcome.

Caffeine
You won't find any caffeinated beverages in the library snack room. If you need a cup of coffee, get one at your hotel or a restaurant before coming to the

Individual Time Planning Calendar for _____
Note: the shaded areas indicate hours that the Family History Library is CLOSED.

TIME	Wed., 7	Thu., 8	Fri., 9 Nov.	Sat., 10	Sun., 11	Mon., 12	Tues., 13	Wed., 14 Nov.
6:30 AM			wake up					
7:00 AM	wake-up		exercise					
7:30 AM	shower		shower					
8:00 AM	breakfast		breakfast					
8:30 AM	find good reader							
9:00 AM	check FHLC for Greene Co., IN							
9:30 AM	Greene Co. Films							
10:00 AM			FamilySearch class		Meet in hotel lobby-brunch			
10:30 AM								
11:00 AM								
11:30 AM	Meet in lobby for lunch							
NOON								
12:30 PM	continue Greene Co. Probate							
1:00 PM	Switch to B1 Ostraby church records							
1:30 PM								
2:00 PM			English Probate class					
2:30 PM								
3:00 PM		snack						
3:30 PM	Fall asleep—go outside							
4:00 PM								
4:30 PM								
5:00 PM								
5:30 PM	dinner	dinner						
6:00 PM			dinner-take TRAX					
6:30 PM	back to library					JSMB computers		
7:00 PM								
7:30 PM			back to library					
8:00 PM					Concert			
8:30 PM	quitting time				Concert			
9:00 PM					Concert			
9:30 PM					Concert			
10:00 PM								
10:30 PM	bed	bed	bed	bed	bed	bed	bed	bed

Figure 13-1 An example of a time-planning chart for use at the FHL.

LATTER-DAY SAINTS ANCESTRY

For researchers with Latter-day Saints ancestry, the library has a special collections section on floor B2. Reference assistance is available, and access to some manuscript collections is obtained via this room. Check with the library for the access guidelines to this area. Additional records with specific Church connections are throughout the library in microform and in books; these have no special access requirements. The Early Church Information File is an index to more than a thousand sources. It includes over 1.5 million names on seventy-five rolls of microfilm. The FHL has a Resource Guide, *Early Church Information File*, with details on this index. Be sure to check with the staff at the FHL, or Family History Centers for assistance also.

The Utah Genealogical Association's *Genealogical Journal* frequently carries articles related to Church sources, including the Mormon Battalion, Mormon-related censuses, and more. Kip Sperry's article "Latter-day Saints Records," in the March/April 2001 issue of *Ancestry*, is another useful resource. The *Mormon Immigration Index*, on compact disc, is an index to over 94,000 Church converts who immigrated to the United States. Some entries are excerpts from diaries and journals about the journey across the ocean and across the United States to Salt Lake City. For more information, check the library's Web site. The FHL has additional information on other sources for researchers with Latter-day Saints ancestry.

Often when researching at the library, a patron finds a previously unknown Church connection via an entry in the International Genealogical Index, a published family history, or another source. Many sources with titles that sound specifically related to Church members may carry information on nonmembers. After all, your Methodist ancestor may have a brother or sister who joined the Church, so a diary or other record from this relative might mention your ancestor. As with all research, and especially when you have a research problem, exhaust all the records for an area, no matter the religion or ethnic group.

library. Check the restaurant list in chapter nineteen for nearby places to buy coffee or soda pop.

Chairs

In the year 2001 the library began replacing the chairs previously used in the building. The new chairs are all comfortable office chairs on rollers, with adjustable height, to make it easier for patrons to work at any workstation or table in the library facility.

Cite Your Sources

Whenever you make a copy from a microfilm, microfiche, or book, immediately note the film, fiche, or book call number on the copy, along with the record or book title, volume number, page number, publisher, date published, and other pertinent details. Remember to note that you copied the item at the FHL. **You may think you'll remember this later, but it is very easy to forget a source.** As your research progresses, you may need to refer to that book or film again. Leave yourself an easy return route to follow. Another way to nudge yourself into documenting your research process well is to use a research calendar or research log. Example of research logs are included in this chapter, and full blank forms are in appendix C. Throughout the library you'll find white slips of paper marked "Quick Reference." These make it easier for you to jot down a complete citation for the record or page you just checked or copied. Fasten the completed slip to your record copy.

Citing Sources

Coins

Researchers used to arrive at the library laden with containers of coins for the copy machines. Since the introduction of copy cards for the copiers, it is no longer necessary to bring coins. The library still has at least one change machine, located in the snack room.

File Folders

We bring empty file folders to the library, and we put record copies directly into a file folder which we immediately label. Until we use the folder, we store it upside down in our carrying case; we can tell at a glance which ones are empty. We also label a file folder for each floor of the library (e.g., "B1") and put in it a to do list and catalog printouts for research on that floor. That way we don't have to flip through all of our papers to see what we need to do next on a specific floor.

Find Call Numbers

Once you have located an item in the FHL catalog, be sure to note whether it indicates it is a United States and Canada, British Isles, or International book or microform. This lets you know which floor you will find the item on. The microfilms and microfiche don't always follow a geographic pattern in the way they are numbered and housed in the drawers on their respective floors. The books are categorized geographically, but the call number is still a helpful locating aid. If you do some browsing on a return visit, note the labels on some book spines which bear numbers, such as 99, 00, 01. These indicate recent additions to the collection and the year of the addition.

Finding Aids

As you work in the library, use the finding aids in the reference areas on the various floors. They provide background information and shortcuts to the collections that may be valuable to you. These finding aids vary from one floor to another. Set aside a little browsing time to use them; this also will provide you with a physical and mental break from work on the microfilm readers. Finding aids are discussed further in chapters eight, nine and ten.

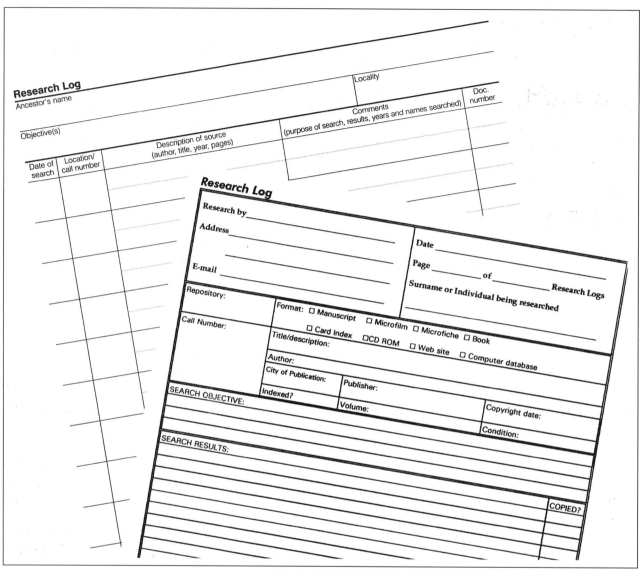

Figure 13-2

Research log examples. *Reprinted by permission. Research log on left © 1999–2000 by Intellectual Reserve, Inc. Research log on the right © 2000 by James W. Warren and Paula Stuart Warren.*

Foreign Languages

If your foreign-language skills are rusty or nonexistent, reference books and word lists in the library can assist you. Chapter ten has more details on these.

Lost?

With so many rows of workstations with film readers in the library, it is easy to forget where you were sitting if you leave to make a copy or retrieve a film. Each row of readers and each microfilm workstation are numbered. When you select a reader, note the row and reader numbers in a notebook you will carry with you or on a piece of paper or index card to put in your pocket. This will come in handy! Some people choose to sit in approximately the same area, row,

Quick Reference

Repository: FAMILY HISTORY LIBRARY 35 N WEST TEMPLE ST SALT LAKE CITY UT 84150-3400	Date

Reference Information

Title

Author

	Book	Microfilm and item number
Call number		Microfiche (and card number)

Publication Information

Published by

Where published (city, state, and country)	Date published

Results

Record this information and the results of your search in your **research log** or your personal computer program. This will help you keep accurate records.

Figure 13-3
An example of the library's Quick Reference note sheets. *Reprinted by permission. Copyright © 1999–2000 by Intellectual Reserve, Inc.*

and reader location each time they visit the library or on each floor to minimize the chance of forgetting where they were sitting.

Maps

As suggested in chapter seven, bring along maps (in a reduced size) of your known ancestral localities in all countries to use for quick reference as you read films or books. It is useful to have those at your work area and for future reference. The library has an extensive map collection. These are especially helpful when you discover a new locality or need to track a new ancestral migration route. The map cases are self-service and have a geographic locality

Citing Sources

NOTES ON FHL CATALOG PRINTOUTS

Another way to help document your work and copies is to make a printout of the catalog entry for the book or record you are using and copying. Jot your research aim and result right on the printout. If you make a photocopy, attach the printout to the copy. Be sure to jot a citation right on the record copy also, in case the printout becomes separated from the copy. Examples of notes that might be added to the catalog entry printout are

Researching Greene Co. Probate for info on Ann and Jeremiah Green

Looking for Albert H. Slaker, who may have bought land pre-1855

Checked the records 1820–1845 in all the "Ws" but didn't see William Warren

---

label. The drawers are labeled to make it easy to find the maps by call number, listed in the library catalog. Make copies of maps for your future use. Reduce or enlarge pertinent sections as you make map copies to make them more readable and useable.

Mark Book Pages for Copying

Warning

Bring along a pocket-size tablet of notepaper to use for marking book pages you want to copy, especially in books without page numbers. **Don't use "sticky notes," as these may leave a residue on the page or tear the page when removed.** Always write down the page numbers you wish to copy; don't tie up a copier while you try to locate the page you wanted to copy. The library supplies small notepaper throughout the facility; use it to mark pages and immediately document the source of each copy.

Microfiche Copying

There are separate copiers for microfiche. Microfiche may have an identifying page or section number to note for copying. If you have a microfiche that looks similar to a photographic negative—white letters on a black or blue background—make sure the copier is set to make a copy from a negative to a positive print. As with the microfilm copiers, you may need to make a few copies to obtain the most readable copy. Ask for assistance in the copy center if you are unsure about how to operate the copier.

Microfilm Copying

Because microfilm often has no frame number, it can be difficult to locate the page you want when you take your film from your reader to a film copier. Write down the page or frame number (if given), the first and last names on a page, and approximately how far into a film you found the page to copy. If the pages are not numbered, look at what's on the top and bottom of the page you want and on the pages before and after. That will help you quickly locate the desired page on the film copier.

When you find a film page to copy, do not rewind your film. Simply take the film on both reels off your film reader and carry them to the copy center. Put the film reels on the copier upside down from the way you had them on the microfilm reader. When you put the two reels on the film copier, you should be close to the page you wish to copy.

Copying microfilm is both an art and a science. You will probably spend a lot of time and money to come to Salt Lake City to find these records; don't go home with unreadable copies because you wouldn't spend a few more dollars in the copiers. Sometimes it can take two, three, four, or more tries to copy a page; you may have to vary the darkness, focus, and zoom to get a readable copy. You may have to copy the darker half of the page at one setting and the lighter half of the page at another. These records are what all your efforts are for, so be patient. Spend the time and a little extra money to get the best copies you can.

Which copier will you need for your film? The machines are labeled as to whether they are better suited for 16mm or 35mm film. The size of the paper is marked on the copier stand. If no staff member is in the copy center to assist, watch other researchers make copies from microfilm and see what types of records are being copied on each machine. Ask a question or two of your fellow researchers. Try several machines to get a feel for how they work and what the copy results look like. If you are at the FHL for more than a couple of days, you will learn which copiers are working best and which ones work for specific types of records.

Remember that the limit is five copies if someone else is waiting to make copies. The FHL staff won't usually remind you, but your fellow researchers might by their sighs or a more direct gentle reminder of the limit. It is easy to get excited about copying an important set of records and forget the limit.

Reminder

Microfilm Readers

Copying comes before *readers* in this chapter, but in the library you use the readers before the copiers. There are more than 500 microfilm readers of several styles in the library. Try a few to see what is most comfortable and effective for you to use. Load a film onto one, and turn the crank. Read a few pages to see if the reader suits your arm strength, vision, and height. You might find that the reader you choose has a turn crank that tests all your strength. If this happens, try others. Test the machines for readability. Some have different light levels and screen positions which may affect film viewing. **If you don't test a reader before you unpack your work materials, you may find yourself at one with a dim or burned-out bulb.** Check first, then set up your research materials.

Tip

No matter which reader you choose, the take-up reel should be the same size as the reel the film is on. This will prevent the film from getting tangled. In other words, if you have a skinny roll of film (16mm), you need a skinny take-up reel. Your film should always thread between the glass plates, and the glass plates should close one on top of the other, otherwise your image will be out

IN THE MORNING

The library opens at 7:30 A.M., and the first couple of hours are often not crowded.

- That's a good time to make copies (particularly if you have a large copying project).

- When you select a film reader, turn on the reader to make sure the bulb is working before you unpack and get all set up.

- Check first for films that weren't in the cabinets or books that weren't on the shelves the previous day. If they still aren't there, ask for help at the library attendant window on that floor.

- Use the computers.

- Take on a quick, easy research task to wake you up.

- Then tackle a tough research project or hard-to-read film—while your mind and eyes are fresh.

of focus. The readers have a focus knob or ring, but this won't help if the film is improperly threaded.

If you are an early arrival at the library, you'll have your choice of readers. Each floor of the library has several left-handed cranking machines and a number of high-magnification machines. If you are unsure about how to operate a machine, ask for assistance at the library attendant window.

Use readers with a label or sign indicating either $42 \times$ or $65 \times$ magnification to read 16mm films or any films you have trouble reading on the regular-magnification readers. Some of the images are very small (our excuse for aging eyesight?). Some readers have adjustable magnification, though these don't always focus well. A few readers are reserved for 16mm film reading only. For some films the catalog entry indicates that a high-magnification reader is needed.

You may take microfilms to another floor to read them, but be sure to return them to the proper floor. Rewind your film onto the reel that it came on, put it back in the correct box, and replace the box in the drawer where you found it.

Missing or Damaged Books

Most of the FHL books are self-service and on open shelves. If you keep checking for a book and don't find it on the shelf, ask about it at the library attendant's window. It may have been pulled for microfilming, binding, or storage. We suggest that if you find a damaged book, you bring it to the attention of the staff at the library attendant's window.

Missing or Damaged Microforms

Most of the film and fiche is self-service. If you check a drawer repeatedly and the film you need is not there, where is it? Someone may be using it for an extended time. It may be a restricted film, or it may have disappeared or been pulled for repair. It may be an item in off-site storage. Ask at the library attendant window; the staff can check on the status of the film. If a replacement film must be ordered, they may be able to supply it before your research trip ends.

If a film or fiche is restricted, it is probably stored in the library attendant window area. The staff can give it to you immediately in exchange for your photo I.D. When you return the restricted item, your I.D. will be returned to you. Some of the most recent filmings of U.S. records are not housed on the second floor, but in an "overflow" area on floor B1. This will change in the future when different film cabinets that hold more films are placed on the second floor and film cabinets are rearranged.

If you have a broken film or one that is too scratched to read, take it to the library attendant's window for repair or replacement. Temporary repair of a broken film may be possible, enabling you to use it immediately.

For a time, many films were held in off-site storage, but most of those have been brought back into the library building. Films listed in the catalog as "Vault" films may or may not be in the library when you visit. You might contact the library in advance to be sure these films will be in the library when you arrive. The FamilySearch Internet section "Preparing to Visit the Library" is one to watch for current information and procedures regarding any films that might not be in the library proper.

Neighborliness

Reminder

- The best advice? The readers and computers are close together; do not wear heavy perfume, hair spray, or aftershave. Such scents in the close confines could adversely affect other researchers and cause them to miss valuable library time. Do shower and wear deodorant. (These suggestions have been echoed by several researchers.)
- Try to keep the aisle clear around your reader so others can walk through the area. Push in your chair before you load film onto your reader or while you are away from your reader.
- Shut the film and fiche drawers tightly so the next researcher walking down the aisle doesn't run into the drawer or catch clothing on it.
- Patience. Bring lots of it with you. The researcher next to you may not be prepared. Some may forget to take only five films at a time or to make only five copies when you are waiting for the copier. Others may not have read this book and so aren't working efficiently, resulting in delays for you. Be patient, smile, offer some limited help, and remember that in this large building you can move away from distractions.
- Patience. Use it on yourself. You can't find every record for every family line during one trip. Work methodically, and try alternate research projects if you have difficulty with one. Try to prevent frustration by changing your pace and surroundings. Relax and enjoy the research.

SATURDAY!

There are exceptions, but Saturday in the library is usually either the busiest day of the week or the slowest. Often, it is the busiest because

- people who work Monday through Friday have only Saturday for a day at the library

- many families and visitors to the Temple Square area come into the library on Saturday

- researchers and group research trips in Salt Lake City for a week often arrive on Sunday and leave the following Sunday. Saturday is their last day in the library, and they rush to maximize those last few hours

As a result, the copiers and the computers in particular often see more activity on busy Saturdays, and you may find the copier lines are longer. Plan accordingly, and do as much of your copying during the week as you can. If you're lucky, you'll be in the library on a slow Saturday when this isn't a problem.

Returning Home

You have been at the library for a week, maybe two. You want to make more copies, but you don't think your suitcase and carry-on bag have enough room. You know that stack of copies is not going to fit in your carry-on bag. Did you bring along an empty, soft suitcase for the copies? In other words, did you pack a spare suitcase inside your large suitcase? Even if you did, you may find that you cannot get it all on the airplane. What should you do? Ship a package to your home. See "Shipping" on page 204 for details.

Working With Professionals

Do not hesitate to hire a professional genealogist for a consultation, either for general help organizing what you have or planning what you should do. It is painful to see people in the library who have spent a week of precious vacation days and hundreds of dollars to make a trip to Salt Lake City, only to frustrate themselves fumbling through records, not knowing what they are looking for. For some additional dollars and an hour or two of their time, they can obtain timesaving advice from a capable professional and make more effective use of the research time in Salt Lake City. More advice on this is in chapter sixteen.

Zilch

Reminder

You have been in the library for three days and the result of your research is *zilch*. Stop and think. **It really isn't zilch. You have systematically ruled out many records and families, haven't you?** We do sympathize with you; we have all had this feeling of finding nothing. This is the time to check out the books and periodicals that you have in your to do folder—those things you would do only if you had time. What about the families you researched several years ago before

---

INDEXES: WHAT'S THERE?

The index you check may cover more years than the actual records at the FHL. Let's use vital records as an example. Even without the actual records for later years, checking the index can help your genealogical budget as you narrow down your options of what records to order from a vital records office in any city, county, state, province, or country.

For example, the District Court vital records for Pipestone County, Minnesota, at the FHL include

Index to Deaths 1878–1945
Register of Deaths 1878–1912
Birth Index 1877–1945
Birth Records 1877–1902

The index covers years into 1945, which means the FHL has many more years of index for these than actual records for this county.

---

the onslaught of the electronic finding aids? Time to review those families and check for them and the related surnames in those easily searchable indexes and abstracts in electronic form.

Redo a census you did several years ago. Recheck one of the probate records. You may find some clues for further research that you had overlooked previously. At any rate, you may be able to obtain a better copy on the newer copiers. Stop researching; take a library class, or just browse the books or periodicals and pick something different to read for a while.

Some of you may say, "I checked the IGI and the Ancestral File and none of my family is there. The result is zilch. What do I do now?" Research, plain and simple. You have to do step-by-step research without the clues you might have found in those two databases.

Tip

HOW TO WORK IN THE FAMILY HISTORY LIBRARY

Working in the FHL is not that difficult. We have heard people say they couldn't possibly visit the FHL because it is too big and there's too much there. Think about it in simpler terms:

- It is a library.

- It has a catalog.

- You should search by subject, place, title, author, and keyword.

- You find your call number in the catalog.

- You use that number to find your book, microform, or map.

These are the same basics steps used at any library. Each library you go to is a bit different from the previous one. The FHL has one special attribute many libraries don't have: It encourages genealogists to visit.

Things may be numbered, cataloged, and shelved in many ways. At any library ask about the systems used. At the FHL, you are fortunate; it has aids you may not find at other libraries:

- Online catalog with extensive instruction

- Classes at the library and elsewhere on the FHL and the catalog

- On-site orientation in Salt Lake City

- Books and articles on the FHL and the collections

- Numerous staff and volunteers to show the way

See, it needn't be as daunting as you think.

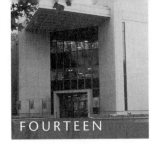

FOURTEEN

I Only Have a Few Hours!

Y ou brought your family to Utah on a skiing vacation, or maybe you are attending a convention on behalf of your employer. Today you have only three hours of skiing or business meetings, and you don't fly home until tomorrow. Maybe you were in Salt Lake City for the Olympics, attended a medal ceremony, and had a free day before the next event you had tickets for. Just two blocks from the medal ceremony site, just one block from the convention center, and less than an hour by bus or car from the ski slopes is the Family History Library in downtown Salt Lake City. You may have heard about it or become intrigued by our description of the place. Can you actually make a short visit to the library and make some headway on a family history project? The answer is a definite *yes*, as long as you have some basic information.

You won't be the only person to have done this. The library staff and regular patrons are used to seeing visitors walk in the door wearing ski clothing or a convention name tag. You can do some family history research even if you have just a few hours. But don't be one of the visitors who walks into the library and says, "I have an hour and want to research my whole family." Realize that after a few hours you will still be in the beginning stages of a wonderful journey to learn more about yourself and your ancestral families.

QUICKLY GATHER FAMILY INFORMATION

Should you stop in and see what the library might hold that relates to your ancestors? Of course you should. If you ask for help in the library, you might have to answer some questions, like when and where your mother was born or what your grandfather's name was and when he came to the United States. The question might lean toward the nationality of your maternal line. Oh, don't you wish you had listened more closely when Grandma told those family stories? You still have ways to get some of this information. Sit down for a short time and make notes from memory on your parents' names and birthplaces and then do the same for their parents, and so on. Jot down the names of their brothers and sisters and what you know about where they were born and where they lived and died. What are their marriage dates and spouses names? If you don't remember exact dates and names, you might note it like this: Grandma Annie Jones (maiden name Griffin?) was born July 1895? Aunt Sylvia, Grandma Annie's sister, was born ca. [circa] 1901 in Clarksville, Arkansas, or Fort Smith, Arkansas.

ORGANIZE BASIC INFORMATION

Stop at the FHL first and get their basic brochure on beginning your family history search. You might purchase an ancestor or pedigree chart at the library, the Family History Discovery Shoppe, or Deseret Book in downtown Salt Lake City. If you don't know what these charts are, ask at the library. Chapter two lists Web sites where such forms are available to download or print. They are easy to fill in and will give you an overview of each family. The forms may vary some, but you will chart the same basic information regardless of the form version. The downtown bookstores also sell basic genealogy how-to guide-books. Check the basic books listed under "Genealogical Research Guides" in appendix B for ideas.

CHECK IN AT HOME

Call, fax, or e-mail other relatives to gather more details. Spend an hour or two talking or e-mailing with your relatives to fill in as much as you can on an ancestor chart or family group sheets. Promise your sister in New Jersey a dinner out if she will gather some details from Mom or other relatives and forward them to you quickly. Tell Cousin Sarah you will send her copies of records you find if she will visit Aunt Bessie and quickly go through her old scrapbooks to get some names, dates, places, and relationships for you to use in your abbreviated search time. Let Cousin Jens in Sweden know that you will be forever grateful for whatever details he can e-mail to you. Armed with those quickly gathered details, you can start your research. Think about focusing on one ancestor or one small family grouping in one or two localities for this short visit. Then go to the library for the short orientation presentation.

Tip

VISIT THE FAMILYSEARCH CENTER

You might consider stopping at the FamilySearch Center in the Joseph Smith Memorial Building where the staff will assist you with Ancestral File, the International Genealogical Index, and other parts of the FamilySearch system. Check the library-related chapters of this guidebook for details on these resources. They are quick and easy resources to try. Many of your ancestors may not be in these indexes. Turn to the library catalog to see what is there for your family localities and surnames. Try to work from the present to the past, one generation at a time, from the known to the unknown. Don't skip generations, and don't start with that oft-told story of the heroic ancestor from the Revolutionary War. Later, your careful, step-by-step research may show that this person was the husband of an ancestor's sister and isn't directly related to you after all. Many genealogists find they have been working on people who become "former ancestors" because the researcher jumped back in time on a probable individual too soon. You need to prove the linkage between each generation to know you are on the right track.

U.S. CENSUS AS THE NEXT STEP

What's your next move after visiting the FamilySearch Center? If you have ancestors who were in the United States by 1920, the federal census is a good place to turn. For the 1920 census, there is an index for all heads of households, whereas the 1930 census (available in the spring of 2002) is only partially indexed. (There are indexes for most other censuses, and these are expanding all the time.) A set of microfilms for the 1920 census and Soundex is housed in the FamilySearch Center. The library and the JSMB have volunteers who will help you understand the Soundex index and the special code which you will need to use for this special index.

For other census years you may find indexes in printed or computerized formats. Be sure to proceed from whatever you find in a census index to the actual census on microfilm. Make a copy of the full census page that lists your parents or grandparents and their families. A machine copy is best, and a hand-written copy on a special form is an alternative. (A volunteer is usually available to help should you need to learn the mechanics of the copiers.) Check at least the pages before and after to see if any other connected families are listed. Make copies of these discoveries also. Repeat the process to check for other families on the 1920 census, then check earlier federal censuses. U.S. federal censuses are compiled every ten years. Don't be surprised if Great-Grandpa Mike doesn't age exactly ten years from one census to the next. Some men hid their ages for varying reasons, some didn't really know how old they were, and in some cases another person may have supplied erroneous information.

WHAT BOOKS MIGHT HELP YOU?

The next step, if you didn't already do it in the FamilySearch Center, might be to see what the library has in microform or in books for some of your ancestral localities or surnames. Does the library have a family history that someone else published on your Copping family from England and Canada? Is there a county history for the county in Ohio where one branch of your family settled? There might be a mini biography of a family member in this book. Are there church records for the Presbyterian church in western Pennsylvania where the other side of the family lived for ten years? You may know that Great-Grandpa's family arrived at the port of Boston in 1859; check the indexes to the Boston passenger arrival records for years around 1859, then proceed to the actual listing of that ship's passengers based on the probable index entry. Though other records may be a more sensible next step, finding ancestors' names on passenger lists seems to be a goal of many beginning genealogists.

Are there birth, marriage, or death records for your U.S. ancestral localities? Especially if there are indexes these are a good place to check for additional information on this quick trip to the library. When records do yield family information, be sure to copy the records or book pages.

Do you have the specific parish name for the place in Sweden where other family members lived for many decades? Check the catalog for the church records. You don't read Swedish? Ask the library reference staff for locations of word translation lists for the main words.

Notes

THINGS TO DO BASED ON WHAT YOU DO OR DON'T KNOW!

- Note names, relationships, dates, and places that you remember.

- Enter details onto family group sheets and ancestor charts.

- Contact relatives by phone or e-mail to gather other details.

- Visit the FamilySearch Center and use the databases.

- Find your family in the 1920 and 1930 U.S. censuses and progress to previous censuses.

- Check for the Research Outlines the library has compiled about doing research in your ancestral country, province, or state.

- Check to see what other guidebooks the library has for your ancestral areas.

- Check the library catalog for your surnames and localities to see what records the library may have for you to check.

What if you don't know many details or the family wasn't able to supply much on short notice? You may find your research a bit more difficult, but you have options. That county history for a place where you do know some ancestors lived might provide details. The census might fill in some more and tell you they were in Pennsylvania before they arrived in Illinois. At the very least check for the many guidebooks listed throughout this book, particularly appendix B. Skim through these to learn more about genealogical records and research techniques, both general and for the specific localities you do know about. You might find that the state historical society or the local genealogical library in that small town in Georgia has indexed more than 100 years worth of obituaries and noted many personal details in the index. Take notes or copy the guidebook page and contact that library when you return home. The guidebook may prove even more helpful if it notes that in 1988 this index was microfilmed and is available at the FHL.

NOTE WHAT YOU FIND

As you find data be sure to pencil it onto the family group sheets and ancestor charts you purchased. Why pencil? Unless you have verified names and dates in all available records, you may find some changes and discrepancies. Remember to jot notes on the copies you make to show you obtained them at the FHL. Copy the title pages of books and other identifying details.

PREPARING TO DO MORE

Now you might wish you had several more days to spend in the library, but, alas, the family vacation or business responsibilities beckon. Plan another trip to Salt Lake City, use a Family History Center where you live, or resolve to learn more about genealogical records and research techniques before proceeding further in your ancestral quest. Check the suggestions on the basics of family history research in chapter two.

FIFTEEN

Group Research Trips

Notes

Often a number of genealogists will join together to research at one or more research repositories. Generally such group research trips have one or more group leaders who may provide a variety of services. The key is to find a group that fits your personality and research needs. Some researchers join a group for the camaraderie of fellow genealogists rather than for specific research help. Salt Lake City and the Family History Library (FHL) are popular destinations for group trips. For many group trips, all the participants travel together; other group trips involve people meeting in Salt Lake City from many different locales. Some group trips are set up simply as means for genealogists to get together in a place such as Salt Lake City without any research assistance other than what the participants provide to each other. Whatever the setup or reason, the fellowship of people who actually enjoy hearing about the faded Latin church record or the five generations mentioned in the probate record is a plus for the group experience.

We designed this chapter to assist both trip planners and researchers choosing a research trip experience in Salt Lake City. Groups trips are offered by genealogical societies, historical societies, ethnic groups, professional genealogists, and other organizations or businesses. Many group trips are excellent experiences for the participants and for the leaders. As with any purchase, be a wise consumer and ask questions to see if the trip arrangements will fulfill your specific needs. Ideally, the trip advertising brochure or flyer should answer most questions.

Several years ago a Salt Lake City newspaper contacted us for information about our experience as FHL group leaders. They were fascinated by the groups traveling to the library from so many places. It was even more interesting to them that many of us were not members of The Church of Jesus Christ of Latter-day Saints. They interviewed us and two of our group's participants. At about this time, the city and its businesses began to fully realize the economic impact genealogists have on the area. Many of us stay in hotels for extended periods of time. Even those who live locally or stay with relatives still spend money in the downtown area on meals, books, supplies, transportation, gifts, clothing, and other things.

Over the past ten years, many genealogists or societies have asked us about

---

GROUP TRIPS AND CONTACT INFORMATION

Jewish Genealogy Trip to Salt Lake City
P.O. Box 99
Bergenfield, NJ 07621
(800) 286-8296
garymokotoff@avotaynu.com or eileenpolakoff@avotaynu.com

National Genealogical Society
4527 Seventeenth St. North
Arlington, VA 22207-2399
(800) 473-0060, ext. 331
http://www.ngsgenealogy.org/edutripsaltlake.htm

New England Historic Genealogical Society
101 Newbury St.
Boston, MA 02116-3007
(888) 286-3447
http://www.nehgs.org
education@nehgs.org

Additional group trips: St. Louis Genealogical Society, Southern California Gene-alogical Society, Genealogical Forum of Oregon, Kansas Council of Genealogical Societies, Dallas Genealogical Society, Heritage Quest, and others. Check with the group for trip schedule, pricing, and other details. Contact details for many societies are at the Federation of Genealogical Society's Society Hall at <http://www.fgs.org>. Some other group trip participants travel to Salt Lake City from Australia, England, France, New Zealand, and Sweden.

---

the group trip experience, from the viewpoints of both joining and leading such a trip. This chapter is the fruit of many years of our labor as group trip leaders and people who find the camaraderie of a group very satisfying. We have also been asked why we chose to lead trips. That answer is easy. We saw the arrivals at the FHL of many groups whose leaders pretty much said to their fellow genealogists, "Well, this is the library. See you later." We saw the lost looks on their faces and knew this was not the way to lead a group. Our group leader experience grew out of such encounters, and we aimed to offer more assistance and pretrip planning ideas. Fortunately, many other groups now do the same.

FOR THE PARTICIPANT

Choose a group that fits your needs. These questions might help your decision:
- Is this your first foray into research at the FHL?
- Will the group you choose offer the pretrip and on-site assistance you need?

- Is there help with hotel and travel planning?
- What consultation or class services are offered once the group is in Salt Lake City?
- Are there arrangements for getting back and forth from the airport, train station, or bus depot?
- How close to the library is the hotel? If it is a few blocks away, what transportation options are offered?
- Is the group leader familiar with the library, especially with all the changes in recent years?

Hopefully, the qualifications of tour leaders and any others assisting will be shared. If the leaders have much experience in leading this type of trip and also have extensive experience in Wisconsin research or passenger arrival records or Swedish research, that may help you decide if this is the trip for you.

Here are more questions and details to consider:

- What are the deadlines for full payment for the trip and related fees? The brochure or flyer should be clear on what the fee does and does not include. The package fee may include airfare, luggage transfer, shuttles, hotel rooms, handouts, newsletters, and consultations. Check to see if the registration materials state what the fee and deadline are for cancellation. If you cancel within the last month before the trip date, you may forfeit the entire deposit.
- Is a roommate service provided? That is, will the group leaders assign you a roommate if you need one or provide a list of others seeking the same so you can make arrangements? Can a nongenealogical spouse or friend come along for a fee? Can extra nights be reserved in the hotel at a discounted rate?
- Is a calendar or listing of the week's events available as a quick reminder for the participants? If you have signed up for the week, you don't want to miss any events.
- Will the group have distinctive name tags so you can recognize each other? This also helps the group leaders and participants get to know others by name. Ask about any get-togethers in Salt Lake City such as classes, meetings, question-and-answer sessions, meals, receptions, continental breakfasts, door prizes, area tours, or anything else you might find enjoyable.
- Is a rooming list provided so you can find others in your group once you check into the hotel? Is a general participants' contact list or maybe even a surname or locality exchange list distributed before departure from home so you can find others with similar research interests? We used to ask participants to send in a small picture of themselves. Several were affixed to a page with the names typed below. These were duplicated on a high-quality copier and shared with all the participants ahead of time so they could see what each person looked like. (Of course, there is always a person or two who sends in a photo from twenty years ago!) This also helped us, as the leaders, to match faces with names of folks that would be with us all week.

Notes

Having listed all these possible amenities, we need to be clear that not all tours can offer all of them. Group tours require many hours, many workers, and expense for the leaders. Decide which amenities are most important for your Salt Lake City experience, and if they are all important, be prepared to pay for these services.

FOR THE LEADERS
Set the Date

The FHL urges group leaders to let the library know about their groups' plans. If many large groups are scheduled for the same dates, you may wish to change your schedule to avoid a busy time. Contact (801) 240-1054 or (800) 453-3860, extension 2-1054, for this information. The FHL Web site has additional information for group visits; click on "Group Visits" at the Library page of <http://www.familysearch.org>.

The ideal is to let the library know your group's plans a year in advance. Of course, shorter notice is permitted, but if you have a trip to advertise, that year in advance is not too soon. The library asks for a three-month minimum notice to help them plan. Why? Suppose five groups all arrived unexpectedly at a time when many library staff were on vacation or attending special training sessions. The library, while it prides itself on having adequate staff on duty to help you, might be too shorthanded in a situation like that. If you and five of your genealogy friends are coming to the library and have experience working at the FHL, you needn't give the library advance notice. If all five of your friends are new to the library and need help with Tennessee or German research and you won't be assisting them, it would be a good idea to let the library know about your group's arrival. Similarly if you are traveling from France with only ten researchers but none of you speaks English very well, contact the library so that reference staff who speak French will be available during your visit to the library.

Even if your group doesn't need much assistance or an orientation, it is still a good idea to let the library know your group is coming. Your group will use books that need reshelving, rest rooms that need cleaning, and restricted films

Tip

Quotes

VOICES OF EXPERIENCE

As one professional researcher remarked, "Some of the visiting groups also create problems because of the high expectations of the members and the poor preparation and limited help offered. Some of these people eventually find their way to a professional who can help them, but many spend the whole week wandering about, almost completely lost. If you, as a professional, are leading a group trip to Salt Lake City, make sure that you fully prepare the visitors and are there on the spot to offer help."

—Vaughn L. Simon, CG, "The Family History Library"

that require assistance from library attendants. All of this affects staffing levels. What if a member of your group becomes ill? The library may need to contact you, the leader, and you may not be in the library. If you have supplied details on where your group is staying, the library can leave a message for you at the hotel. No matter how small and experienced your group is, you might contact the library about your arrival to make sure you will not be visiting the same weeks as eight large or inexperienced genealogy groups!

If your group requires special assistance, such as signers or interpreters, the library will need to schedule staff and volunteers who can handle those duties. Several years ago we were at the library with a group when hundreds of researchers from another country arrived. Many of them did not speak English and required interpreters. The library had not been forewarned. As usual, the library went the extra mile to assist them by calling in people from various library and Church offices to assist. (Area restaurants, on the other hand, were overwhelmed!)

If a group will largely be doing one type of ethnic research, let the library know; that will affect reference counter staffing for that area.

When you notify the library your group is coming, ask them to provide an extended orientation session for your group. Occasionally two groups might be scheduled together for this. A library staff member will present information on the library, the catalog, library guidelines, and more. If your group is primarily doing research in one country's records, the person assigned to give the orientation may have expertise in that area. This means scheduling specific staff members to be available when your group is at the library. Classrooms in the library are used for many purposes and require advance scheduling.

The Salt Lake Convention & Visitors Bureau offers free assistance to group trip planners. This might consist of hotel referral, area travel literature and maps, and information on events that might be of interest to your group. They may be able to help you get discount coupons from area merchants.

For More Info

Salt Lake Convention &
Visitors Bureau Group
Trip Information
kpettey@saltlake.org
(800) 541-4955

Speaking of Dates

What dates are best for group trips? Some favor summer in Salt Lake City and don't mind the dry heat. Some groups chose January, when the library was less crowded; now, lots of people travel to the library in January. Spring and fall months are busy group trip times. Actually the library is usually busy, though not overcrowded, most of the year. The time between Thanksgiving and Christmas is the exception. The days preceding and following major U.S. holidays are less crowded, but this may not be the best time for trip participants. Some groups prefer the Sunday-to-Sunday schedule. More and more are choosing midweek to midweek. Years ago our group voted on the week it preferred. The popular choice was Wednesday to Wednesday or Thursday to Thursday. Airfares are usually cheaper midweek. Because the library is closed Sunday, this schedule forces the participants to have a day to reorganize and relax, and Sunday evening was a great time for a group party. First-time researchers at the FHL especially need that day to regroup.

Hotels

Many hotels in Salt Lake City welcome research groups. If enough rooms are rented, groups may receive a discount on room rates, an amount deducted from the entire bill, or a free room for the leader. A meeting room or classroom may be available; some hotels charge an extra fee for this. Some hotels offer regular shuttle service to transport the group participants to and from the airport or train station.

There will generally be a contract for the group leader to sign agreeing to the fees and number of rooms to be rented. Deadlines must be met in order to assure the room rentals at the agreed-to fee. The leaders need to stay in contact with the hotel, provide rooming lists as needed, and handle many other details. It is also important for the leader to be sure that participants who require nonsmoking rooms or a refrigerator for medicines end up with what they need. It is to the group's advantage if the leaders have actually stayed at the hotel before and are familiar with the services and staff.

Set Fees and Handle Other Details

If you will lead a trip as part of your professional genealogical business, check with your insurance agent about liability insurance. Societies and organizations should do the same. The participants need to sign a conditions and responsibility statement so they understand the trip's guidelines and limitations.

Important

What should the participants' cost be? Will it cover the leaders' airfare, hotel room, meals, printing and postage for trip-related group mailings, name tags, telephone calls, printer cartridges, paper, envelopes, and more? Will the fee cover a wage for the leaders, who are basically on call for the entire week? Leaders must understand that this is their job for the week and they may only be able to do their own research before or after the group week or in the evenings. Do you have enough leaders among your society volunteers that the job can be divided among many hands—each person volunteers a certain number of hours to work while in Salt Lake City? If so, more of the profit from the trip can go into the society's educational coffers. If you need to hire additional consultants from the professional genealogical community in Salt Lake City or instructors/lecturers, be sure to include these costs in the overall fee.

Set a cancellation deadline that will give you time to try and fill any canceled trip slots. The cancellation fee should be high enough that registrants will not take lightly a decision to cancel. Twenty-five dollars to fifty dollars is a suggested range. You will have already paid for printing, telephone calls, and hotel deposits.

Be clear about what the trip package price does and does not include. It likely will not include meals and tips, laundry service, telephone calls, beverages, and more.

Have you thought about whether the occupancy level of your group's rooms will be more than two people? Your hotel contract may limit this or add a significant extra person fee. We discourage putting more than two people in a room because as group leaders we have been called upon to settle arguments!

Your advertising should state whether there is a limit on the total number of people for the trip. Decide if you will assign a roommate or simply supply names to contact for those who desire a roommate but have no specific person in mind.

Be clear about what hours of assistance will be available from the group leaders in the library. If you need to raise prices to cover increased costs, explain this to your past participants. If you can keep prices the same from one year to the next, champion that in your advertising.

The Business End

Business? Yes, a group research trip with money involved is essentially a business proposition. If you or your organization offers a group trip and takes participants' money and reservations, you need to provide what you have advertised. If you advertise one-on-one assistance in the library, will you have enough leaders to do this? Have the leaders had enough recent experience in this library to provide the knowledgeable assistance participants expect? Think about how you will handle situations such as accidents, illnesses, "problem" people, or other unforeseen circumstances.

Who Is in Charge?

Before you agree to lead such a trip, be clear about who is in charge. Make sure the leaders' names and qualifications are mentioned in the advertising. If you are a leader and more than one person has this job, who has the final say on things? Who pays the bills? If the trip is sponsored by a society, are the officers and the trip leaders in agreement on who has the responsibility and authority?

Travel

If all the participants are coming from one area, will travel arrangements be included in the package price? If the participants are coming to Salt Lake City from various locations, they will likely make their own travel plans. The advertising brochure might list a suggested travel agent. Set a clear time by which the participants should arrive in Salt Lake City.

At the Library

A good way to introduce your group to the library is to offer short orientation tours. Assign a knowledgeable leader to groups of four to five people and have then do a quiet walk-through of the library. Point out the reference-book shelves, microfilm and microfiche cabinets, elevators, computer catalogs, rest rooms, book stacks, copy centers, reference counters, classrooms, and other highlights. Do this for each floor.

Another helpful tour is an equipment orientation session. Have a leader show four or five participants how to use the computers, the various film and fiche readers and copiers, and paper copiers. For these library tours and equipment orientations, use a sign-up sheet with times and meeting places clearly stated.

Many groups offer one-on-one consultations to participants. Use a sign-up sheet to schedule appointments. A time limit, such as a half hour, is useful. Some groups offer assistance on a first come, first served basis. The group should be informed about where the consultants for that day will be sitting.

Group leaders should work with participants so they do not cause extra work for library staff or unnecessarily disturb other researchers. A few groups seem to appear in the library and receive no assistance from the leaders who came with them. The duties of a group leader might include brushing up on research for New York or Poland if your group has significant interests in those areas. You may need to bolster spirits of a depressed researcher who "isn't finding anything" and tells everyone this. You may need to be a travel agent and help someone find an alternate flight when theirs gets canceled.

You might issue a daily newsletter for your group while you're visiting the library. This can provide reminders of classes, consultations, mini tours, lunch or dinner gatherings (with times and meeting places), and hotel departure information. If someone has a birthday or anniversary during the week, you might mention this. Place the newsletters under the group registrants' hotel room doors at night or early in the morning.

Idea Generator

In the City

Make sure your group members have an orientation to the area around the library. A short group tour in Temple Square and the nearby downtown area is a good idea. Point out and discuss Temple Square, the Visitors Information Center, how to get to the library from the hotel, where to get on the light rail, and how to find the malls and various restaurants. As in the library, keep these groups small. Remember that participants will not all hear, walk, or absorb instructions at the same pace.

Group lunches are a good way to assemble the group and refresh overworked minds. There are two food courts in the malls near the library, and group members can choose their own food and then sit together. This can be a good question-and-answer time, or the group might prefer general conversation. Go before or after the noon hour to ensure you can all sit together.

Other Group Events

An opening or closing reception is a good way to begin and end the week together. On our groups' Sunday breaks from the library, many participants began the day by attending the Mormon Tabernacle Choir performance in the morning. Then many would walk or take cabs to one of the local Sunday brunches with us.

That evening we had a party. We served light refreshments, including items for those with special diets. We often used themes. If your trip is around Halloween, Valentine's Day, or another such date, your theme is ready-made. We had time for questions and answers, conversation, and some door prize drawings. Door prizes were items such as a genealogical guidebook, a packet of genealogical forms, a gift certificate to a downtown Salt Lake City restaurant, and a gift certificate toward part of the registration fee for the next year's trip. After

Idea Generator

several years of trips, some of the regulars began to donate door prizes or photo award prizes.

We also asked the participants to bring various things. One year it was participants' baby photos: We placed them out on a table (with no names visible), and everyone had to match the baby photo with the adult participant. Another year we asked them to bring unusual photos of ancestors or related things. People brought photos of ancestors in caskets and pictures of events, houses, and more. Yet another year we asked them to bring ancestral family group pictures. Two or three of the participants were asked to judge each year's pictures. We gave prizes for the sweetest smile, the most sour-faced person, the cutest baby, and other categories. We gave children's candies with catchy names to match the award.

The Sunday evening gathering was a good opportunity for people to share a research find in the library. It was also an opportunity for conversing and making new friends. Before long the participants from California, Texas, Virginia, Minnesota, and Wisconsin had started new genealogical friendships. Many of those who came along on these trips remain our friends. We hope the group research trip experience will have the same results for all of you.

COUPON FOR 1996 WARREN GROUP RESEARCH TRIP DEPOSIT

This coupon is good for $25.00 off the $100.00 deposit fee for the 1996 Warren Group Research Trip. To redeem, sign this coupon, and send it with a check for $75.00 and the completed Registration Form from our 1996 brochure. This coupon is not transferable to another person, only one coupon is redeemable per eligible person, and it is valid only for the 1996 Warren Group Research Trip. The coupon is good only until the trip fills up or for registrations postmarked by 1 May 1996, whichever comes first.

Registrant's Signature_____

Date_____

Figure 15-1
Example of an incentive coupon for group trip participants.

Will They Come Back?

The way a trip is planned and whether it works for the participants will influence repeat reservations. To help ensure that your group's participants sign up for the next group trip to Salt Lake City, consider giving them discount coupons for the next trip. Registration at the previous year's prices might bring repeat business. At least give them the next year's dates immediately so they can mark their calendars. If they had fun, they will likely come back with your group; even some people who did not have positive research results will return. If they learned a lot about research and the library, ruled out some research avenues, and felt good about the experience, it will have been a positive experience. Their preparation for the next trip will be different based on what they learned. Advertise early, and keep in contact with past participants. We all need a bit of encouragement to make us feel a part of the group.

SIXTEEN

Working With a Professional Researcher

B efore you decide that this chapter might not apply to you, ask yourself a few questions. Do you have unlimited research time? Have your research plans always yielded success? If you live in the Salt Lake City area, you are fortunate to have the Family History Library close by. How many times in the last year have you scheduled blocks of time to research at the library and actually accomplished that task? What arrangements did you have to make for child care, dinner preparation, or a vacation day?

Many people who live even within an hour's drive of the library say they just don't get there often enough. For those who live farther away, how much does a plane ticket to Salt Lake City cost? How much would the gas cost if you drove? What are the hotel costs involved? If you travel from a distance and stay with family, what is the cost of the gifts you would bring to them or the restaurant meals you might treat them to as a way of expressing your thanks? No matter where you live, costs and arrangements are involved.

This chapter pertains to all researchers; we all need help with our research at one time or another. When we visit a major repository for the first time, we often hire a local professional to show us the ropes and give us a jump start on the research collection and facility.

ASSISTANCE YOU MIGHT NEED

Consider using the services of a professional genealogist for research before you arrive at the FHL. A research plan for your on-site visit could be devised. **The professional might be able to rule out some records and narrow the scope of items you need to check once you arrive.** She might be one on-site in your ancestral home who will check records not available at the FHL. This research, which could be in any country, could aid in your pretrip preparation.

At times it makes sense to have another set of eyes review your family history materials and give fresh suggestions on the next steps to take. Frequently the answer to a research problem is not as difficult as you might think. That professional who has not had your Griffin family problem staring her in the face

Timesaver

for the last two years might be able to break through some of your difficult problems.

The professional might be able to read the language in which your microfilmed ancestral records are written. This would save you time before and during your trip as you attempt to read the records in an unfamiliar language. That professional, or another one, may be familiar with the style of writing in the time period or geographic area in which your ancestor lived. If you don't hire the professional for the on-site help in the library, one may still be available to translate the records you find.

If it has been a while since you visited the FHL, the professional can reacquaint you with the library, provide updates on the collection, offer equipment orientation, or give you other timesaving tips. This is especially important due to equipment, layout, and collection changes at the library in recent years. If you have never been to the FHL and will not be coming with a group, consider hiring a professional to provide orientation services and a mini tour of the library. These could be tailored to your specific research needs.

A word of caution: The library has a firm rule prohibiting professional researchers and others from soliciting clients or selling materials in the library. Contact the professional in advance, or make an appointment to meet him outside the library grounds to make arrangements.

Warning

If You Live Near Salt Lake City

Consider hiring a professional genealogist who is familiar with the library to do some of the research you just never get around to doing. Hire one of these researchers to spend some time working with you at the library helping you to maximize your time. Perhaps you can start with a quick update on the library facilities and collections, then move on to one-on-one research time.

If You Live Elsewhere

If you will spend some of your valuable budget and time to travel to the FHL, you need to maximize your work there. Having a professional researcher work side by side with you for a few hours or more is a wise choice for many people. These few hours can save time and frustration and allow you to proceed with the research more quickly. Compared to the cost of your airline ticket and hotel room, these few hours are a bargain.

CONTACT A PROFESSIONAL RESEARCHER

Should you expect a researcher to be free to meet with you or do your advance research on the schedule you need? The researcher likely has a set schedule, so advance contact is important. In the Salt Lake City area you will find firms that have multiple researchers available. Contact the researcher or firm to inquire about availability, research fees, reimbursable expense, credentials, geographic or subject areas of expertise, and other details that may be important to you. If dealing with a firm, ask for these details as they would relate to the person with whom you would be working. Be prepared to hire the person for their set

Money Saver

minimum amount of time, which may be anywhere from one hour to several hours. **When you actually hire the researcher, be sure you have a clear, written statement about the costs involved, and make clear your hour or dollar limits.** It is also up to you to explain what you have already accomplished to avoid duplicate research.

See "Sites for Professional Organizations" and appendix B for contact information for some of the following:

- The Association of Professional Genealogists has published and online directories of its worldwide members. They also have a brochure titled *So You're Going to Hire a Professional Genealogist*. This information is included on their Web site. The Association of Professional Genealogists has a Salt Lake chapter.
- The Board for Certification of Genealogists also has published and online rosters of its associates.
- International Commission for the Accreditation of Professional Genealogists (ICAPGen). The Accredited Genealogist program formerly administered by the FHL has been transferred to the ICAPGen. Lists of accredited researchers are online.
- A genealogical or historical society in your ancestral area may have a list of researchers for hire.
- Advertisements or lists appear in genealogical periodicals.
- Look for listings from specific ethnic organizations and publications.
- Talk to other genealogists to see if they have hired a professional researcher whom they might recommend.
- Read chapter eleven in Sharon DeBartolo Carmack's *The Genealogy Sourcebook* for a good discussion on working with a professional genealogist.

Internet Source

SITES FOR PROFESSIONAL ORGANIZATIONS

Association of Professional Genealogists: http://www.apgen.org

Board for Certification of Genealogists: http://www.bcgcertification.org

International Commission for the Accreditation of Professional Genealogists: http://www.icapgen.org or www.infouga.org

CHOOSE A PROFESSIONAL RESEARCHER

If your research problem is confined to a specific geographic area, time period, or language, check the directories of researchers to find one who specializes in your area or time period or reads and translates the foreign language. Some researchers relish the chance to show you the vast records at the FHL and help you zero in on what might aid your research. Others excel in analyzing the information you already have gathered and laying out a research plan for you. Some professional researchers specialize in family health history or a specific ethnic group. If the directory is not clear, ask the professionals about their areas of expertise.

WORK WITH THE PROFESSIONAL RESEARCHER

Once you have spent money to hire a researcher, be willing to listen and learn. Take the suggestions offered and do the work, even if it seems time-consuming or has more steps than you were planning to do. The professional with expertise in a particular area gives you advice for a reason; he knows the records and research procedure. That person may know about resources you are unfamiliar with, including new accessions at the FHL. Remember that this professional will have knowledge of your research needs. If your research project isn't finished when you leave the FHL, the researcher might be available to continue the work.

PART FIVE

Making the Most of Your Trip to the Beautiful Salt Lake City Area

SEVENTEEN

Salt Lake City Basics, A to Z

Why leave the library and visit Salt Lake City and the surrounding area of Utah? Thousands of skiing and snowboarding enthusiasts know why, as do convention goers, sports buffs, symphony lovers, hikers, vacationers, and those who stand in awe of the natural beauty of the state.

Salt Lake City lies between the Wasatch Range and the Oquirrh Mountains. And then there is the genealogy connection: The Family History Library in Salt Lake City is visited by an average of 2,400 people each day. It is common for someone attending a convention or other meeting in the Salt Palace Convention Center or a hotel to steal away from a session to do some family history research in the library. So why do these folks come to Salt Lake City and the library? If you have been there or lived there, you know why. If you have never been to the library, one visit is all it will take to convince you that you need to return more than once. How does a genealogist who is also a skier decide what to do on a winter's day in Salt Lake City?

Salt Lake City has a fascinating history that is appropriate for the home of the world's largest family history research collection. We recommend a little pretrip reading to acquaint you with Salt Lake City's past. The first settlers, the Native Americans, were there for thousands of years before Brigham Young and other members of The Church of Jesus Christ of Latter-day Saints arrived on 24 July 1847. Today Salt Lake County is home to almost 825,000 people with a diverse culture. The Great Salt Lake, just west of the city, is another impressive sight.

This guide deals mainly with current information for visitors to a city that is clean and just as busy as other cities of similar size. Visitors are amazed at how wide the streets are and how long each city block is. Unlike many urban areas that have lost many of their stores and restaurants, downtown Salt Lake City has two enclosed malls, other shops, and a variety of restaurants.

The architecture is stunning, with an impressive mix of historic buildings and newer construction. Whether you call it the Crossroads of the West, "This is the Place," Zion, or the Saintly City, Salt Lake City is a spectacular place to visit. For those of us who don't live near mountains, the vistas of the mountains are breathtaking. The sunrises and sunsets are not to be missed.

If a city can host the 2002 Winter Olympic Games with thirty-five hundred athletes and officials from about eighty countries, followed by the Paralympics with eleven hundred athletes, officials from thirty-five nations, and all the thousands of spectators, it can handle genealogists. Each year the area hosts hundreds of conventions, some with thousands of attendees. It should be a snap to host the twenty-four hundred genealogists who research in the city each day!

Getting around in the city and area gets easier all the time. This book is written with the scheduled November 2001 opening of the new TRAX line on 400 South in mind. All telephone area codes are 801 unless otherwise noted.

Accessibility

Salt Lake City is a very accessible city. The airport, the FHL, the hotels, the downtown shopping malls, and many restaurants are handicapped accessible. The sidewalks have curb cuts for wheelchairs and motorized carts. Some of the downtown street corners have pedestrian signals that chirp for north-south and cuckoo for east-west to let sight-impaired people know which way is safe to walk. Check with individual restaurants on accessibility of the dining areas and the rest rooms. Some people choose motorized carts, scooters, or wheelchairs to make getting around easier. Rental agencies for these are listed in the yellow pages under "wheelchairs & scooters."

Airport

The Salt Lake International Airport is a modern facility only ten minutes from the heart of downtown. It is served by many airlines and is a hub for Delta Air Lines. The airport is undergoing a multiyear expansion and upgrade that will showcase the surrounding scenic mountains. It can be a busy and sometimes crowded airport. Allow plenty of time to check in and get to your gate for departure.

Near the baggage carousels are areas with advertising and direct-line courtesy telephones for many hotels. Call your hotel to verify whether shuttle service is provided. If it is provided, the hotels will likely ask on which airline you arrived and tell you the door number at which you will be picked up. There are also taxis and other services for transportation to area hotels and motels, as well as several car rental companies.

Altitude and Dryness

The city's elevation is 4,330 feet (1,320 meters). Some visitors find it difficult to climb steps or walk a distance, or they tire more easily while in Salt Lake City. This may be due to the altitude. If you have heart or lung problems or other health concerns, check with your physician for precautions to take. Pace yourself accordingly. Use the elevators in the library and shopping malls if you aren't used to the elevation. We have heard it takes up to six months for a

Salt Lake City Access and Selected Salt Lake Valley Places of Interest

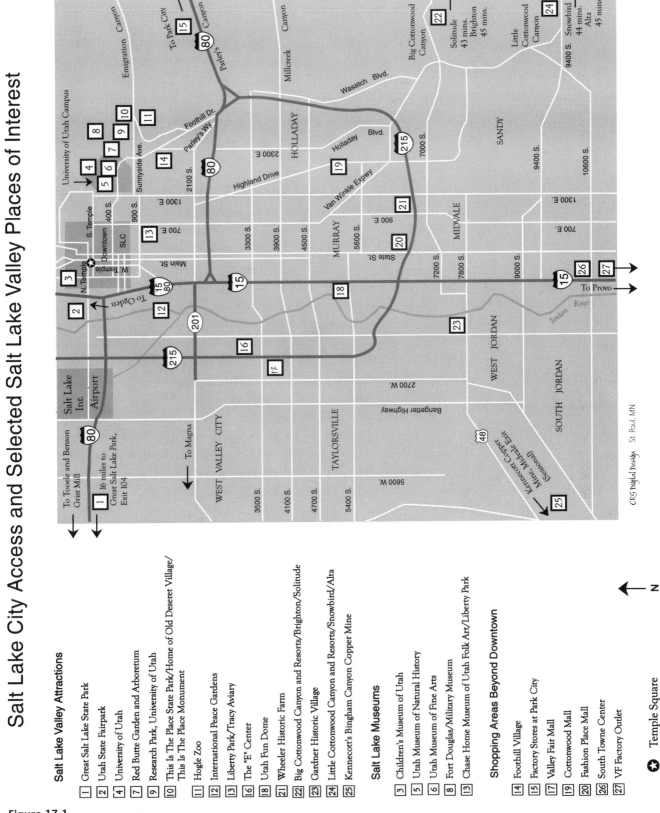

Figure 17-1
Salt Lake City Access and Salt Lake City places of interest map. *Map prepared by Carol Barrett*

Salt Lake Valley Attractions

1. Great Salt Lake State Park
2. Utah State Fairpark
4. University of Utah
7. Red Butte Garden and Arboretum
9. Research Park, University of Utah
10. This Is The Place State Park/Home of Old Deseret Village/ This Is The Place Monument
11. Hogle Zoo
12. International Peace Gardens
13. Liberty Park/Tracy Aviary
16. The "E" Center
18. Utah Fun Dome
21. Wheeler Historic Farm
22. Big Cottonwood Canyon and Resorts/Brighton/Solitude
23. Gardner Historic Village
24. Little Cottonwood Canyon and Resorts/Snowbird/Alta
25. Kennecott's Bingham Canyon Copper Mine

Salt Lake Museums

3. Children's Museum of Utah
5. Utah Museum of Natural History
6. Utah Museum of Fine Arts
8. Fort Douglas/Military Museum
13. Chase Home Museum of Utah Folk Art/Liberty Park

Shopping Areas Beyond Downtown

14. Foothill Village
15. Factory Stores at Park City
17. Valley Fair Mall
19. Cottonwood Mall
20. Fashion Place Mall
26. South Towne Center
27. VF Factory Outlet

★ Temple Square

Tip

person to become completely acclimated to the higher altitude. Alcohol's effects are intensified by the high altitude. **Pack hand lotion and lip moisturizer to combat the dryness.** Due to the dryness and altitude, you may also experience nosebleeds. Some people find they are more thirsty when they visit, and this may be due to the dryness or different drinking water.

Liquor Laws

More liberal than in the past, Utah's liquor laws still limit the number of locations of on-site liquor sales and the times when liquor may be served. Three different types of eating and drinking establishments in Utah are restaurants, private clubs, and taverns. The legal drinking age in Utah is twenty-one. At many restaurants, adults can order beer, mixed drinks, or wine with a meal after noon and until midnight. Private clubs can serve alcohol from 10:00 A.M. to 1:00 A.M., and do not need to serve food with the alcohol purchased. For about five dollars you can purchase temporary memberships that allow several people to enter a private club. Visitors may also be hosted by other members of the club and enter without charge. Some larger hotels have private clubs for their hotel guests. Taverns are open to the public and may or may not serve food. Most taverns only serve beer with a 3.2 percent alcohol content. Check the telephone directory (Utah government section) for the location of downtown-area state wine and liquor stores; these are closed on Sundays and holidays. Grocery and convenience stores sell 3.2 beer.

Newspapers and Magazines

At least once or twice while you are in Salt Lake City you should find out what else is going on in the world beyond the microfilm reader. At the same time you can determine what day and date it is, as immersion in research often causes people to forget these! The *Salt Lake Tribune* <http://www.sltrib.com> and the *Deseret News* <http://www.deseretnews.com> are the two major daily newspapers. In the area near the library, newspaper boxes are located near JB's Restaurant in the hotel next door to the library, at Dee's Restaurant, in Crossroads Plaza mall, on nearby streets, and in some hotel gift shops. The bimonthly *Salt Lake: Magazine of the Mountainwest* is available at newsstands. There are several other weekly and alternative newspapers. The free *Salt Lake City Weekly* is available at bookstores, restaurants, <http://www.avenews.com>, and other locations and carries descriptions of restaurants, area events, and services. Once a year it compiles "The Best of Utah" for these and other categories.

The Borders bookstore in Crossroads Plaza carries newspapers from other major cities in the United States and elsewhere.

Parking

Two large fee-basis parking lots for FHL patrons are located behind the library with entrances on 200 West between South and North Temple streets and on North Temple between West Temple and 200 West streets. Other parking in the area is available in ramps and underground. The larger hotels have parking ramps; the one at the Plaza Hotel next to the library has daily parking rates. There are a few surface parking lots in the library vicinity and some short-term parking meters. The Joseph Smith Memorial Building has underground parking with an entrance on South Temple Street. The ZCMI Center Mall and Crossroads Plaza have parking ramps. People coming from large cities usually find the daylong rates quite reasonable.

Parks

A good way to extend your lunch hour and relax is to get carryout food and walk or drive to a park. (The deli counters at larger grocery stores sell take-out food.) Some of the parks have good walking paths or other points of interest that can give your mind a break. Some researchers say they won't give up valuable research time, but you will be more alert and your thinking process will be sharper after some exercise. Some of the parks you might venture to are

- City Creek Park and Brigham Young Memorial Park, Second Street and Second Avenue (two and a half blocks from the library): This park offers a mill wheel, a stream, a pond, and walking paths in the midst of the city.
- Liberty Park and Tracy Aviary, 1300 South 589 East: walking and running paths, large children's playground, picnic tables, and almost five hundred birds in the aviary.
- Memory Grove Park/City Creek Canyon, 135 East North Temple: walking and jogging paths that extend into the mountains.
- Red Butte Gardens and Arboretum, 300 Wakara Way (in the University of Utah area): In addition to the extensive botanical gardens and walking trails, the Red Butte Gardens hosts musical events.
- This is the Place Heritage Park and Old Deseret Village, 2601 East Sunnyside Avenue (800 South): Admission is charged. This park marks the end of the trail for the pioneers who came to the Salt Lake Valley. Reenactments by costumed volunteers enhance your visit.

Photo Opportunities

Be sure to bring your camera or purchase a disposable camera to take advantage of the scenery and buildings. If you stay in a hotel with many stories you might be able to take photos of the city and the mountains from the hotel itself. The area outside the library is great for pictures. Temple Square and the plazas between the Square and the JSMB and the Church Office Building are full of flowers and greenery and must be among the most photographed areas in Salt Lake City. Of course, the buildings in Temple Square and downtown are themselves ideal subjects for pictures. This whole area is decorated at Christmas. Venture to the observation areas discussed later in this chapter under "Views of the Valley and Mountains." North of the capitol area are lookout areas for picture taking. City Creek Park is another pretty place, and the area outside Abravanel Hall and the Salt Palace are often photographed. Rent a car and drive into the mountains for even more photo spots. Photo-finishing services are available in the two downtown malls.

In the library be sure to ask permission before you take someone's picture. Camera flashes can disturb someone intently studying a microfilmed record.

Radio

Salt Lake City is home to just about every type of radio station. We bring along our radios and headsets to wear while we do our frequent walking. (Well, it should be frequent.) This includes talk, rock, oldies, religious, and others. Check the magazines and information guides in your hotel for lists of radio stations, format, and dial location. In some hotels you may find poor-quality reception of some radio stations. Stations and content include

570	AM	KNRS	syndicated talk
910	AM	KALL	news and talk
1010	AM	KIQN	news and talk
1160	AM	KSL	news, talk, sports, traffic
1280	AM	KDYL	news and talk
1320	AM	KFNZ	all sports
88.3	FM	KCPW	National Public Radio
89.1	FM	KBYU	classical
90.9	FM	KRCL	worldwide information and music
94.1	FM	KODJ	oldies
100.3	FM	KSFI	easy listening
104.3	FM	KSOP	country
106.5	FM	KOSY	easy listening; Saturday evenings show tunes run starting at 9:00 P.M.

Safety

While Salt Lake City is a safe city and is not as large as New York City or Paris, it nonetheless has its share of concerns including street crime and homeless people. Area businesses suggest that donations be made to area homeless shelters and food shelves rather than directly to panhandlers. One worthwhile outlet for donations, recommended by several area organizations, is Traveler's Aid, 210 South Rio Grande, Salt Lake City, UT 84101.

Tip

Researchers generally stay in the heart of the busy tourist area, and common sense dictates going out after dark in pairs or via taxicab. **We advocate (for both men and women) wearing a hidden pouch, a belt bag, or a fanny pack for your money, I.D., and credit cards, rather than carrying a purse or just a wallet.** This is also a good hands-free option for working in the library. If you must bring a purse, put it in a locker at the library; do not hang it over the back of your chair. If you are with a group visiting the library, you might wish to remove your name tag when out on the street.

Salt Palace Convention Center

This beautiful, modern building is one of the busiest places in Salt Lake City. The Utah Genealogical Association has used the facilities for educational events, and in September of 2000 the Federation of Genealogical Societies and the Utah

Genealogical Association hosted the annual FGS Conference there. This event drew two thousand genealogists, speakers, and vendors to the city.

The center faces West Temple Street, and visitors are drawn to the six-story glass-encased tower, which is lit at night. The center accommodates a wide variety of events from machinery shows to upscale meetings and banquets. It is within a block of the FHL and close to downtown shopping and many hotels and restaurants. It is adjacent to Abravanel Hall, where stage and musical events take place. The main entrance near the tower houses a large visitor information center.

Seasonal Outdoor Activities

Regardless of the season, there is always something to do in the Salt Lake valley. You can take a bus or rental car to the ski slopes. Ski rental services are in the mountains, Salt Lake City, and even the airport. Snowboarding is popular here. In the summer there are concerts at many locations, including Gallivan Center downtown (36 East 200 South). Try winter ice skating (with skate rental) at Gallivan Center. Don't break that microfilm-reeling arm, though.

The spectacular holiday lights in Temple Square shine at night from the day after Thanksgiving until early January. There are more lights on the Church Office Building Plaza, Main Street Plaza, and elsewhere downtown. Christmas music accompanies the lights.

Take a pioneer trolley ride in the Temple Square area in summer, or play golf on the many courses. There are more city and area tours in spring, summer, and fall than in winter. You can find outdoor dining all over the valley in the warm months. The zoo, water parks, amusement parks, and more can occupy children and adults. Check the "Sunday Options" and "Tours" sections near the end of chapter twenty for more suggestions.

Senior Citizens' Discounts

If you have achieved this age category, don't forget to ask merchants and restaurants if they offer senior citizens' discounts. Some restaurants have early bird dining specials for senior citizens.

Street Numbering

Salt Lake City's street numbering system makes navigation easy once you understand it. Temple Square is the heart of the system. Most street names indicate how far north, south, east, or west they are located from Temple Square. For example, 300 South lies three blocks south of Temple Square and runs east to west. If the address you want to reach is 500 West 300 South, the building is five blocks west and three blocks south of Temple Square. There are some exceptions: 100 East is State Street; what might be called East Temple is Main Street; and part of 300 South is Broadway. You may also hear someone say Fifth South instead of 500 South. The individual blocks are longer than in most cities.

For an address such as 629 East 400 South that location is on 400 South between 600 East and 700 East. Some neighborhoods have different street names and are not as wide as those described above. The avenues northeast of the downtown area are good example of this. You will find streets designated by letters and numbers, such as C Street and Fifth Avenue.

Telephone Numbers

The quick reference sheet at appendix A lists telephone numbers that you may need before or during your trip to Salt Lake City.

Television

Some hotels carry only regular network channels, some add a few basic cable channels, and others offer all the cable channels; check with your hotel for details. Those who drive to Salt Lake City might want The Weather Channel, as weather changes can come quickly to the mountain areas. The late-night news is on at 10:00 P.M. as in the central time zone, not 11:00 P.M. as in the eastern or Pacific time zone (see "Time Zone" below). At least one channel has a 9:00 P.M. newscast. Some of the local stations are

KUTV	Channel 2	CBS affiliate
KTVX	Channel 4	ABC affiliate
KSL	Channel 5	NBC affiliate
KUED	Channel 7	PBS affiliate
KBYU	Channel 11	PBS affiliate
KSTU	Channel 13	FOX affiliate
KJZZ	Channel 14	Independent
KAZG	Channel 24	UPN

Time Zone

Reminder

Most people doing research at the library for more than one day tend to lose track of the time and what day or date it is! **Salt Lake City is in the mountain time zone.** This means that when the library closes in January at 10:00 P.M. in Salt Lake City, it's 9:00 P.M in California, 11:00 P.M. in Minnesota, and midnight in New York. Of interest to those coming from other countries, it would be 5:00 A.M. in London, England; 6:00 A.M. in Paris, France; and 4:00 P.M. in Sydney, Australia (all the next day). Salt Lake City observes daylight saving time from the first Sunday in April to the last Sunday in October. (This is a time change in which the time is set one hour ahead in April to allow for more daylight hours. In October the clocks are set back one hour.)

Tourist Information

Tourist information is available in hotel lobbies, in literature racks by hotel gift shops, and from bell captains. The Salt Lake Convention & Visitors Bureau (see chapter twenty) is located at 90 South West Temple, the first block south of the library. There are several free seasonal tourism publications.

Transportation: Local
Light-Rail

In December of 1999 the light-rail TRAX system began operating in Salt Lake City. The main line runs from the Delta Center downtown along South Temple, turns south on Main Street, and runs to 10000 South in Sandy, Utah, fifteen miles away. The entire ride takes thirty-five to forty minutes, and the wait for a train is ten to thirty minutes depending upon the time of day. There are sixteen stations, and eleven have free park-and-ride lots; many of these fill early in the morning. TRAX gives visitors in the downtown area increased access to restaurants, shopping, hotels, and attractions. It allows researchers who stay at south valley motels and relatives' homes to easily access the library without parking concerns, as a station is a half block from the library. To reach the library from the TRAX station, exit and cross South Temple at the corner, walk past the right side of JB's Restaurant and continue walking north a half block. The library entrance will be on your left.

In late 2001, an additional line is scheduled to open on 400 South in the downtown area. It will travel east on 400 South from Main Street up the hill to 500 South to the Rice-Eccles Stadium at the University of Utah. This east-west line connects with the north-south line at Main Street. A total of four stations are on this new line, providing easy access to additional hotels, restaurants, office supply stores, the city library, grocery stores, and the Marriott Library at the University of Utah.

TRAX is a wonderful way for visitors to travel, but construction of additional lines does mean varying degrees of disruption. Check the times for your station and destination to be sure you will arrive when you need to. Connecting buses and taxicabs are often waiting at the stations in the south valley.

Cost

The cost for the light-rail is one dollar for two hours, with off and on privileges. An all-day pass is two dollars. Each station has ticket dispensers that accept coins and bills. A downtown free-fare zone spans 500 North Temple to 500 South and 200 East to 400 West Temple and includes the state capitol area. You must board and exit within this area. The Courthouse Station is the southernmost station in the free-fare zone. These fees and the free-fare zone also apply to the bus service, but not to special ski buses. TRAX service uses the honor system, but you will pay a fine if you don't have a ticket when periodic checks are made. Special fares are available for senior citizens, disabled riders, and students. Schedules and fare amounts are posted at each station.

For safety reasons it is illegal to walk on the light-rail tracks or to walk across them to cross the street, except at street corners. Jaywalkers may be ticketed and pay a fine. To board the TRAX train, push the large button near the door of the train car to open it.

Bus Service

Bus routes radiate out all over the Salt Lake Valley. Transfers can be used interchangeably for TRAX and the bus service; the fares are the same. The bus lines have some free park-and-ride lots also. Bus schedules are often available in hotels, at the Visitors Information Center in the Salt Palace, and at shopping malls.

Information Locations

The Utah Transit Authority (UTA) has a transportation information center in the ZCMI Center Mall downtown, on the light-rail line. For route and schedule information you may call RIDE-UTA or check online (see appendix A). These are also good places to check for details on ski buses.

Accessibility

Both the TRAX cars and some buses are handicapped accessible. UTA also provides Paratransit service for residents with disabilities that may be used by visitors for up to twenty-one days a year. For eligibility details contact the UTA Paratransit customer service office at 287-4659 or check the UTA Web site.

Other Transportation

Shuttle companies with taxis, limousines, and vans operate from the airport to hotels all over the valley, and many hotels have their own shuttle service. Some of these services are available for hire or for other needs with prior reservation. Many car rental companies operate at or near the airport, and some hotels have car rental offices on-site. This is an easy way to rent a car for a day or two and give yourself a chance to see the area.

Taxicab service operates twenty-four hours a day, seven days a week. There are several cabstands in the downtown area (especially at the major hotels), and cabs may be flagged down. A taxi ride from the airport to downtown is about thirteen to fifteen dollars.

Transportation: TRAX Stops

TRAX station stops are clearly labeled, and large maps at the stations and on the trains show the stops. Why should you check out the TRAX system? We have listed some of the businesses that are within two blocks of the stations on both routes. Other stops are largely industrial, but in time construction will change the array of services available.

For More Info

Utah Transit Authority (888) RIDE-UTA <http://www.rideuta.com>; City Cab: 363-5014; Ute Cab: 359-7788; Yellow Cab: 521-2100 (area code 801, unless otherwise noted)

NORTH-SOUTH LINE

Delta Center (301 West South Temple; northern free-fare zone boundary)
    Delta Center, home of the Utah Jazz and other events
    Wyndham Hotel
Temple Square (132 West South Temple)
    Abravanel Hall, center for Utah Symphony concerts and other events
    Family History Library
    Salt Palace Convention Center
    Temple Square
    several hotels and restaurants
City Center (15 South Main Street)
    Crossroads Plaza
    Payless Drug
    Joseph Smith Memorial Building
    ZCMI Center Mall

Gallivan Plaza (239 South Main Street)
Judge Cafe
Sam Weller's Books
Lambs Restaurant

Courthouse (between 400 and 500 South; southern free-fare boundary)
Little America Hotel and restaurants

Ballpark (1300 South)
Franklin Covey Field, home of the Salt Lake Stingers baseball team

Central Pointe (2100 South)
Office Depot
several fast food restaurants

Fashion Place West (6400 South)
Fashion Place Mall and surrounding stores and restaurants (a short bus ride away)

Midvale Fort Union (7200 South)
several hotels and motels
fast-food and other restaurants

Sandy Civic Center (10000 South)
South Towne Center Mall, which has 150 stores, restaurants, services, and movie theaters (walk or ride a bus) several hotels, motels, and restaurants.

EAST-WEST LINE

Library Station (between 200 and 300 East)
Salt Lake City Main Library
several restaurants, including Sizzler

Trolley Square Station (between 600 and 700 East)
Chase Suite Hotel
Chili's Restaurant
Chuck-a-Rama Restaurant
Dee's Restaurant
Fred Meyer Grocery Store
Ruby River Steakhouse
Staples office supply store
Starbucks Coffee
Wild Oats Food Market

900 East Station
Office Max office supply store
Training Table Restaurant
several other restaurants

Stadium Station
University of Utah and Marriott Library
University of Utah football stadium

Transportation: Nonlocal

Salt Lake City is served by Interstates 15 and 215 (north-south) and Interstate 80 (east-west) and state highway 89. Amtrak serves Salt Lake City from the east and west at the station located at 340 South 600 West, just seven blocks from the library. A Greyhound bus depot is located one block from the library at 160 West South Temple. Some genealogical group tours from the western United States arrive via bus.

Driving to Salt Lake City? We drive for one or two of our trips there each year. It is a full two-day drive. We've even made this drive in winter; we expect weather delays and build that into our travel itinerary. The value of the drive? We take turns driving; while one of us drives the other one either naps or organizes to do items for the FHL. Some wonderful research repositories are also along the way in Des Moines, Iowa; Lincoln, Nebraska; and Cheyenne, Wyoming.

If you wish to drive to Salt Lake City and arrive near the library, follow these directions (entrances are subject to change due to freeway construction).

From the north on I-15, take the Sixth North exit to downtown.

From the south on I-15, take the Sixth South exit.

From the west on I-80, take the North Temple exit.

From the east on I-80, take the I-15 interchange to the Sixth South exit.

From the airport, take the North Temple exit from the airport area and stay on North Temple to the downtown area. Signs will direct you to the city center or Temple Square area from all these exits.

Views of the Valley and Mountains

The twenty-sixth floor of the Church office building has two observation decks that are open to the public on weekdays. The views are magnificent, and this is an ideal spot for picture taking. The Joseph Smith Memorial Building has great views from the observation decks and restaurants on the tenth floor. The mountainous area north of the capitol building, located at the north end of State Street, provides another site for viewing and photographing. It is possible to see State Street stretching straight south for many miles.

Weather Forecasts

Radio station 1160 AM, KSL, features regular news and weather updates. Salt Lake City has affiliates of all the major television networks with regular newscasts and weather features. Many hotels feature the twenty-four-hour Weather Channel (online at <http://www.weather.com>.)

When listening to the weather forecasts, visitors are often confused by the variances in snowfall and temperature predictions. The valley, the benches, and the mountains often vary considerably. The benches are the gently sloping areas between the flat valley and the mountains. You will hear forecasts for the Wasatch Front and for Dixie. Dixie is southern Utah, and **the Wasatch Front forecast covers Salt Lake City.**

Tip

The average January temperature is in the thirties with some temperatures in the twenties, and the summertime temperatures are in the eighties and nineties. You might also find temperatures in the fifties in January and some snow in the mountains in May. If you don't live there and you hear about many inches of snow falling, keep in mind that the majority of it is likely in the mountains, not in the city. The summertime humidity is usually low.

Zoo

You were probably thinking that we couldn't come up with something for the letter Z. The Hogle Zoo is well known and can provide a nice respite from staring at a microfilm reader. See "Musical, Sporting, and Entertainment Events" in chapter twenty for information on the zoo.

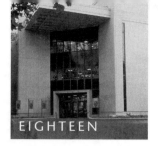

EIGHTEEN

Accommodations

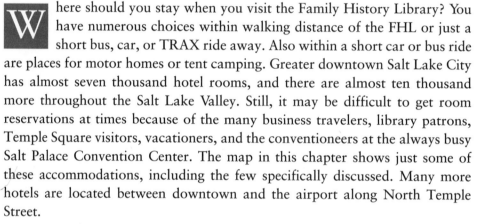

Where should you stay when you visit the Family History Library? You have numerous choices within walking distance of the FHL or just a short bus, car, or TRAX ride away. Also within a short car or bus ride are places for motor homes or tent camping. Greater downtown Salt Lake City has almost seven thousand hotel rooms, and there are almost ten thousand more throughout the Salt Lake Valley. Still, it may be difficult to get room reservations at times because of the many business travelers, library patrons, Temple Square visitors, vacationers, and the conventioneers at the always busy Salt Palace Convention Center. The map in this chapter shows just some of these accommodations, including the few specifically discussed. Many more hotels are located between downtown and the airport along North Temple Street.

Money Saver

Plan your trip well in advance, and be sure to ask about special genealogy rates. Some researchers like to stay very close to the library; others choose to stay several blocks away and get their exercise by walking to the library. Several hotels offer a scheduled shuttle service to and from the library in the morning and evening.

The *Salt Lake Visitors Guide*, available from the Salt Lake Convention & Visitors Bureau, has addresses and telephone numbers for many hotels and motels, long-term rental accommodations, and some campgrounds; it provides excellent guide maps. Contact information for most of these can also be found via the Salt Lake Convention & Visitors Bureau Web site. You'll find some bed-and-breakfasts and all-suite hotels in this and other guides. For the large hotels you might ask about the view from specific sides of the hotel. Various views include the city, the mountains, or the Utah state capitol building, which is lighted at night.

For further details, inquire directly about the availability of city and airport shuttles and room amenities. Even though we list amenities in the pages that follow, please verify these with your hotel. The costs of local and long-distance calls change frequently. We have often found that cable TV offerings are not created equally, so if you desire particular channels, it is best to inquire directly. If you plan to check your e-mail it is also wise to check on the hotel fees for

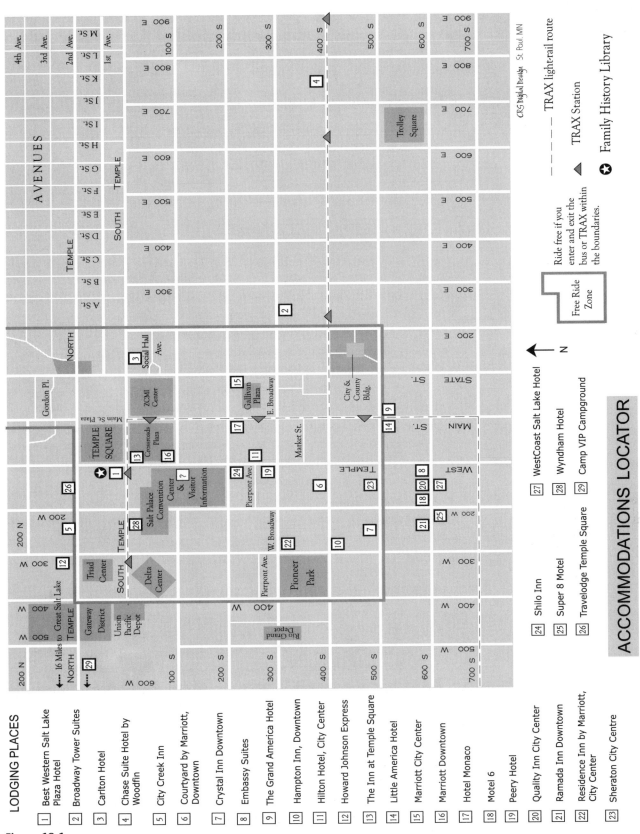

ACCOMMODATIONS LOCATOR

24	Shilo Inn	27	WestCoast Salt Lake Hotel
25	Super 8 Motel	28	Wyndham Hotel
26	Travelodge Temple Square	29	Camp VIP Campground

LODGING PLACES

1. Best Western Salt Lake Plaza Hotel
2. Broadway Tower Suites
3. Carlton Hotel
4. Chase Suite Hotel by Woodfin
5. City Creek Inn
6. Courtyard by Marriott, Downtown
7. Crystal Inn Downtown
8. Embassy Suites
9. The Grand America Hotel
10. Hampton Inn, Downtown
11. Hilton Hotel, City Center
12. Howard Johnson Express
13. The Inn at Temple Square
14. Little America Hotel
15. Marriott City Center
16. Marriott Downtown
17. Hotel Monaco
18. Motel 6
19. Peery Hotel
20. Quality Inn City Center
21. Ramada Inn Downtown
22. Residence Inn by Marriott, City Center
23. Sheraton City Centre

24. Shilo Inn
25. Super 8 Motel
26. Travelodge Temple Square
27. WestCoast Salt Lake Hotel
28. Wyndham Hotel
29. Camp VIP Campground

Figure 18-1

Map prepared by Carol Barrett

--- TRAX light-rail route

▲ TRAX Station

✪ Family History Library

dialing in to your provider. Be sure you understand the exact location of the hotel you choose. Similar and changing names for some hotels have caused some genealogists to think they would be staying closer to the library than they actually were.

The next entries are overviews of a few lodging facilities in Salt Lake City.

Best Western Salt Lake Plaza Hotel

122 West South Temple, Salt Lake City, UT 84101-1402
(800) 366-3684, (801) 521-0130, (801) 322-5057 Fax
http://www.plaza-hotel.com
Check-in: 3:00 P.M.; checkout: noon
Room amenities: Coffeemaker, data port, voice mail, iron and ironing board. Most rooms are nonsmoking.
Other features: Refrigerators in some rooms, coin-operated laundry, restaurant, room service, complimentary airport shuttle, meeting rooms, small exercise room with hot tub, outdoor pool, gift shop, three-dollar parking per night, extended cable TV. Fee for phone calls. Adjacent to the library. Located at a TRAX station. The Plaza frequently offers special genealogy rates.

Broadway Tower Apartments and Suites

230 East Broadway (300 South), Salt Lake City, UT 84111
(801) 534-1222, (801) 359-3624 Fax
This is one example of a rental unit. Short- and long-term accommodations in one- and two-bedroom suites with separate kitchen, living/dining room, bedrooms and balcony. Stays for more than two weeks are greatly discounted. Seven blocks to the FHL. About one block to TRAX on 400 South.
Suite amenities: Kitchenware, microwave, refrigerator, stove, toaster, coffeemaker, data ports, and cable TV.
Other features: Fitness center, coin-operated laundry, and meeting space. Market and pharmacy next door.

Camp VIP

1400 West North Temple, Salt Lake City, UT 84116-3236
(800) 226-7752, (801) 328-0224, (801) 355-1055 Fax
http://www.campvip.com
Check-in: after noon; checkout: noon
RV and tent sites, "pull-thrus," convenience store, self-service laundry, showers, playground, shade trees, outdoor pools, whirlpool, restaurant. Complimentary coffee in office. UTA bus routes 43 and 50 go by the camp and stop a half block from the library on North Temple. To return, the bus stop is on North Temple in front of the Church conference center. It is neither on a TRAX line nor within walking distance of the library.

The Carlton Hotel

140 East South Temple, Salt Lake City, UT 84111-1102
(800) 633-3500, (801) 355-3418, (801) 355-3428 Fax
Check-in: anytime; checkout: noon
Room amenities: Extended cable/satellite TV, VCR/movies.
Other features: Weekly rates available. Cafe, exercise room, meeting room,

and coin-operated laundry. Complimentary services: Shuttle service to library and airport, made-to-order breakfasts, local calls, parking, coffeemaker, refrigerator, iron and ironing board, and hair dryer by request. Three blocks from the FHL, somewhat uphill. About two blocks to a TRAX station.

Crystal Inn Downtown

230 West 500 South, Salt Lake City, UT 84101

(800) 366-4466, (801) 328-4466, (801) 328-4072 Fax

http://www.crystalinns.com

Check-in: 2:00 P.M.; checkout: noon

Room amenities: Large, bright rooms with coffeemaker, iron and ironing board, microwave and refrigerator, dataports, voice mail, hair dryer, extended cable TV.

Other features: Hot breakfast buffet, indoor pool and fitness center, whirlpool, coin-operated laundry, ATM, meeting rooms, small convenience store, complimentary newspaper, local calls, airport shuttle, and parking. Restaurants nearby. Seven blocks to the FHL. Three blocks to a TRAX station.

The Inn at Temple Square

71 West South Temple, Salt Lake City, UT 84101-1511

(800) 843-4668, (801) 531-1000, (801) 536-7272 Fax

http://www.theinn.com

Check-in: 3:00 P.M.; checkout: noon

Room amenities: Refrigerator, iron and ironing board, data port, voice mail, hair dryer, basic cable TV.

Other features: Renovated, classical look in smoke-free hotel, meeting rooms, restaurant, room service. Complimentary services: Large continental breakfast, airport shuttle, local calls, valet parking, and pass to full-service gym one block away. Less than one block to the FHL and to a TRAX station.

Peery Hotel

110 West Broadway (110 West 300 South), Salt Lake City, UT 84101-1913

(800) 331-0073, (801) 521-4300, (801) 575-5014 Fax

http://www.peeryhotel.com

Check-in: 3:00 P.M.; checkout: noon

Room amenities: Hair dryer, coffeemaker, iron and ironing board, data port, voice mail, extended cable TV.

Other features: Historic hotel renovated in 1999.

Two restaurants and gift shop.

Complimentary services: Day passes to full-service gym two blocks away, library and airport shuttle, breakfast buffet.

Available on a fee basis: Meeting rooms, parking, refrigerator, and room service.

Four blocks to the FHL. Almost two blocks to a TRAX station.

Travelodge at Temple Square

144 West North Temple, Salt Lake City , UT 84103-1507

(801) 533-8200, (801) 596-0332 Fax

Check-in: 2:00 P.M.; checkout: 11:00 A.M.

Room amenities: Coffeemaker, data port, and extended cable TV.

Other features: Iron and ironing board and hair dryer upon request. All showers. No refrigerators or airport shuttle. On bus line to airport. Restaurant across the street. Complimentary parking, local calls, and continental breakfast. One block to FHL. About a block to a TRAX station.

Wyndham Hotel

215 West South Temple, Salt Lake City, UT 84101-1333

(800) 553-0075, (801) 531-7500, (801) 328-1289 Fax

http://www.wyndham.com/saltlakecity

Check-in: 3:00 P.M.; checkout: noon

Room amenities: Coffeemaker, iron and ironing board, data port, voice mail, hair dryer, and extended cable TV.

Other features: Steak house and lounge, meeting rooms, ATM, large exercise areas and indoor pool, gift shop, many nonsmoking rooms, and room service.

Available on a fee basis: Parking, airport shuttle, microwave, and refrigerator. Two blocks to FHL, slightly uphill. One block to TRAX station.

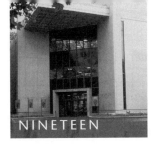

NINETEEN

Restaurants

D owntown Salt Lake City and the nearby area have hundreds of places to eat, with something for every craving and budget. The yellow pages for Salt Lake City contain about thirty pages of restaurant and pizza listings. Published travel guides, the restaurant listings provided by the Salt Lake Convention & Visitors Bureau, hotel bell captains and concierges, Salt Lake City residents, and fellow library visitors are good sources for recommendations on where to eat. The daily newspapers, the weekly *Salt Lake City Weekly*, and the bimonthly *Salt Lake: Magazine of the Mountainwest* carry restaurant descriptions and reviews, *Salt Lake City Weekly* carries a rotating list of restaurants by cuisine, such as Chinese, Italian, vegetarian, and others.

The selection of restaurants in or near downtown Salt Lake City is based on referrals and our personal preference. The restaurant locator map carries these and others. We have had excellent burgers, fish, ribs, and steak, and great Chinese, Italian, and Mexican meals in downtown Salt Lake City. There are nice delicatessens and sandwich shops within a few blocks of the Family History Library; some only operate Monday through Friday. Chain fast-food restaurants are within walking distance and TRAX boundaries of the library. Most of the downtown hotels have one or more restaurants. More restaurants are in the new Gateway area at the western edge of downtown. If you want to rely on a name and menu you know, you'll find many of the national restaurants in the greater downtown area. We would appreciate hearing about other places that you discover and would recommend. Also, please let us know about restaurants you would not visit again. All Salt Lake City restaurants are smoke free.

VENTURE OUT

Why such an emphasis on eating? Many genealogists are almost as passionate about eating as they are about their research! As you can tell throughout this book, we are strong advocates of getting out of the library and exploring the city. What better way than to pick a new place to eat every so often?

If you are part of a large tour or conference group, you may find that many places are not eager to seat large groups all at once. We encourage researchers

Tip

to venture out together in smaller groups and walk or take a cab, bus, or TRAX to try some of the many restaurants in Salt Lake City.

Some people bring an insulated lunch bag, purchase a few light groceries supplies locally, and eat in the library's snack room. If you pack your lunch, go outside in the fresh air to eat. We strongly recommend getting away from the building for a while to help refresh the brain!

GETTING THERE

If you walk to a restaurant, remember that Salt Lake City blocks are long. (You might define walking distance differently than we do.) Trying a couple of the restaurants beyond walking distance gives you a break from the library and a look at more of the city. Cabs are inexpensive in Salt Lake City, especially when shared, and there is good bus and light-rail service. With the scheduled completion in late 2001 of the TRAX line on 400 South, more restaurants will be easily accessible. When there are events at the Salt Palace, Abravanel Hall, or the Delta Center, some of the downtown restaurants are quite busy before and after the events.

PRICE RATING

Our price ratings are for food, nonalcoholic beverages, and tax (per person); they do not include the gratuity.

$	under $5, fast-food prices
$$	$5–$10
$$$	$10–$15
$$$$	$15–$20
$$$$$	$20+

The following are some of our favorite restaurants, a few old standbys, and some recommended by other folks who actually leave the library for a meal. (The area code for all phone numbers is 801.)

1. **Al Forno's Ristorante**, 239 South 500 East, 359-6040
   Italian specialties including pasta, veal, chicken, and crusty bread. Almost a mile from the FHL and a few blocks from the TRAX line. Hours: Monday-Friday 11:30 A.M.–2:30 P.M., Monday-Thursday 5:00 P.M.–9:30 P.M., Friday-Saturday 5:00 P.M.–10:00 P.M. Closed Sunday. $$$–$$$$

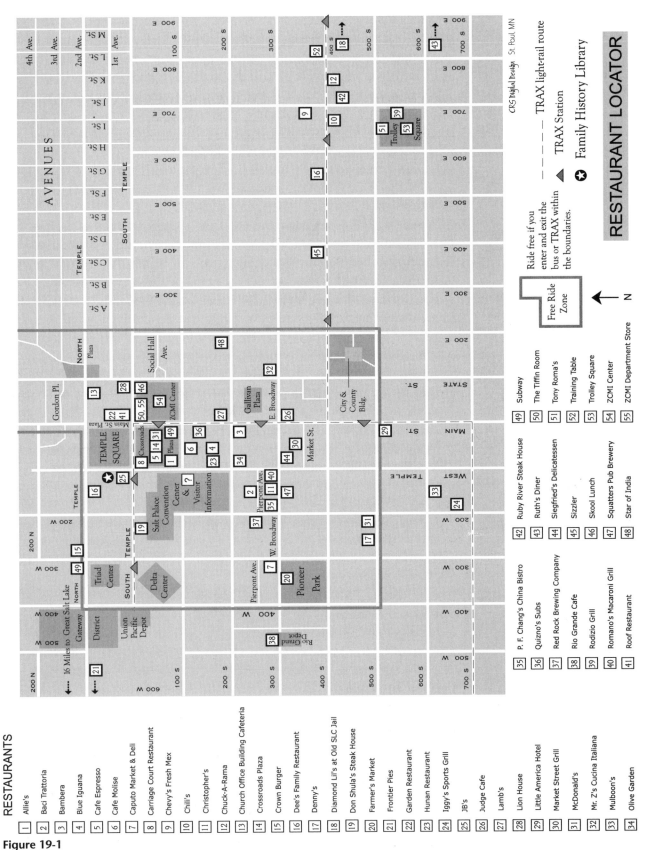

Figure 19-1

Map prepared by Carol Barrett

2. **Allie's Pantry**, 75 South West Temple (in the Marriott hotel), 531-0800
Allie's has a regular menu, a buffet for many meals, and a brunch on some Sundays. Table service is at a leisurely pace, which makes the buffet a good choice if you want to get back to the library. It is one block from the library. There is more likely to be buffet service when the hotel is full or there are major downtown events. Hours: Monday-Sunday 6:30 A.M.–2:00 P.M. and 5:00 P.M.–11:00 P.M.; Sunday brunch 11:00 A.M.–2:00 P.M. $$$–$$$$

3. **Baci Trattoria**, 134 West Pierpont, 328-1500
Italian and Mediterranean specialties, wood-fired pizza. Three blocks from the FHL. Hours: Monday-Friday 11:30 A.M.–3:00 P.M., Monday-Saturday 5:00 P.M.–11:00 P.M. $$$–$$$$$

4. **Bambara**, 202 South Main Street (in the Hotel Monaco), 363-5454
Excellent food and service. It does get quite busy, but try to get a table by the big arched windows or where you can watch the centralized open kitchen. Almost five blocks from the FHL and just a block from the TRAX line. Hours: Monday-Friday 7:00 A.M.–10:00 A.M. and 11:30 A.M.–2:30 P.M.; Saturday-Sunday 8:00 A.M.–10:00 A.M. and brunch 10:00 A.M.–2:00 P.M.; Monday-Thursday 5:30 P.M.–10:00 P.M.; Friday-Saturday 5:30 P.M.–11:00 P.M.; Sunday 5:30 P.M.–9:30 P.M. $$$–$$$$$

5. **Blue Iguana**, 165 South West Temple, Arrow Press Square, 533-8900
Downstairs restaurant in pleasant atmosphere within walking distance for many people. You may need to ask exactly where it is! Two blocks from the library. Upscale Mexican. Sister to the Red Iguana at 736 West North Temple. Hours: Monday-Thursday 11:30 A.M.–9:00 P.M.; Friday-Saturday 11:30 A.M.–10:00 P.M.; Sunday 4:00 P.M.–9:00 P.M. $$$–$$$$

6. **Cafe Espresso**, located on the upper level of Borders Books in Crossroads Plaza, 355-6899
Offers coffee, tea, sodas, smoothies, croissant sandwiches, bagels, soups, and some bakery items. Try to get a table by the window for a view of Temple Square. Hours: Monday-Saturday 9:00 A.M. to 10:00 P.M.; Sunday 11:00 A.M.–7:00 P.M. $$

7. **Cafe Molise**, 55 West 100 South, 364-8833
Exposed brick walls in this upscale Italian restaurant give it a special feeling. Outside tables in the summer. Within walking distance of the library. Hours: Monday-Friday 11:30 A.M.–2:00 P.M.; Monday-Thursday 5:30 P.M.–9:00 P.M.; Friday-Saturday 5:30 P.M.–10:00 P.M. $$$–$$$$

8. **Caputo's Market & Deli**, 308 West 300 South, 531-8669
Tony Caputo's is busy at lunchtime. Daily sandwich and hot Italian specials. With the adjoining Caputo's Pioneer Park Marketplace, it features hot take-out Italian food, an Italian market, a bakery, fresh fish, and produce. It is a short hike to this restaurant, but part of the return trip (on a full stomach) is uphill. Outdoor seating in season. Hours: Monday-Friday 9:00 A.M.–7:00 P.M.; Saturday 9:00 A.M.–5:00 P.M.; Sunday 10:00 A.M.–2:00 P.M. $$–$$$

9. **Carriage Court Restaurant**, 71 West South Temple (in The Inn at Temple Square), 531-7200

An upscale restaurant with an elegant atmosphere. The dinner rolls are excellent, as is the other food. Try to get a window table for great people watching. No alcohol. Hours: Monday-Friday 11:00 A.M.–2:30 P.M.; Monday-Saturday 5:00 P.M.–10:00 P.M.; Sunday 5:00 P.M.–9:00 P.M. $$$–$$$$

10. **Chevy's Fresh Mex**, 358 South 700 East, 517-4500

    Fresh Mexican food, fresh fish, homemade tortillas. Chain restaurant. Not within walking distance of the FHL, but on the 400 South TRAX line. Hours: Monday-Thursday 11:00 A.M.–11:00 P.M.; Friday-Saturday 11:00 A.M.–1:00 A.M.; Sunday 11:00 A.M.–9:00 P.M. $$–$$$$

11. **Chili's**, 644 East 400 South, 575-6933

    A national chain with a varied menu. Weekend evenings can get very crowded. It is not within easy walking distance from Temple Square, but it is on the 400 South TRAX line. Hours: Sunday-Thursday 11:00 A.M.–10:00 P.M.; Friday-Saturday 11:00 A.M.–11:00 P.M. $$–$$$

12. **Christopher's Seafood & Steak House**, 110 West Broadway (300 South), 519-8515

    Popular steak, pasta, chicken, and seafood restaurant in the Peery Hotel, three blocks from the library. Early bird and Sunday specials. Hours: Monday-Friday 11:30 A.M.–3:00 P.M.; Monday-Thursday 4:30 P.M.–10:00 P.M.; Friday-Saturday 4:30 P.M.–11:00 P.M.; Sunday 4:30 P.M.–9:00 P.M. $$$$

13. **Chuck-A-Rama**, 744 East 400 South, 531-1123

    Similar to an Old Country Buffet or Hometown Buffet, Chuck-A-Rama is an inexpensive, all-buffet restaurant with island serving stations. It has an extensive salad bar. At the dinner hour there is often a waiting line. Totally new building and decor in 2000. It is not within easy walking distance from the library, but it is on the TRAX line. Hours: Monday-Saturday 11:00 A.M.–9:00 P.M.; Sunday 11:00 A.M.–8:00 P.M. $$

14. **Church Office Building Cafeteria**, 50 East North Temple

    The cafeteria has a tremendous variety of hot and cold foods, including a salad and fresh fruit bar, all at reasonable prices. No caffeinated beverages are served. Library visitors must obtain a complimentary cafeteria pass in the library's lobby. A slightly uphill two-block walk. Hours: 7:00 A.M.–8:30 A.M., Monday-Friday 11:30 A.M.–1:30 P.M. Closed Saturday and Sunday. $–$$

15. **Crossroads Plaza**, 50 South Main St., 363-1558

    The lower mall level has the Richards Street food court with about fifteen different fast-food, sandwich, and specialty food shops. Others on upper levels include hamburgers, hot dogs, pasta, pizza, Oriental, Mexican, roast beef, healthy sandwiches, cinnamon rolls, bagels, chicken, specialty coffees, ice cream, fruit drinks, and cookies. If you are with a group, everyone can buy the meal of their choice, then sit together to discuss their research. To splurge on a sinfully delicious breakfast or snack, try a roll from Cinnabon. The place is packed at the noon hour, and most genealogists eat an early or late lunch here since it is a block from the library. Hours: The food court is open Monday-Saturday 10:00 A.M.–9:00 P.M. and Sunday noon to 6:00 P.M. A few places open early for breakfast. $–$$

16. **Crown Burger**, 118 North 300 West, 532-5300
    Hamburgers, french fries, grilled cheese, chicken, and more. A fast-food type of restaurant within walking distance of the library. Hours: Monday-Saturday 10:00 A.M.–10:30 P.M.; closed Sunday. $–$$

17. **Dee's Family Restaurant**, 143 West North Temple, 359-4414
    Dee's is a local chain, a Denny's-like restaurant. Located on the same square block as the library. The menu ranges from basic breakfast items to hamburgers, sandwiches, and full meals. Hours: Sunday-Thursday 6:00 A.M.–2:00 A.M.; Friday-Saturday open 24 hours. $$

18. **Denny's Restaurant**, 250 West 500 South, 355-1210
    Part of the national chain. A bit of a walk from the library. Hours: Open 24 hours. $$

19. **Diamond Lil's at the Old Salt City Jail**, 460 South 1000 East, 359-6090
    The unique decor and dining right in the old jail make this a fun experience. A dinner restaurant serving steaks, seafood, chicken, and ribs. The original Diamond Lil's is at 1528 North West Temple. Neither are within walking distance. The Jail location is relatively near a TRAX stop, but it is a steep uphill walk. Jail hours: Sunday-Thursday 4:00 P.M.–9:00 P.M.; Friday-Saturday 4:00 P.M.–10:00 P.M. $$–$$$$

20. **Farmers Market**, 300 South 300 West, Pioneer Park, 364-4885
    Fresh fruit and vegetables, breads, pastries, sandwiches, beverages, crafts, flowers, and entertainment. Not a quick walk from the library. Hours: Every Saturday 8:00 A.M.–1:00 P.M. mid-July through mid-October. $–$$

21. **Frontier Pies**, 735 West North Temple, 521-4700
    Open for all three meals, it offers a varied menu, reasonable prices, and is an excellent place to splurge on pie! (Or take a piece back to your room for a late snack.) You'll need a car or cab for this one. Hours: Monday-Thursday 7:00 A.M.–10:00 P.M.; Friday-Saturday 7:00 A.M.–11:00 P.M.; Sunday 7:00 A.M.–9:00 P.M. $$

22. **Garden Restaurant**, 15 East South Temple (in the Joseph Smith Memorial Building), 539-1911
    This popular lunch and dinner spot has a great view from many tables and an overall bright and airy feeling, especially when the retractable roof is open. The food is good, and the service is pleasant. Hours: Monday-Friday 11:00 A.M.–3:30 P.M. and 5:00 P.M.–9:00 P.M.; Friday and Saturday 5 P.M.–10:00 P.M. $$–$$$

23. **Hunan Restaurant**, 165 South West Temple, 531-6677
    Mandarin-Szechuan cuisine. We have eaten in the restaurant and used the take-out service, and we enjoy the food. Recommended by several of our research trip participants, too. In the south side of the Arrow Press Square Building, two blocks from the library. Hours: Monday-Friday 11:00 A.M.–9:30 P.M.; Saturday 4:00 P.M.–9:30 P.M. $$

24. **Iggy's Sports Grill**, 677 South 200 West, 532-9999
    Burgers, salads, fish, pasta, chicken, ribs, appetizers. Friendly service. You will be surrounded by sports on large screen TVs. On the TRAX line, but not near a station. Take a cab or car to Iggy's. Hours: Monday-Thursday

11:30 A.M.–10:30 P.M.; Friday 11:30 A.M.–11:00 P.M.; Sunday 10:00 A.M.–9:00 P.M. $$–$$$.

25. **JB's Restaurant**, 122 West South Temple, 328-8344

Adjoins the Best Western Salt Lake Plaza Hotel, next to the library. A family style restaurant, similar to Denny's, with reasonable prices and adequate but not fancy food. Service is sometimes slow, but it has improved in recent years. It is sometimes quite busy when there are conventions or sporting events in the area. JB's has a bakery case and self-service coffee for quick breakfasts; there is also a breakfast buffet. A soup and salad bar option is available for a quick lunch and dinner. Another place frequented by genealogists. Hours: Sunday-Thursday 6:00 A.M.–11:00 P.M.; Friday-Saturday 6:00 A.M.–midnight. $$

26. **Judge Cafe**, 8 East Broadway (300 South), 531-0917

Array of breakfast items, sandwiches, burgers, salads, soups, pastas, and espressos. Utah Jazz memorabilia. A bit more than three blocks from the library and close to the TRAX line. Hours: Monday-Friday 7:00 A.M.–2:00 P.M. $$–$$$

27. **Lambs**, 169 South Main Street, 364-7166

A Salt Lake landmark since 1919, the traditional decor is known to many library patrons. Within walking distance and serving all three meals, it has reasonable prices and good food. Sandwiches, salads, lamb, liver, seafood, and beef. Excellent desserts and noted for its rice pudding. Near Sam Weller's bookstore on the TRAX line. Hours: Monday-Friday 7:00 A.M.–9:00 P.M.; Saturday 8:00 A.M.–9:00 P.M.; closed Sundays. $$$–$$$$

28. **Lion House Pantry Restaurant**, 63 East South Temple, 363-5466

This popular à la carte cafeteria-style restaurant with home-style cooking is located on the ground floor of a restored building that was home to part of Brigham Young's family. No coffee is served. It is within walking distance of the library. Hours: Monday-Saturday 11:00 A.M.–2:00 P.M.; Friday and Saturday evenings 5:00 P.M.–8:30 P.M. After Thanksgiving through December, open for dinner Monday-Saturday 5:00 P.M.–8:30 P.M. $$$

29. **Little America Hotel**, 500 South Main, 363-6781

Little America has a good coffee shop and dining room. It is known for an extensive Sunday brunch which is served in the main ballroom. Reservations are taken only for large groups. Not within easy walking distance of the library area for everyone, but it is at a TRAX stop. A very good smaller brunch is served daily in the dining room, including Sundays. Hours: Every day; coffee shop 5:00 A.M. to midnight; dining room 5:00 P.M.–11:00 P.M.; ballroom brunch 10:00 A.M.–3:00 P.M. $$–$$$$

30. **Market Street Grill**, 48 Market Street, 322-4668

Located several blocks from the library in an area with several other fine restaurants. Excellent fresh fish is the specialty. Evening early bird specials. Serves a good, full breakfast menu. Many area movers and shakers eat here. Hours: Monday-Thursday 6:30 A.M.–10:00 P.M.; Friday 6:30

A.M.–11:00 P.M.; Saturday 7:00 A.M.–11:00 P.M.; Sunday brunch 9:00 A.M.–3:00 P.M.; Sunday dinner 3:00 P.M.–10:00 P.M. $$$$–$$$$$

31. **McDonald's**, 50 South Main, Crossroads Plaza, 322-0362
Lower level of the mall near the other food court restaurants. Serves breakfast. Another McDonald's is at 210 West 500 South (phone: 364-1614). Both operate every day. $

32. **Mr. Z's Cucina Italiana**, 111 East Broadway (300 South), 994-2002
Pasta, both traditional and specialty Italian dishes, at reasonable prices with pasta and salad lunch specials. Outdoor dining in season. About five blocks from the library and a block from a TRAX station. Hours: Monday-Thursday 9:00 A.M.–10:00 P.M.; Friday 9:00 A.M.–11:00 P.M.; Saturday 9:00 A.M.–11:00 P.M.; Sunday 10:00 A.M.–9:00 P.M. $$–$$$$

33. **Mulboon's**, 161 West 600 South (in the WestCoast Salt Lake Hotel on the top floor), 530-1313.
The restaurant has a beautiful view of the valley and the mountains. The offerings are not cheap, but not the highest priced either. A long walk to this one. Hours: Monday-Thursday 5:00 P.M.–10:00 P.M.; Friday-Saturday 5:00 P.M.–11:00 P.M.; Sunday brunch 10:00 A.M.–2:30 P.M. $$$–$$$$

34. **Olive Garden**, 77 West 200 South, 537-6202
Good food and service at this national chain. Reasonable prices. Within walking distance of the library for most people. If you drive, there is an underground parking ramp; enter from 200 South. Hours: Sunday-Thursday 11:00 A.M.–10:00 P.M.; Friday-Saturday 11:00 A.M.–11:00 P.M. $$$–$$$$

35. **P.F. Chang's China Bistro**, 174 West 300 South, 539-0500
Extremely popular chain restaurant with wide choices in a variety of Chinese cuisines, but with a modern twist. A good place to go with a group and share entrees. Several blocks from the library; not near a TRAX stop. Hours: Sunday-Thursday 11:00 A.M.–11:00 P.M.; Friday-Saturday 11:00 A.M.–midnight. $$$–$$$$

36. **Quizno's**, 132 South Main, 532-2225
Submarine sandwiches. Almost three blocks from the library and near a TRAX station. Hours: Monday-Friday 8:00 A.M.–5:00 P.M. $$

37. **Red Rock Brewing Company**, 254 South 200 West, 521-7446
A microbrewery serving lunch and dinner. It's light and airy, and it's very busy on Friday and Saturday nights. The menu includes burgers, upscale sandwiches, pasta, pizza, and salads. The food is excellent. About four blocks from the library and not near a TRAX stop. Hours: Sunday-Thursday 11:00 A.M.–11:00 P.M.; Friday and Saturday 11:00 A.M. to 1:00 P.M.; Saturday and Sunday brunch 11:00 A.M.–3:00 P.M. $$–$$$$

38. **Rio Grande Cafe**, 270 South Rio Grande (450 West), 364-3302
Located in the old Rio Grande railroad depot, this popular restaurant has delicious Mexican food. While you wait for your food, have some chips and watch the toy train go round far above your head. Drive or take a cab—not an area to walk to. Hours: Monday-Friday 11:00 A.M.–2:30 P.M. and Saturday 11:30 A.M.–2:30 P.M.; Monday-Saturday 5:00 P.M.–9:30 P.M. and Sunday 4:00 P.M.–9:00 P.M. $$$–$$$$

39. **Rodizio Grill,** Trolley Square, 220-0500

    A popular Brazilian restaurant with extensive hot food and cold salad bars. A place to go when you are really hungry. Order the "Full Rodizio" to sample all the various grilled meats and vegetables served at your table on long swordlike skewers. A few blocks from the TRAX line. Hours: Sunday-Thursday 11:00 A.M.–10:00 P.M.; Friday and Saturday 11:00 A.M.–11:00 P.M. $$–$$$$

40. **Romano's Macaroni Grill,** 110 West Broadway (300 South; in the Peery Hotel), 521-3133

    Italian specialties served by good staff after you watch food prepared in the open kitchen. A short walk from the library. Hours: Sunday-Thursday 11:00 A.M.–10:00 P.M.; Friday and Saturday 11:00 A.M.–11:00 P.M. $$$–$$$$

41. **Roof Restaurant,** 15 East South Temple (in the Joseph Smith Memorial Building), 539-1911

    Dinner service atop the JSMB. The view is spectacular. The buffet has a variety of food, and the desserts are nice. Reservations are recommended. No liquor service. Hours: Monday-Thursday 5:00 P.M.–9:00 P.M.; Friday-Saturday 5:00 P.M.–10:00 P.M.; closed Sunday. $$$$$

42. **Ruby River Steak House,** 435 South 700 East, 359-3355

    Mesquite-grilled steaks are a specialty. They also serve seafood, chicken, and ribs. If you have to wait for a table, buckets of peanuts tide you over. Too far to walk, but it's on the TRAX line. Hours: Monday-Thursday 11:00 A.M.–10:00 P.M.; Friday 11:00 A.M.–11:00 P.M.; Saturday 4:00 P.M.–11:00 P.M.; Sunday 4:00 P.M.–9:30 P.M. $$$–$$$$$

43. **Ruth's Diner,** 2100 Emigration Canyon, 582-5807

    It is a diner, but one with a long history. It has diner food plus some trendier items. Wonderful breakfasts, sandwiches, chicken, desserts, and more. You'll need a car and a map for this, but it's worth it. When it's hot in the city, it is cool in this area (especially on their patio) surrounded by mountains. Hours: 8:00 A.M.–9:00 A.M. every day; breakfast served till 4:00 P.M. $$–$$$$

44. **Siegfried's Delicatessen,** 69 West 300 South, 355-3891

    This spot has been recommended by some of our group trip participants for its German food. Just three blocks south of the library. It also has a food market area. Hours: Monday-Saturday 11:00 A.M.–4:00 P.M.; food market: Monday-Friday 9:00 A.M.–6:00 P.M.; Saturday 9:00 A.M.–5:00 P.M. $$–$$$

45. **Sizzler,** 371 East 400 South, 532-1339

    Features steak, seafood, chicken, and big salad bar. Similar to a Bonanza or Western Sizzlin'. Not fancy, but a good array of food and an often crowded restaurant. Not within walking distance, but a car, cab, or TRAX will get you there. Hours: Sunday-Thursday 11:00 A.M.–9:00 P.M.; Friday-Saturday 11:00 A.M.–10:00 P.M. $$–$$$

46. **Skool Lunch,** 60 East South Temple, 532-5269

    Located on the South Temple Street side of the ZCMI Center Mall. This breakfast and lunch spot offers bagels, croissants, toast, muffins, and breakfast sandwiches. For lunch there are thick deli sandwiches, soups, quiche, salads, fresh baked breads and breadsticks. For dessert there are brownies, cookies, and cakes. Hours: Monday-Friday 7:00 A.M.–4:00 P.M. $$

47. **Squatter's Pub Brewery**, 147 West 300 South (in the Salt Lake Brewing Company building), 363-2739
Serving burgers, pasta, salads, and more. Friday and Saturday evenings are very busy. Squatter's has an outdoor patio and seasonal menu choices. A few blocks south of the library. Hours: Monday-Saturday 11:30 A.M.–12:30 A.M.; Sunday brunch 10:30 A.M.–3:00 P.M. and dinner till 10:30 P.M. $$$–$$$$

48. **Star of India Restaurant**, 177 East 200 South, 363-7555
Vegetarian, lamb, chicken, seafood and other choices. A few blocks' walk from the library and just more than a block to a TRAX station. Hours: Monday-Saturday 11:30 A.M.–2:30 P.M.; Monday-Thursday 5:30 P.M.–10:00 P.M.; Friday-Saturday 5:30 P.M.–10:30 P.M.; Sunday 5:00 P.M.–9:30 P.M. $$–$$$

49. **Subway**, 103 North 300 West, 363-8148
Hours: Monday-Friday 10:00 A.M.–9:00 P.M.; Saturday 11:00 A.M.–9:00 P.M.
Subway, 10 West 100 South, 364-6229
Hours: Monday-Thursday 10:00 A.M.–6:00 P.M.; Friday-Saturday 10:00 A.M.–5:00 P.M.; closed Sunday. Submarine sandwiches. Both of these are within walking distance. $–$$

50. **The Tiffin Room**, ZCMI Center Mall, 579-7300
On the fourth floor of the Meier & Frank department store. The Tiffin Room has a varied menu, good service, and reasonable prices for good food. It reminded us of what department store restaurants used to be. Hours: Monday and Friday 11:00 A.M.–7:00 P.M.; Tuesday-Thursday and Saturday 11:00 A.M.–5:00 P.M. $$–$$$

51. **Tony Roma's**, Trolley Square, 537-RIBS (537-7427)
Famous for ribs, steak, and chicken, but mostly for those good ribs. A few blocks from the TRAX line. Hours: Monday-Thursday 11:00 A.M.–10:00 P.M.; Friday-Saturday 11:00 A.M.–11:00 P.M.; Sunday noon to 9:00 P.M. $$–$$$$

52. **Training Table**, 809 East 400 South, 355-7523
Hamburgers, sandwiches, and salads. Order by telephone at your table and pick up your food at the counter. Too far to walk, but on the TRAX line. Hours: Monday-Thursday 11:00 A.M.–11:00 P.M.; Friday-Saturday 11:00 A.M. to midnight; Sunday 11:00 A.M.–9:00 P.M. $$–$$$

53. **Trolley Square**, 600 South 700 East, 521-9877
A unique shopping center, located in the old trolley barns, has several restaurants, including Tony Roma's, Hard Rock Cafe, The Pub's Desert Edge Brewery, Rodizio Grille, and The Old Spaghetti Factory. We have walked there, but it is a *long* walk from the Temple Square area. It is a few blocks from the TRAX line. The restaurants are open long hours. $–$$$$

54. **ZCMI Center Mall**, South Temple at Main Street (kitty-corner from Temple Square), 321-8745

    Just two blocks from the library, the ZCMI food court, The Park, is similar to Crossroads Plaza's. It offers additional choices and a change of setting, which is light and airy. Selections include baked potatoes, hamburgers, submarine sandwiches, other sandwiches, pizza, pasta, Oriental, Mexican, frozen yogurt, soups and chowders, and other choices. Hours: Food Court: Monday-Friday 10:00 A.M.–9:00 P.M.; Saturday 10:00 A.M.–7:00 P.M.; closed on Sunday. $–$$

Several bagel shops, coffeehouses, juice bars, and microbreweries are also within a short walk, TRAX ride, or drive from the library. Several pizza companies deliver directly to hotels (see the yellow pages), and Metro Gourmet (288-4100) delivers from more than thirty restaurants.

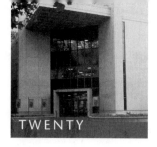

TWENTY

Attractions and Services

This chapter has some natural overlap with chapter seventeen, "Salt Lake City Basics, A to Z." Be sure to check both chapters to learn about many of the activities and services the city and area have to offer. The area code for all telephone numbers listed is 801 unless noted otherwise. As with the earlier chapter, this is written with the scheduled November 2001 opening of the new TRAX line on 400 South in mind. (We hope that does happen!)

Bookstores

Many genealogists gravitate to bookstores whenever they visit a different area. Salt Lake City is no exception. The downtown and suburban shopping areas have the bookstores found in most malls. Borders Books & Music is in the Crossroads Plaza less than a block from the Family History Library and is open seven days a week. Barnes and Noble is located on 400 South at 600 East. The yellow pages have listings for several used bookstores, most of which are in the downtown area. Local bookstores include

- **Sam Weller's Books**
  254 South Main Street (anchor store), 328-2586, <http://www.samwellers.com>
  Reaching this store from the FHL is made easier for many genealogists by the light-rail line stops nearby. It has one of the largest and finest used book collections in the West. Hours: Monday-Friday 9:30 A.M.–9:00 P.M.; Saturday 9:30 A.M.–7:00 P.M.

- **Deseret Book**
  26 South State Street in the ZCMI Center Mall (downtown location), 328-8191, <http://deseretbook.com/retail>
  This is a general bookstore with popular books, genealogy books, some software, supplies, and a large section of Latter-day Saints publications. It is just two blocks from the library. Hours: Monday-Friday 10:00 A.M.–9:00 P.M. and Saturday 10:00 A.M.–8:00 P.M.

- **The Family History Discovery Shoppe**
  Located on the lower level of Crossroads Plaza, 596-1030, <http://www.heritageconsulting.com>

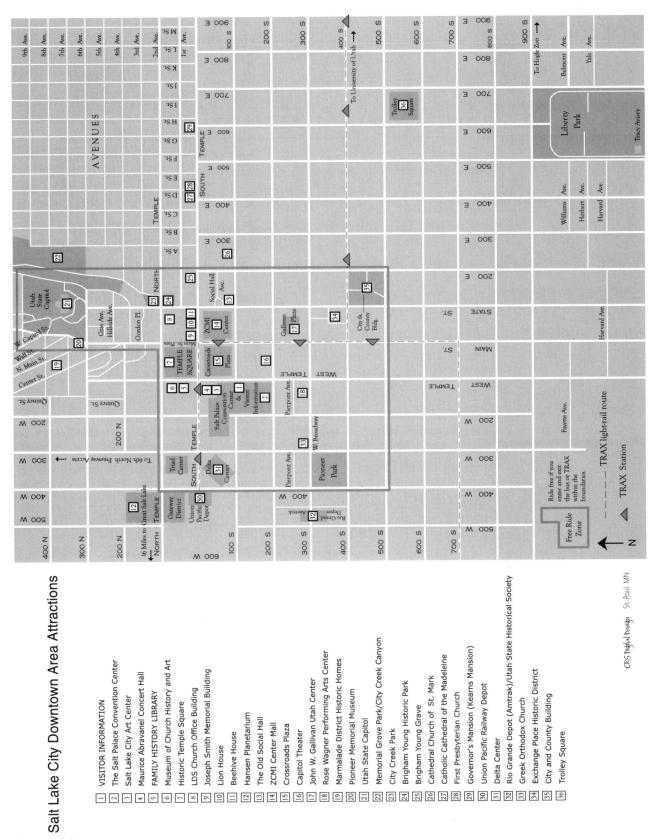

Salt Lake City Downtown Area Attractions

1. VISITOR INFORMATION
2. The Salt Palace Convention Center
3. Salt Lake City Art Center
4. Maurice Abravanel Concert Hall
5. FAMILY HISTORY LIBRARY
6. Museum of Church History and Art
7. Historic Temple Square
8. LDS Church Office Building
9. Joseph Smith Memorial Building
10. Lion House
11. Beehive House
12. Hansen Planetarium
13. The Old Social Hall
14. ZCMI Center Mall
15. Crossroads Plaza
16. Capitol Theater
17. John W. Gallivan Utah Center
18. Rose Wagner Performing Arts Center
19. Marmalade District Historic Homes
20. Pioneer Memorial Museum
21. Utah State Capitol
22. Memorial Grove Park/City Creek Canyon
23. City Creek Park
24. Brigham Young Historic Park
25. Brigham Young Grave
26. Cathedral Church of St. Mark
27. Catholic Cathedral of the Madeleine
28. First Presbyterian Church
29. Governor's Mansion (Kearns Mansion)
30. Union Pacific Railway Depot
31. Delta Center
32. Rio Grande Depot (Amtrak)/Utah State Historical Society
33. Greek Orthodox Church
34. Exchange Place Historic District
35. City and County Building
36. Trolley Square

Figure 20-1

Map prepared by Carol Barrett

This business offers a wide range of products and services including genealogical books, software, maps, supplies, research consultations, research for clients, and classes. Hours: Monday-Saturday 10:00 A.M.–9:00 P.M., Sunday noon to 6:00 P.M.

Cash Machines (ATMs)

ATMs are located in several banks within a couple blocks of the FHL and in the nearby Crossroads Plaza and ZCMI Center Mall. For guests many hotels will cash checks up to a specified amount.

Child Care

Important

We often hear parents repeatedly hushing young children or telling them to sit still in the FHL. While genealogy is definitely something in which to involve the entire family, it is difficult for a young child to sit quietly and still for several hours. Their attention span just isn't the same as someone older who can sit for hours at a microfilm reader. **To be fair to a child who is too young to assist in the research, and in consideration of other researchers, we suggest finding a relative, friend, or service to care for the child.** The parent will be more productive in research, and the child will be happier.

There are many full-time child care facilities in Salt Lake City, but researchers needing drop-in child care may have difficulty finding such a service; open spots fill quickly. Consult the hotel staff and the telephone directory for child care services that will come to a hotel to care for children. There are also services that rent equipment such as car seats, cribs, and strollers.

The Salt Lake Convention & Visitors Bureau notes a child care referral service that provides services to visitors on an individual basis and tailored to the needs of the specific family. This includes either drop-in care or on-site babysitting. Contact Child Care Resource and Referral at 537-1044.

Churches

While Salt Lake City is known for the strong membership of the Church of Jesus Christ of Latter-day Saints, there are many other choices for worship. Contact the front desk or bell captain at your hotel or check the telephone directory for information on nearby places of worship. The denominations include Buddhist, Episcopalian, Greek Orthodox, Jewish, Lutheran, Methodist, Presbyterian, Quaker, Roman Catholic, Southern Baptist, Unitarian, and others.

For example, The Cathedral of the Madeleine, a Roman Catholic church, is located at 331 East South Temple (phone: 328-8941). Sunday Masses are 6:00 P.M. Saturday and 8:30 A.M., 11:00 A.M., and 6:00 P.M. Sunday. The sound of the cathedral bells of this magnificently refurbished cathedral is spectacular. The Episcopal Cathedral of St. Mark, at 231 East 100 South, is the oldest non-Mormon church in Utah.

Computer Rental and Access

Some people choose to travel without their laptop computer; they bring their notes along on a disk and rent a laptop computer during their library visit.

Some services are listed below, and others are listed in the telephone directory. Ask about daily and weekly rates and whether delivery service is provided. Some of the larger hotels have business centers with on-site computer availability and laptop computer rental services. If you are not familiar with several kinds of computers and word processing programs, this option may be a time-consuming process as you familiarize yourself with the rental unit.

COMPUTER RENTALS

- Burgoyne Computers & Services, 421 South 400 East, phone 531-2100, fax 531-2120, http://www.burgoyne.com

- Desktop Visual Products, 411 West 400 South, phone 359-5808

- Kinko's, 19 East 200 South, phone 533-9444. Offers on-site rental computers and printers with both Internet and e-mail access.

For More Info

Convenience Stores
See the "Groceries" section of this chapter.

Convention & Visitors Bureau
It is definitely worth your time to walk the half block south from the library to the Salt Lake Convention & Visitors Bureau's visitor information center at 90 South West Temple. You'll find brochures, maps, and an extensive gift shop. Their *Salt Lake Visitors Guide* has clear maps. It includes information on area restaurants, tours, skiing, lodging, shopping, museums, history, and more. The Salt Lake Convention & Visitors Bureau also has sites at the airport. The Salt Lake Convention & Visitors Bureau can also assist with hotel reservations anywhere in the Salt Lake Valley.

For those planning a trip through the rest of Utah, the Utah Travel Council and its publications will be helpful. See the Web site at <http://www.utah.com>. Phone numbers to contact them are (801) 538-1030, (800) 200-1160 and fax (801) 538-1399.

For More Info

Salt Lake Convention & Visitors Bureau. Phone (800) 541-4955; fax (801) 355-9323; e-mail slcvb@ saltlake.org. Web site http://www.visitsaltlake .com.

Copies
Most of your photocopying will likely be done in the library, but you may need to make copies outside of library hours. For copying, fax service, or on-site computer time and printer rental, you will find several copy stores around the city which offer these services. A twenty-four-hour Kinko's is located within a few blocks of the library at 19 East 200 South (phone: 533-9444). Parking is scarce here, but a parking garage is behind it; enter on the east side of the store. Kinko's validates for parking during the day, and evenings are free. The Staples, Office Depot, and Office Max stores (see the "Office Supplies" section of this chapter) also have self-service copiers; these have ample parking.

Exercise

While some researchers are determined to be in the library fourteen hours a day, we advocate taking mental and physical breaks. You will be more effective at your research if you do. Many hotels near the library have exercise rooms and pools for their guests. Crossroads Plaza and ZCMI Center Mall open in the early morning, so you can partake in the great American tradition of mall walking. It's a great way to exercise and avoid hot, chilly, rainy, or snowy weather. Of course, you can walk around the malls anytime during open hours, or you can walk outdoors. Metro Sports Club in the ZCMI Center Mall has a wide variety of exercise equipment and an indoor lap pool. It is open Monday through Saturday and has weekly and monthly rates for visitors. The cafe next to it offers bagels, muffins, coffee, soup, salads, and sandwiches for lunch and dinner. (The phone number is 364-8803.)

Just a few blocks from the library is the Utah College of Massage Therapy at 25 South 300 East (phone: 521-3330). Several genealogists we know say this is *the* way to relax and release a lot of the tension and strain from viewing microfilm or sitting at a computer for long hours. Other massage and spa services are in the downtown area.

Supplies

Genealogical Supplies

Did you run out of the forms you brought along or forget to pack them? If you need genealogical reference books, software, forms (including ancestor charts, family group sheets, and research logs), informational sheets, and more, check out the copy center areas in the FHL, Deseret Book in the ZCMI Center Mall, and the Family History Discovery Shoppe in the Crossroads Plaza. Forms may also be printed from a variety of Web sites. See more information on such sites in chapter two.

Groceries

Many genealogists bring breakfast and snack items such as fruit, instant oatmeal, and granola bars with them to Salt Lake City. Others like to purchase these, other food items, and bottled water once they arrive. Gift shops with a few convenience items are generally located in hotel lobbies, and a number of hotels are close to the library. Within a short walk or cab ride are several other options:

- **Maverik Country Store**
  206 West North Temple (a block from the library). This small convenience store/gas station carries soda, milk, juice, cereal, bottled water, paper goods, chips, cookies, candy, and other items. Open twenty-four hours.
- **Neighbors Market**
  44 North State Street (on the east side of State Street between North and South Temple, across from the Church office building), 355-8061. The market is on the street level of the Gateway apartment building. It is a small deli and grocery store and carries frozen foods, fresh fruit, dairy products, paper goods, canned items, and snack foods such as chips and

pretzels. The store was clean and the staff friendly on our last visit. Hours: Monday-Saturday 7:00 A.M.–10:00 P.M.

- **Rite Aid Pharmacy**
  72 South Main (between South Temple and 100 South; on the TRAX line), 531-0583. In addition to toiletries and medical items, you'll find stationery items. The grocery section includes canned fruit, apples, bananas, packaged muffins, cookies, crackers, soda, granola bars, cereal, milk, juice, bottled water, ice cream, paper plates, plastic silverware, and paper towels. Hours: Monday-Friday 7:30 A.M.–7:00 P.M.; Saturday 9:00 A.M.–6:00 P.M.; closed Sunday.
- **Wild Oats Market**
  645 East 400 South (on the 400 South TRAX line), 355-7401
  A full-service natural and organic foods store with a deli department. Hours: Monday-Saturday 10:00 A.M.–10:00 P.M., Sunday 10:00 A.M.–9:00 P.M.

Many researchers find it convenient to take a taxicab to a larger, full-service grocery store:

- **Fred Meyer**
  455 South 500 East, 328-6003 (grocery department) This is a big, clean combination grocery and discount department store that is on the 400 South TRAX line. The large grocery department includes an extensive deli. The rest of the store includes toiletry and health items, clothing, hardware, stationery, and more. Hours: Every day 7:00 A.M. to midnight. Pharmacy hours are shorter.
- **Smith's Food & Drug Center**
  402—6th Avenue, 328-1683
- **Smith's Food & Drug Center**
  876 East 800 South, 355-2801
  The Smith's stores also have stationery, toiletry, and health items and are open 24 hours a day. The pharmacy hours are shorter.

Mailboxes

Mailboxes are located near the entrance to the FHL and on many street corners. See the "Post Office" section of this chapter for more information.

Medical Care

Salt Lake City is a major metropolitan area with many well-known and award-winning large medical facilities for both adult and child care. Should you need medical or dental care while in Salt Lake City, you will find a wide array of assistance. Emergency care, after-hours clinics, and urgent care facilities are available. Consult the telephone directory or the front desk at your hotel. For emergencies, dial 911. If an emergency occurs in the library, contact a staff member or library security in the main lobby for assistance.

Before your trip, check with your health care provider and health insurance company to locate providers in Salt Lake City and see if your insurance coverage is for specific facilities only.

The large hospitals include LDS Hospital, Primary Children's Medical Center, Salt Lake Regional Medical Center, St. Mark's Hospital, University of Utah Hospitals & Clinics, and the Veterans Affairs Medical Center.

Museums and Art Galleries

Several museums and art galleries are within a short distance of the FHL, and more are in the Salt Lake Valley—almost thirty in all. Many arts festivals take place in the valley, as well. Information can be obtained through your hotel's bell captain or the Salt Lake Convention & Visitors Bureau.

- The Children's Museum of Utah (will be moving to the Gateway district), (801) 328-3383, http://www.childmuseum.org
  This is a hands-on, interactive museum for all ages.
- Museum of Church History and Art, 45 North West Temple, (801) 240-3310
  Adjacent to the FHL. Has Mormon cultural and historical exhibits which can be enjoyed by everyone. Open every day.
- Pioneer Memorial Museum, 300 North Main Street, (801) 538-1050
  Free museum with an excellent collection of memorabilia on four floors plus a carriage house. Sponsored by the Daughters of Utah Pioneers.
- Salt Lake Art Center, 20 South West Temple, (801) 328-4201
  Contemporary art gallery and gift shop one-half block from the library.
- Social Hall Heritage Museum, 51 South State (east end of ZCMI Center Mall), (801) 321-8745
  View of archeological dig of early Salt Lake City pioneer life.
- Utah Museum of Fine Arts, 1650 East South Campus Drive (on the University of Utah campus), (801) 581-7049, <http://www.utah.edu/umfa>
  Five thousand years of world art in permanent and changing exhibitions. Open every day, including Sunday afternoon.
- Utah Museum of Natural History, 1390 East President's Circle (200 South University Street; on the University of Utah campus), (801) 581-6927

Musical, Sporting, and Entertainment Events

Salt Lake City is the home of many musical and sporting events and venues. The daily newspapers carry extensive advertising for these. When we were leading groups to the FHL, a contingent within our group made a tradition of attending the symphony or another musical event at Abravanel Hall each year. Some individuals from another group we have been a part of attend a Utah Jazz basketball game or go skiing.

- The Capitol Theater, 50 West 200 South, box office (801) 355-2787
  Housed in a 1912 Vaudeville theater which has been painstakingly refurbished, the theater hosts many cultural events including ballet, opera, and Broadway shows.
- Pioneer Theatre Company, 300 South 1340 East, box office (801) 581-6961
  Utah's resident professional theater company presents plays and musicals in the Pioneer Memorial Theater on the University of Utah campus.
- The Utah Symphony's home in Abravanel Hall, 123 West South Temple,

is one block from the FHL. For further information on the symphony's season and other events at Abravanel Hall, call the general ticket office at (801) 355-2787 or check <http://www.utahsymphony.org>.

- Hogle Zoo, 2600 East Sunnyside Avenue, (801) 582-1631
  This large zoo will satisfy family members who do not spend the day at the library. A child-size train ride and a petting zoo are two of many highlights.
- The Salt Lake City Stingers baseball team is a AAA minor league team. Games are played at Franklin Covey Field from April to September. Franklin Covey Field is located at 77 West 1300 South, one block from a TRAX station. (Phone (801) 485-3800 or check the Web site at <http://www.buzz baseball.com>.)
- The Utah Grizzlies team is Salt Lake City's International Hockey League franchise. They play from October to April at the E Center (3200 South Decker Lake Drive, West Valley City, Utah 84119), a skating venue for the 2002 Winter Olympics. (Phone (801) 988-PUCK or visit on the Web site at <http://www.utahgrizz.com>.)
- The Utah Jazz NBA basketball team plays home games at the Delta Center, 301 West South Temple, three blocks from the FHL and at a TRAX station. (Phone (801) 355-DUNK. See the Web site at <http://www.utahjazz.com>.)
- The Utah Starzz, the WNBA team, play from June to August at the Delta Center. (Phone (801) 325-STAR or visit the Web site at <http://www.utah starzz.com>.)

Office Supplies

Genealogists always need paper, pens, pencils, binders, and file folders. Fortunately, there are several options for purchasing these items. Some supplies are available at the Rite-Aid pharmacy in Crossroads Plaza and at Office & Things in the ZCMI Center Mall. A Staples is located at 400 South 600 East, and an Office Max is located at 410 South 900 East; both are near TRAX stations. An Office Depot is at is 281 West 2100 South, near the Central Pointe TRAX Station, 2100 South.

Supplies

Options for Sunday or the Non-Genealogist

What do you do when the library is closed on Sunday? No, it is not open seven days a week. How about church, a city or area tour, a Mormon Tabernacle Choir performance, a movie or bowling, a walk around downtown, a cruise on the Great Salt Lake, Sunday Brunch, a nap, research material organization session, a call to the folks back home, sending postcards back home, a skiing or shopping trip, a sporting event, or one of a hundred other activities? Rent a car and drive into the mountains or to the outlet stores in Park City. Eat at one of the many Park City restaurants and maybe spend a few dollars in the shops there. Drive forty-five minutes south to Provo and give yourself a tour of the Brigham Young University Campus. Visit the extensive university library and the large Family History Center which is open some Sunday afternoons. Back in Salt Lake City, visit the University of Utah's Marriott Library or the Utah

Museum of Fine Arts on campus. Drive a few miles west and actually see the Great Salt Lake.

What about the rest of Utah? How about more golfing, hiking, a dinosaur museum, National Parks, picnic spots, spectacular scenery, splashing at a water park? Some of the ski resorts are open in the summer. That's where you can enjoy the scenery. Nearby is Evanston, Wyoming, where you can take in some horse racing. Just less than two hours west via I-80 on the Utah/Nevada line is Wendover, Nevada, and its several large casinos and hotels; special tour buses operate to Wendover from Salt Lake City. The Wendover Area Chamber of Commerce & Tourism Web site is at <http://www.wendover.org>, and the phone number is 877-WENDOVE, ext. 311. The quick reference sheet in appendix A has contact details for further tourism information. Many of these attractions should fill the time of that nongenealogist traveling companion. Be sure to verify hours and days when these attractions operate.

Post Office

A full-service post office is on the second floor of the ZCMI Center Mall, two blocks from the library. The main downtown post office is at 230 West 200 South. The Airport Mail Center, 320 North 3700 West, is a full-service station open seven days a week. It is at the entrance to the Salt Lake International Airport Complex. You might want to use the post office to ship some of your things back home. A stamp vending machine is on the first floor of the library.

Shipping

Money Saver

Have you made more copies or bought more gifts than you had planned? Does the thought of trying to juggle the extra items on the airplane seem daunting? **Ship home some of the lighter clothing you brought along.** This option gives you the freedom to make a few extra record copies to bring home in your carry-on bag. You can ship from Quick Connections (in the lower level of Crossroads Plaza), which offers a packaging and mailing service seven days a week. The store is open Monday through Saturday until 9:00 P.M. and also on Sunday afternoons. The phone number is 328-1099. Another option for shipping is the full-service post office in the ZCMI Center Mall, open Monday through Saturday.

Shopping

Most things you might need will be within walking distance of the library at the downtown malls—Crossroads Plaza and ZCMI Center Mall—and other nearby stores. The ZCMI Center Mall is the home of the ZCMI (Zions Cooperative Mercantile Institution) department store, the first department store in the United States. The store name changed to Meier & Frank in 2001, but the mall name remains the same. In these malls and stores, you will find books and toys; barber shops, beauty salons, and spas; card and gift shops; a post office; clothing, jewelry, and shoes; luggage and sporting goods; food courts and restaurants; stationery stores; specialty shops; candy stores; photo developing; and eyeglass repair. The Gateway area at the western edge of downtown has more stores.

With the success of the light-rail on Main Street, more downtown shops are opening. Some stores in Salt Lake City (including ZCMI Center Mall) are closed on Sundays, but Crossroads Plaza, Trolley Square, and suburban malls are open. There are several pockets of antique shops in the downtown area. The general sales tax rate in Salt Lake City is 6.60 percent. Ask at mall information counters for coupon booklets good toward food, services, and products.

Genealogists interested in scrapbooking will find many supply stores throughout the city. There are many additional shopping malls and discount department stores in the greater Salt Lake Valley. The unique Trolley Square can be reached by cab, bus, or TRAX from Temple Square. It features shops and restaurants in the renovated Salt Lake City trolley barns which were built in 1908 to house and service the city's first trolley cars. Trolley Square was renovated in the early 1970s and is a National Historic Site. Genealogists will appreciate the preservation at Trolley Square.

- Crossroads Plaza, 50 South Main Street; (801) 531-1799, <http://www.crossroadsplaza.com>. Parking garage, food court, Nordstrom's, Mervyn's, and many other stores.
  Hours: Monday-Saturday 10:00 A.M.–9:00 P.M. Sunday noon to 6:00 P.M.
- Mormon Handicraft, 15 West South Temple (on the street level of the Gateway Tower West building between Crossroads Plaza and ZCMI Center Malls), 355-2141 (800) 843-1480. This unique gift shop carries thousands of unique handmade gifts.
  Hours: Monday-Friday 10:00 A.M.–9:00 P.M.; Saturday 10:00 A.M.–7:00 P.M.
- Trolley Square, 602 East 500 South, (801) 521-9877. Restaurants, movie theaters, specialty stores, some upscale clothing stores, and more. Some restaurants have longer hours. Surrounded by free parking on-site and across both 500 South and 600 South Streets.
  Hours: Monday-Saturday 10:00 A.M.–9:00 P.M.; Sunday noon to 5:00 P.M.
- ZCMI Center Mall, 36 South State at South Temple and Main Streets, (801) 321-8745, <http://www.zcmimall.com>. Parking garage, food court, services including a post office, and many stores.
  Hours: Monday-Friday 10:00 A.M.–9:00 P.M.; Saturday 10:00 A.M.–7:00 P.M.; closed Sunday.

Tipping

Courtesy tipping for van and cab drivers, bellmen, maids, and waitpersons is an individual choice. Typical amounts are one dollar per bag for the bellman, one to two dollars per day for the maid, one to two dollars for the shuttle driver, and 15 to 20 percent of the bill for cab drivers and waitpersons. Due to the weight of the suitcases and bags of most genealogists (all those books and papers!), the tip might be greater for bellmen and cab and shuttle drivers.

Tours of the City and Area

At the Salt Lake Convention & Visitors Bureau visitor information center, the Utah Heritage Foundation, and the Utah Travel Council, look for the excellent guidebook *Historic Downtown Salt Lake City Walking Tour*. This is a good history and personal walking tour guide. Horsedrawn carriages, operated year-round and available in the downtown area, are another way to see some of the sights.

A guided tour is a perfect way to rest and let someone else show you the city and the valley and tell you their history. Brochures are available in the hotels for several guided tours of the city and the surrounding area's sights. Tour sites include the Great Salt Lake, Fort Douglas, Temple Square, Hogle Zoo, the capitol area, ski areas, open-pit copper mines, Park City, and the University of Utah. Tours on Sunday are not as plentiful as those on other days of the week, but they are definitely worthwhile. Some tours do not operate during the winter months. Tours depart from many of the downtown hotels. Your hotel's bell captain may be able to assist you with a reservation.

Winter in the Canyons

A note about driving in Salt Lake City's environs: The road to Park City is a busy, four-lane interstate highway. Every effort is made to keep it open even in the worst winter weather. It can still be snow packed, and tire chains or snow tires are required. Routes to other ski areas can be steep and winding, and tire chains may be required when the roads are snow packed. These are all beautiful year-round, but they can be a bit treacherous in the winter. Some of the hotels post ski and driving conditions.

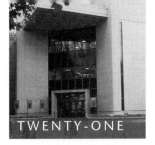

TWENTY-ONE

Temple Square

T his ten-acre site is the number one tourist attraction in Salt Lake City and is a center of activity for The Church of Jesus Christ of Latter-day Saints. The square is open to the public and attracts between five and six million visitors annually. The gardens are breathtaking, the architecture is impressive, and it is a peaceful place to walk. Tours are offered frequently and in many languages. Special services are offered for those with hearing impairments. The Salt Lake Temple with its six tall spires is an impressive building that can be seen for miles; it is not open to the general public. The Temple was begun in 1853 and completed in 1893. It is built of granite hauled from just southeast of the city. There are two visitors centers within the square. At the east side of Temple Square is a two-acre plaza area, formerly part of downtown's Main Street. This area has greenery, a reflecting pool, and places to sit and relax. From the day after Thanksgiving until early January, the square, plaza, and nearby area are home to thousands of Christmas lights.

VISITORS CENTERS

Temple Square has two visitors centers where information can be obtained on Temple Square tours, The Church of Jesus Christ of Latter-day Saints, and area activities. The north visitors center is the place to view the film *Legacy*, which is a powerful story of the Church and its members' westward trek for religious

---

MORMON TABERNACLE CHOIR PERFORMANCES

The choir rehearses in the Tabernacle most Thursday evenings from 8:00 P.M. to 9:30 P.M., and visitors may come in for all or part of this free event. The choir broadcast on Sunday morning is a free, live performance from 9:30 A.M. to 10:00 A.M. You should be there early, however, since the doors to the Tabernacle close at 9:15 A.M.

Notes

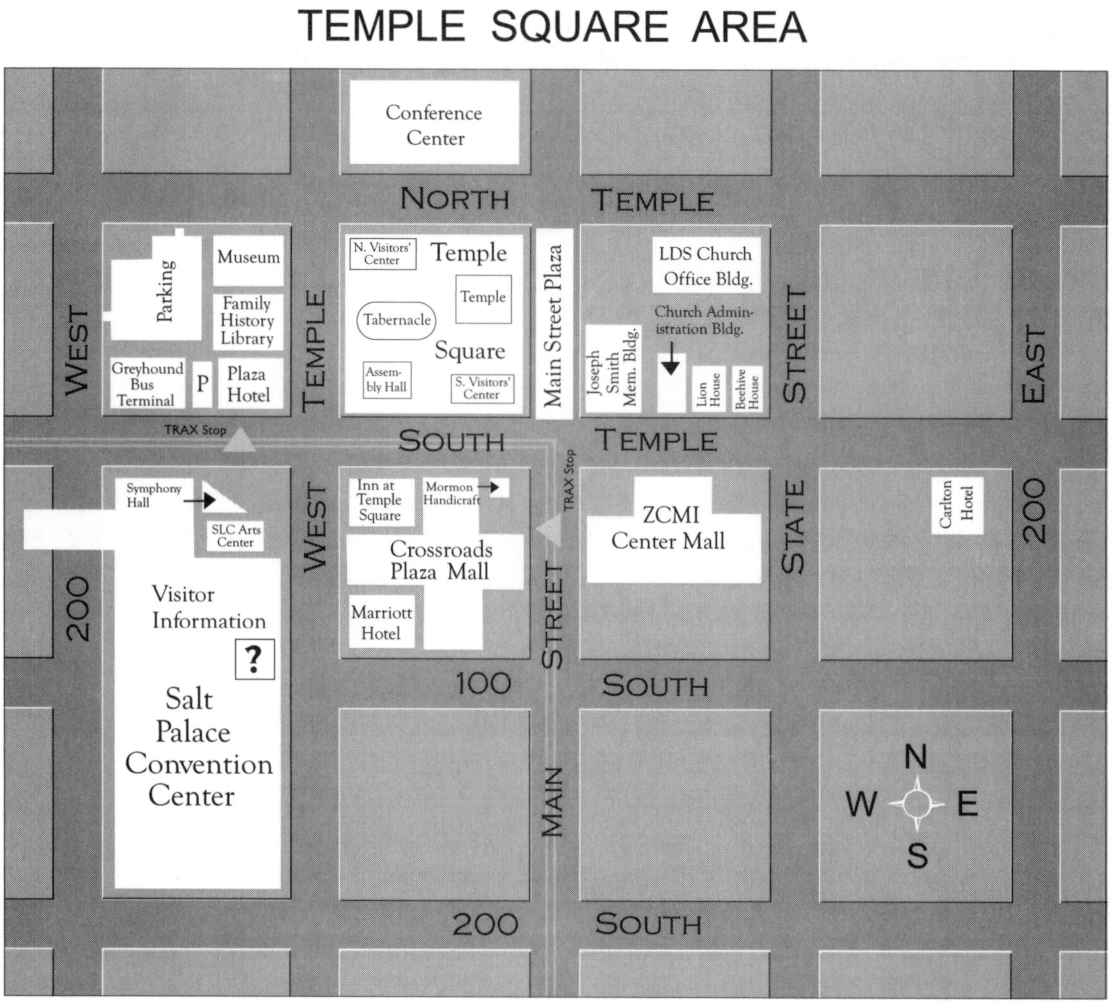

TEMPLE SQUARE AREA

Figure 20-1
Map prepared by Carol Barrett

CRS Digital Design   St. Paul, MN

freedom. The film lasts almost one hour. Both Church members and nonmembers have enjoyed this film, and many return to view it again.

MUSICAL OFFERINGS

The Mormon Tabernacle Choir performs in the domed Tabernacle, and the Assembly Hall has other concerts and musical events. Organ recitals are given Monday through Saturday in the Tabernacle at noon. Many researchers find the noontime events a peaceful interlude in a busy research day.

Information on the world-renowned adult choir's performances can be obtained through your hotel's bell captain, the Salt Lake Convention & Visitors Bureau, or the visitors center in Temple Square. The choir rehearses in the Tabernacle most Thursday evenings from 8:00 P.M. to 9:30 P.M., and visitors may come in for all or part of this free event. The choir broadcast on Sunday morning is a free, live performance from 9:30 A.M. to 10:00 A.M. However, you should arrive early since the doors to the Tabernacle close at 9:15 A.M. The performance is carried live on Salt Lake television station KSL, channel 5. The acoustics in the Tabernacle are amazing and afford great pleasure listening to both the 325-member adult choir and the organ, which has 11,623 pipes. On occasion, the choir is gone to perform elsewhere.

OTHER AREA BUILDINGS

Across West Temple Street are the Family History Library and the Museum of Church History and Art. Both of these buildings are open to the public. Between the museum and the library is a restored log cabin which was built in 1847 by Utah pioneers. This is surrounded by trees, flowers, and low retaining walls that offer a nice place to relax and take a break.

The next block east from the Square holds the Joseph Smith Memorial Building (detailed in chapter twelve), the Beehive House, and Lion House. In the same block, at 50 East North Temple, is the Church office building. It offers guided tours and two twenty-sixth floor observation decks which operate during daytime hours Monday through Friday.

The Beehive House at South Temple and State Streets was Brigham Young's home built in the mid 1850s. It has been beautifully restored and is open for tours seven days a week. The beehive symbolizes industriousness and working together; it is also the state symbol. The adjacent Lion House houses the Pantry, a pleasant and popular cafeteria-style restaurant.

At the corner of State Street and South Temple is Eagle Gate. This impressive monument spanning the street is a re-creation of the eagle that once stood at the entrance to Brigham Young's private estate.

Across North Temple Street from the Square is the Church's massive Conference Center, which opened in April 2000. It holds 21,000 people, has a custom-built pipe organ, rooftop gardens, waterfalls, and underground parking. Additional Christmas lights add to the beauty of this large building.

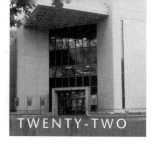

TWENTY-TWO

Other Area Research Repositories

Tip

A s with any state, the local public libraries, historical societies, and college and university libraries will have much material for genealogical research. Sometimes the staff at these facilities may not realize the importance of their materials in the research process. We suggest checking publications such as *The Genealogist's Address Book*, *American Library Directory*, and *Directory of Special Libraries and Information Centers* and online directories for addresses of other repositories. In some cases these guides will also give general information on the holdings of the specific facility. Next see if you can check the library's holdings via an online catalog. Many of these will have Utah-specific materials including newspapers, manuscripts, and microforms. Some will have holdings with a broader base. For example, many historical societies have publications of similar societies in other counties and states.

We always say that genealogists who drive through a city and neglect to stop at the public, university, or other library might be missing something vital to their own family history. **Though the special collections department may have more limited hours than the rest of the library, the surprising collections make stopping worthwhile.**

On the other hand, some of these repositories are open during hours when the Family History Library is not. The hours for facilities listed below are general; please call ahead to verify the current hours and holiday schedules.

Brigham Young University (BYU)

Harold B. Lee Library

Provo, UT 84602

(801) 378-2927 (Note: In 2002, the Provo area code will change to 385.)

http://www.lib.byu.edu

Hours: Monday-Friday 7:00 A.M. to midnight; Saturday 8:00 A.M. to midnight; in summer the library closes at 10:00 P.M.

Located just forty-five miles south of Salt Lake City, this university library has extensive reference, map, and history divisions. Special collections include Mormonism and western Americana. The collection represents materials related to many countries. The county history collection for the United States is superb.

It also houses a Family History Center called the Utah Valley Regional Family History Center (see below).

Utah Valley Regional Family History Center

2250 Harold B. Lee Library

Brigham Young University

Provo, UT 84602

(801) 378-6200

http://www.lib.byu.edu/dept/uvrfhc/

Hours: Monday-Saturday 8:00 A.M.–9:45 P.M.; Second and Fourth Sundays 9:00 A.M.–6:45 P.M.

The Lee Library building houses the Utah Valley Regional Family History Center. This FHC has an extensive on-site collection of microforms and books. This FHC's materials are cataloged in the BYU library catalog. The FHC has many in-house finding aids. The actual FHC is on an underground level in a new wing of the BYU library.

The Church of Jesus Christ of Latter-day Saints
Historical Department/Church Archives

Church Office Building

50 East North Temple

Salt Lake City, UT 84150

This church archives has many manuscripts, publications (newspapers and journals), and records. The manuscripts include many diaries of the early Mormon settlers and of the journeys taken to Utah.

Salt Lake City Public Library, Main Building

209 East 500 South

Salt Lake City, UT 84111-3280

(801) 524-8200

http://www.slcpl.lib.ut.us

Hours: Monday-Thursday 9:00 A.M.–9:00 P.M.; Friday-Saturday 9:00 A.M.–6:00 P.M.

Has some newspapers for other large cities. A new library building will open on this same block (at the corner of 200 East and 400 South) in late 2002 and will feature books, computers, a cafe, gardens, and more. This library is on the TRAX line on 400 South.

University of Utah
J. Willard Marriott Library

295 South 1500 East

Salt Lake City, UT 84112

http://www.lib.utah.edu

Hours: Monday-Thursday 7:00 A.M. to midnight; Friday 7:00 A.M.–8:00 P.M.; Saturday 9:00 A.M.–8:00 P.M.; Sunday 11:00 A.M. to midnight. Hours are more limited in the summer and between semesters. Special Collections hours: Monday-Thursday 8:00 A.M.–9:00 P.M.; Friday 8:00 A.M.–5:00 P.M.; Saturday 9:00 A.M.–5:00 P.M.; closed Sunday

The Special Collections department has an extensive manuscript collection for Utah and the West, including Native Americans. Many of the manuscripts are records of western mining companies. The Marriott Library is known as a

Internet Source

LINKS TO UTAH ONLINE LIBRARY CATALOGS

Utah's online library offers linkage to many library information sites and catalogs <http://pioneer.lib.ut.us/libraries.html>. The Utah State Library Division has other links to Utah public and academic libraries <http://www.state.lib.ut.us/directories.html>.

large government documents depository. The library has many of the reference tools and indexes typically found in major libraries and an excellent map collection. This library is on the TRAX line, and the nearest stop is a couple of blocks away at the Rice-Eccles Stadium.

Utah State Archives

Archives Building, State Capitol Area

Near 400 North Main

P.O. Box 141021

Salt Lake City, UT 84114-1021

(801) 538-3012

http://www.archives.state.ut.us

Hours: Monday-Friday 8:00 A.M.–5:00 P.M.

Records of Utah local, county, and state government are preserved by the state archives. Some materials have been microfilmed and are available via interlibrary loan. Some special items include military burial records, naturalization records, and vital records. An article by Elizabeth Perkes on "Genealogical Research at the Utah State Archives" appeared in the *Genealogical Journal* 28 (number 1, 2000): 40–45.

Utah State Historical Society

Utah History Information Center

300 South 455 West (in the historic Rio Grande Depot at 300 Rio Grande Street)

Salt Lake City, UT 84101

(801) 533-3535; (801) 533-3501 for hours

http://www.history.utah.org

Hours: Monday-Friday 10:00 A.M.-5:00 P.M.; Saturday 10:00 A.M.–2:00 P.M.

The collection's Utah focus includes an extensive manuscript collection, many printed state and county histories, newspapers, photographs, indexes, clippings files, and maps. It also includes Mormon history, WPA records, and western history. The society publishes the *Utah Historical Quarterly* and other publications. Databases include Utah burials and cemeteries and are online.

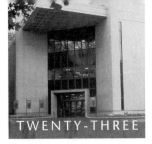

TWENTY-THREE

Now What? After Your Trip

We return home from our trips to Salt Lake City tired, but revitalized, by the days spent in search of ancestral information. When a trip is over, the reality of priorities that accumulated while we were away seems to take over. In spite of that, set aside a little genealogical time in those first days back to take care of some important things.

Reminder

A FEW FIRST STEPS

- Write thank-yous.

- Review what you brought home.

- Write a summary of your trip as you update your charts and time lines.

- Make copies of documents to file and share.

- File documents.

- Pass along the story of your trip.

Do those tasks before the discoveries and the enthusiasm of that trip to Salt Lake City are lost in the press of day-to-day concerns. (If you're a Utah resident for whom the trip is a short one, think about doing some of these things, too.)

THINGS TO KEEP IN MIND

Most folks come home from Salt Lake City with two important things: new information and a renewed enthusiasm for genealogical research. Feed and water both of these to keep them growing! Now that you've seen the library and how things work, you'll be able to plan an effective return trip. You will also appreciate all the other ways in which you can access information from the library without going to Salt Lake City and hopefully will make use of them.

START PREPARING FOR THE NEXT TRIP

Reread chapter seven of this book, which covers preparing for a trip. Many of the suggestions there will assist you in deciding what direction to go with the new information you bring back from Salt Lake City. For example, if you've tracked your ancestors' migration back to an earlier location, learn more about that area. Locate and read the genealogical and historical periodicals that deal with that locality to learn more about the records, repositories, history, and social history of that vicinity. Track down articles and books written about the genealogy and family history of other families in that area to see how other genealogists traced families from that locality. Even if they are families not directly connected to yours, you may pick up problem-solving strategies or clues about resources by reading the results of their research.

RETURN SOMETHING TO THE FAMILY HISTORY LIBRARY

Idea Generator

We are often asked what is the best way someone can show their appreciation for the help and access to the wonderful facility and collection at the Family History Library. **We feel there are three appropriate and practical ways of doing that.**

Say "Thank You"

Of course, you can do this in person, and frequently, during your trip to the library. Take one step further and spend a few minutes writing a simple one-page letter to the library director. Express your appreciation to the library staff and volunteers for their help and to the Church for their support that makes free access to the facility and the collection possible. If particular resources or individuals helped you, or if you have suggestions, mention them briefly. A written thank-you is encouraging and rewarding to anyone, and none of us gives one as often as we should. Address your thank-you to the library director, who will share its contents appropriately with staff.

David E. Rencher, Director
Family History Library
35 North West Temple Street
Salt Lake City, UT 84150-3400

Consider Making a Donation

If you appreciated the free access you had to the largest genealogical collection in the world, consider making a donation to the library. The library does not solicit financial donations, but they are gratefully accepted as long as no restrictions are placed on the use of the funds. The cost of operating the FHL, its 3,400 Family History Centers worldwide, and the worldwide microfilming and preservation operation is paid by the members of The Church of Jesus Christ of Latter-day Saints. Additional financial donations to the library from its patrons enable the Family and Church History Department to do that much more to acquire additional resources for use by all researchers.

DONATING MATERIALS TO THE FHL

Are you donating to the FHL a book or booklet you have prepared? If you hold the copyright, consider granting permission for the library to microfilm the book. That will enable the film to circulate to Family History Centers, and your work will be more widely read and utilized. This will also ensure that your work is preserved in the security of the Granite Mountain Vault where the master microfilms of material the Church has filmed are stored. Books are not stored there, but microfilm is as well protected from future natural or man-made disasters as it can be.

The two-page library guide *Donations to the Family History Library* clearly outlines the what and how of making a donation to the library collections. That information is available on the FamilySearch Internet Web site <http://www.familysearch.org>.

Contribute to the Library Collection

If you know of an available genealogical or historical book that is not part of the library's collection, consider purchasing and donating it. Make your own family history data part of the FHL collection. If you computerize your genealogical data, consider uploading that on the FamilySearch Internet site for the Pedigree Resource File. If you produce a family history book or booklet, if you index or abstract a set of records, or if you compile other genealogical data, donate a copy to the library. That will preserve the results of your research and make them more available to other researchers, who may be able to share additional information with you in the future.

Last Words

The end of a research trip is not the end of the genealogical journey; it is just the beginning. Think about all the different resources we've mentioned briefly in this book and all the finding aids and indexes and guides being added every year to those already in existence. Consider the wealth of information from other researchers being made available on the thousands of Internet sites that have genealogical data. New clues for your research abound; just take the time to look for them. Remember that genealogical societies, conferences, seminars, and classes afford you endless opportunities to learn more about the sources and methods for finding your family history. If you take advantage of those opportunities, you will continue to know more tomorrow than today about your family and also how to research them.

Of course, not all the rolls of microfilm in the FHL pertain to areas or subjects connected to your ancestors. The collection is so deep and rich, however, that few of us ever exhaust the material that realistically could hold clues for our ancestral search. No matter how many rolls of film you looked at in Salt Lake City, remember that the library holds about another two million microfilm rolls that you

A FEW LAST VOICES OF EXPERIENCE

"Be sure and label all your research notebooks (or whatever you bring) with your name, address, phone number, and e-mail address. The FHL is great about returning any notebooks left behind, but they need to know where to send the materials."

—Donna Turbes

"For me as a Swede, the attraction might not be the Swedish records. I feel very much at home on B1, but this is the opportunity to try those American records I have read about and browse the book collection and sample some of those scholarly journals. It also gives me a possibility to try to find something on my elusive Germans."

—Elizabeth Thorsell

"I take a hot pot, instant soup, [and] snack food with me so I can have a quick meal and get right back to research. Then there is room for some of the paper in the suitcase on the way home. I go over to Crossroads Mall and get a six-pack of caffeinated soda and other snacks."

—Nancy Emmert

Tip:

Having trouble reading difficult or faint handwriting on a census or other record? Place a sheet of yellow (or pastel) paper on the microfilm reader.

"I do mostly client work while in Salt Lake City, but when I get stonewalled, frustrated, tired, I turn to some personal research."

—Roger Joslyn

"My research strategy was to concentrate on films that were fairly quick to check while postponing those that needed to be read completely until I got home (making a list of those as I went along, to order through the FHC). I felt this made the best use of time to get the most . . . films possible."

—Sue Kratsch

"There is usually more than one way to approach a genealogical search. If one source does not produce a record, try another. And another. Think it through. Learn the history of the areas you are researching to determine what might have influenced record keeping in a given place and time period."

—Donna Turbes

"We used the pack-and-mail service in Crossroads Mall and were very pleased with the way this helped tidy things up at the end of the trip. It decreased the amount of heavy papers and books that we had to pack and carry ourselves on the homeward . . . trip. It also meant that I felt I could make more photocopies and buy more resource books because I did not have to worry about toting everything myself. This meant that I carried home some background information that I might have skipped otherwise—and I was glad later that I had the info."

—Deborah Swanson

haven't used—yet. And just think, a year from now the library will have added some four thousand books and about eighteen thousand rolls of microfilm to its collection. Regardless of what you found, or didn't find, during your trip to the FHL or FHC, start making plans to travel there again. We hope to meet you there!

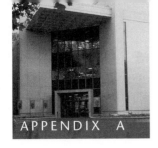

Salt Lake City Quick Reference Information

City Emergency Number

Fire, Medical, Police   Call 911

Hours

Family History Library

Monday	7:30 A.M.–5:00 P.M.
Tuesday-Saturday	7:30 A.M.–10:00 P.M.
Sunday	Closed

Joseph Smith Memorial Building

FamilySearch Center

Monday-Saturday	9:00 A.M.–9:00 P.M.
Sunday	Closed

Crossroads Plaza (mall)

Monday-Saturday	10:00 A.M.–9:00 P.M.
Sunday	Noon to 6:00 P.M.

ZCMI Center Mall

Monday-Friday	10:00 A.M.–9:00 P.M.
Saturday	10:00 A.M.–7:00 P.M.
Sunday	Closed

TRAX (light rail)

Monday-Friday	5:30 A.M. to midnight
Saturday	6:30 A.M. to midnight
Sunday	Limited hours

Useful Addresses

- Family History Library
  35 North West Temple St., Salt Lake City, UT 84150-3400
  (801) 240-2331   http://www.familysearch.org
- Joseph Smith Memorial Building
  15 East South Temple St., Salt Lake City, UT 84150
  (801) 240-4085

- Salt Lake Convention & Visitors Bureau
  90 South West Temple St., Salt Lake City, UT 84101-1406
  (800) 541-4955   (801) 521-2822   http://www.visitsaltlake.com
- Utah Travel Council
  300 N. State St., Salt Lake City, UT 84101
  (801) 538-1900   http://www.utah.com
- Utah Heritage Foundation
  485 N. Canyon Rd.
  P.O. Box 28, Salt Lake City, UT 84110-0028
  (801) 533-0858   http://www.utahheritagefoundation.com
- Other helpful connections
  http://www.utah.citysearch.com
  http://www.downtownslc.org
  http://www.skiutah.com

Other Telephone Numbers and Web Sites

Utah Transit Authority
    Call RIDE-UTA or (888) RIDE-UTA
    http://www.rideuta.com
Taxicabs:

City Cab	(801) 363-5014
Ute Cab	(801) 359-7788
Yellow Cab	(801) 521-2100

Daily Newspapers

Deseret News
    http://www.deseretnews.com
The Salt Lake Tribune
    http://www.sltrib.com

Travel Information

Road Conditions	(801) 964-6000
Weather	(801) 467-8463
Airline Flight Information:	
America West	(800) 247-5692
American	(800) 433-7300
Continental	(800) 525-0280
Delta	(800) 221-1212
Frontier	(800) 432-1359
Northwest	(800) 225-2525
Southwest	(800) 435-9792
United	(800) 241-6522
Vanguard	(801) 826-4827

Salt Lake City Access and Selected Salt Lake Valley Places of Interest

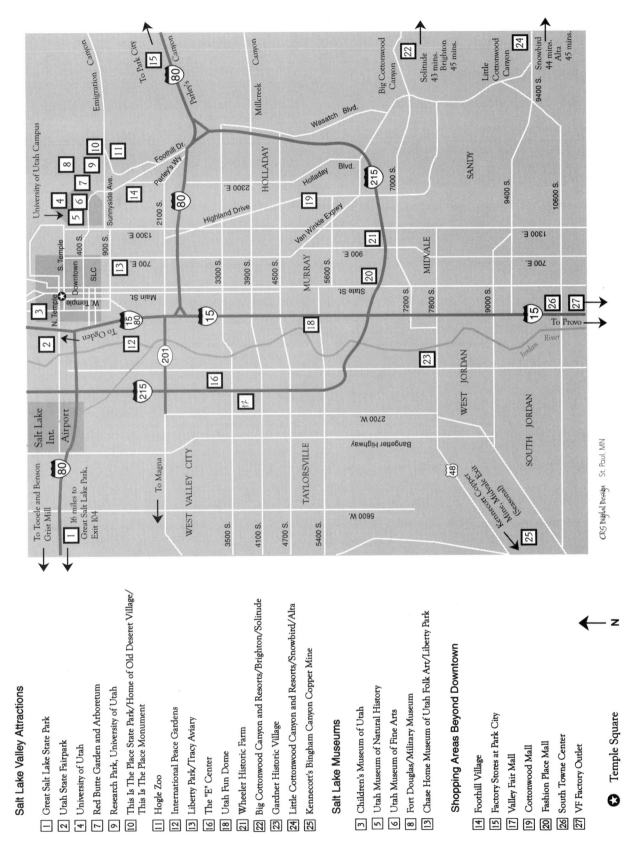

Salt Lake Valley Attractions

1. Great Salt Lake State Park
2. Utah State Fairpark
4. University of Utah
7. Red Butte Garden and Arboretum
9. Research Park, University of Utah
10. This Is The Place State Park/Home of Old Deseret Village/ This Is The Place Monument
11. Hogle Zoo
12. International Peace Gardens
13. Liberty Park/Tracy Aviary
16. The "E" Center
18. Utah Fun Dome
21. Wheeler Historic Farm
22. Big Cottonwood Canyon and Resorts/Brighton/Solitude
23. Gardner Historic Village
24. Little Cottonwood Canyon and Resorts/Snowbird/Alta
25. Kennecott's Bingham Canyon Copper Mine

Salt Lake Museums

3. Children's Museum of Utah
5. Utah Museum of Natural History
6. Utah Museum of Fine Arts
8. Fort Douglas/Military Museum
13. Chase Home Museum of Utah Folk Art/Liberty Park

Shopping Areas Beyond Downtown

14. Foothill Village
15. Factory Stores at Park City
17. Valley Fair Mall
19. Cottonwood Mall
20. Fashion Place Mall
26. South Towne Center
27. VF Factory Outlet

★ Temple Square

Map prepared by Carol Barrett

CRS Digital Design   St. Paul, MN

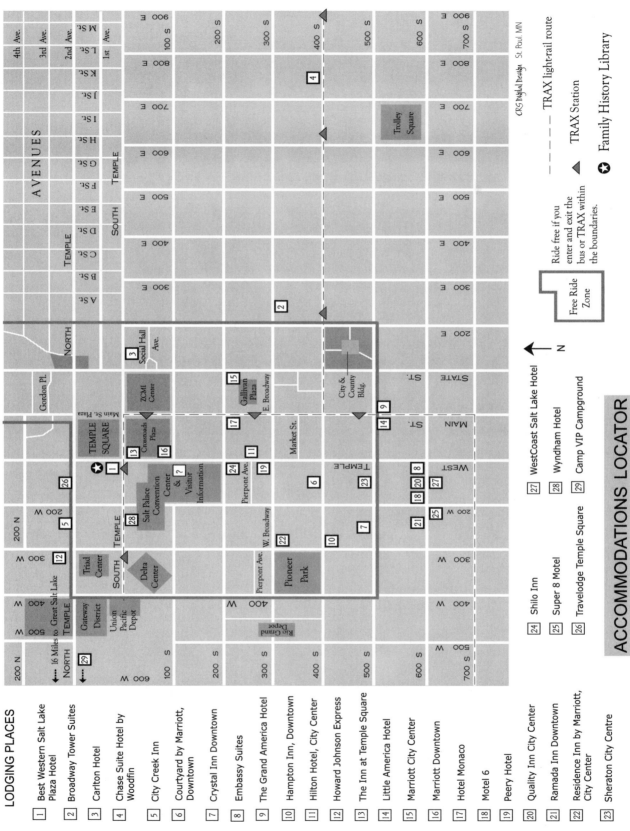

CRS Digital Design St. Paul, MN

– – – – TRAX light-rail route

◀ TRAX Station

✪ Family History Library

Ride free if you enter and exit the bus or TRAX within the boundaries.

Free Ride Zone

N ←

ACCOMMODATIONS LOCATOR

LODGING PLACES

1. Best Western Salt Lake Plaza Hotel
2. Broadway Tower Suites
3. Carlton Hotel
4. Chase Suite Hotel by Woodfin
5. City Creek Inn
6. Courtyard by Marriott, Downtown
7. Crystal Inn Downtown
8. Embassy Suites
9. The Grand America Hotel
10. Hampton Inn, Downtown
11. Hilton Hotel, City Center
12. Howard Johnson Express
13. The Inn at Temple Square
14. Little America Hotel
15. Marriott City Center
16. Marriott Downtown
17. Hotel Monaco
18. Motel 6
19. Peery Hotel
20. Quality Inn City Center
21. Ramada Inn Downtown
22. Residence Inn by Marriott, City Center
23. Sheraton City Centre
24. Shilo Inn
25. Super 8 Motel
26. Travelodge Temple Square
27. WestCoast Salt Lake Hotel
28. Wyndham Hotel
29. Camp VIP Campground

Map prepared by Carol Barrett

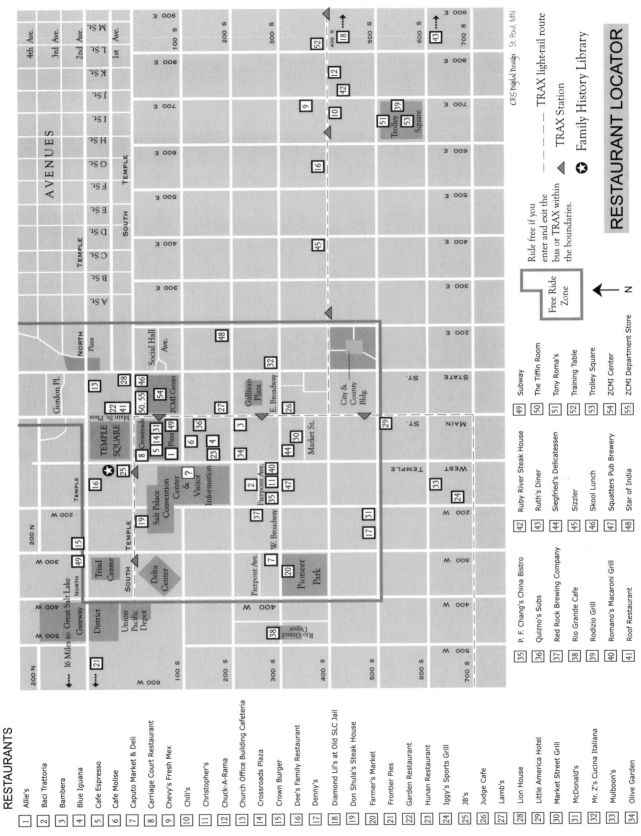

Map prepared by Carol Barrett

RESTAURANTS

1	Allie's
2	Baci Trattoria
3	Bambera
4	Blue Iguana
5	Cafe Espresso
6	Cafe Molise
7	Caputo Market & Deli
8	Carriage Court Restaurant
9	Chevy's Fresh Mex
10	Chili's
11	Christopher's
12	Chuck-A-Rama
13	Church Office Building Cafeteria
14	Crossroads Plaza
15	Crown Burger
16	Dee's Family Restaurant
17	Denny's
18	Diamond Lil's at Old SLC Jail
19	Don Shula's Steak House
20	Farmer's Market
21	Frontier Pies
22	Garden Restaurant
23	Hunan Restaurant
24	Iggy's Sports Grill
25	JB's
26	Judge Cafe
27	Lamb's
28	Lion House
29	Little America Hotel
30	Market Street Grill
31	McDonald's
32	Mr. Z's Cucina Italiana
33	Mulboon's
34	Olive Garden

35	P. F. Chang's China Bistro
36	Quizno's Subs
37	Red Rock Brewing Company
38	Rio Grande Cafe
39	Rodizio Grill
40	Romano's Macaroni Grill
41	Roof Restaurant
42	Ruby River Steak House
43	Ruth's Diner
44	Siegfried's Delicatessen
45	Sizzler
46	Skool Lunch
47	Squatters Pub Brewery
48	Star of India
49	Subway
50	The Tiffin Room
51	Tony Roma's
52	Training Table
53	Trolley Square
54	ZCMI Center
55	ZCMI Department Store

CRS Digital Design   St. Paul, MN

RESTAURANT LOCATOR

— — — TRAX light-rail route
◄ TRAX Station
✪ Family History Library

Ride free if you enter and exit the bus or TRAX within the boundaries.

Free Ride Zone

N

Salt Lake City Downtown Area Attractions

Map prepared by Carol Barrett

1. VISITOR INFORMATION
2. The Salt Palace Convention Center
3. Salt Lake City Art Center
4. Maurice Abravanel Concert Hall
5. FAMILY HISTORY LIBRARY
6. Museum of Church History and Art
7. Historic Temple Square
8. LDS Church Office Building
9. Joseph Smith Memorial Building
10. Lion House
11. Beehive House
12. Hansen Planetarium
13. The Old Social Hall
14. ZCMI Center Mall
15. Crossroads Plaza
16. Capitol Theater
17. John W. Gallivan Utah Center
18. Rose Wagner Performing Arts Center
19. Marmalade District Historic Homes
20. Pioneer Memorial Museum
21. Utah State Capitol
22. Memorial Grove Park/City Creek Canyon
23. City Creek Park
24. Brigham Young Historic Park
25. Brigham Young Grave
26. Cathedral Church of St. Mark
27. Catholic Cathedral of the Madeleine
28. First Presbyterian Church
29. Governor's Mansion (Kearns Mansion)
30. Union Pacific Railway Depot
31. Delta Center
32. Rio Grande Depot (Amtrak)/Utah State Historical Society
33. Greek Orthodox Church
34. Exchange Place Historic District
35. City and County Building
36. Trolley Square

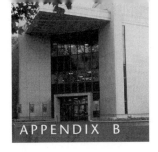

Helpful Reference

This section is designed to accompany the many reference suggestions listed throughout the guide. In addition to the references listed in this section, others are cited within individual chapters. To make it easier for you to find specific items, the reference categories are:

- Census
- Daughters of the American Revolution
- Ethnic and Locality Resources
- Family History Library Information Guides
- Family History Library Publications
- Genealogical Research Guides
- Language and Handwriting
- Libraries and Genealogical Societies
- Military
- Miscellaneous
- National Archives Guides and Microfilm
- Passenger Lists and Naturalization Records
- Salt Lake City and Area Guides
- U.S. Locality Guides
- Works Projects Administration

This section includes a selected bibliography of helpful books and some other resources. We urge you to do some creative browsing in libraries and online catalogs, check reviews, pay attention to publications suggested by other lecturers and writers, and talk to other genealogists to seek out additional items. Some of these books have extensive bibliographies that lead you to other resources. Guidebooks may hold some of the answers you seek or further information on a specific record or locality.

Where can you find these books? Check at libraries with genealogical or historical collections. This includes the Family History Library. Attend a genealogical society meeting or seminar, and you may find one or more vendors of genealogical books and software. Many vendors have Web sites where you can order books directly. With the growing popularity of genealogy, many mainstream bookstores worldwide now offer a selection of genealogical titles. Some of the books cited are out of print, but they are available in many libraries.

The general reference areas on each floor of the FHL have many more guidebooks for specific localities and topics. The list below is only a small portion of the guidebooks available to help you focus on research in a specific ancestral area. We suggest that you consult many of these prior to your visit to the FHL. The information you glean will help you be better prepared for both the city and library. Also check genealogical newsletters and journals for city, county, and state genealogical societies and for specific ethnic groups. The contents are valuable for research hints and reviews of related books. Listen to audiotapes of specific lectures about doing research at the FHL, doing research in the Hamburg Passenger lists, reading Norwegian, what's new in Jewish research, and many other topics. Even better, attend genealogical seminars and conferences to add to your genealogical knowledge.

CENSUS

Bakeman, Mary Hawker. *A Guide to the Minnesota State Census Microfilm.* Roseville, Minn.: Park Genealogical Book Co., 1992. [Includes the FHL call numbers.]

Buckway, G. Eileen, comp. *U.S. 1910 Federal Census: Unindexed States: A Guide to Finding Census Enumeration Districts for Unindexed Cities, Towns, and Villages.* Salt Lake City: Family History Library, The Church of Jesus Christ of Latter-day Saints, 1992.

Buckway, G. Eileen, and Fred Adams. *U.S. State and Special Census Register: A Listing of Family History Library Microfilm Numbers.* Rev. ed. 2 vols. Salt Lake City: Family History Library, The Church of Jesus Christ of Latter-day Saints, 1992. [Also on nine microfiche.]

Dollarhide, William. *The Census Book: A Genealogist's Guide to Federal Census Facts, Schedules, and Indexes.* Bountiful, Utah: Heritage Quest, 1999.

Lainhart, Ann S. *State Census Records.* Baltimore: Genealogical Publishing Co., 1992.

Smith, Leonard H. Jr., comp. *United States Census Key 1850, 1860, 1870.* Bountiful, Utah: American Genealogical Lending Library, 1987.

Thorndale, William, and William Dollarhide. *Map Guide to the U.S. Federal Censuses, 1790–1920.* Baltimore: Genealogical Publishing Co., 1987. [Useful for census year boundary changes.]

DAUGHTERS OF THE AMERICAN REVOLUTION

Grundset, Eric G., and Steven B. Rhodes. *American Genealogical Research at the DAR, Washington, D.C.* Washington, D.C.: National Society of the Daughters of the American Revolution, 1997.

Kirkham, E. Kay. *An Index to Some of the Bibles and Family Records of the United States: 45,000 References As Taken From the Microfilm at the*

Genealogical Society of Utah. Vol. 2. Logan, Utah: Everton Publishers, 1984.

———. *An Index to Some of the Family Records of the Southern States: 35,000 Microfilm References From the N.S.D.A.R. Files and Elsewhere.* Vol. 1. Logan, Utah: Everton Publishers, 1979.

Lacy, Ruby. *D.A.R. Records on Microfilm Available in Salt Lake City Genealogical Society Library.* 4 vols. Ashland, Ore.: R. Lacy, 1978, 1979.

Stemmons, John D., and E. Diane Stemmons. *The Cemetery Record Compendium: Comprising a Directory of Cemetery Records and Where They May Be Located.* Logan, Utah: Everton Publishers, 1979.
This book contains more cemeteries than just those on the Genealogical Records Committee films.]

———. *The Vital Record Compendium: Comprising a Directory of Vital Records and Where They May Be Located.* Logan, Utah: Everton Publishers, 1979. [This book contains more vital records sources than just those on the Genealogical Records Committee films.]

ETHNIC AND LOCALITY RESOURCES

Carmack, Sharon DeBartolo. *A Genealogist's Guide to Discovering Your Immigrant & Ethnic Ancestors.* Cincinnati: Betterway Books, 2000. [This guide has more ethnic background and bibliographic citations to ethnic research guides and social history than we are able to include here.]

African American

Burroughs, Tony. *Black Roots: A Beginner's Guide to Tracing the African American Family Tree.* New York: Fireside Div. of Simon & Schuster, 2001.

Taylor, Marie. *Family History Library Bibliography of African-American Sources: As of 1994.* Salt Lake City: Family History Library, The Church of Jesus Christ of Latter-day Saints, 2000.

Woodtor, Dee Parmer. *Finding a Place Called Home: A Guide to African-American Genealogy and Historical Identity.* New York: Random House, 1999.

Native American

Byers, Paula K., ed. *Native American Genealogical Sourcebook.* Detroit: Gale Research Inc., 1995. [Part of the Gale series on ethnic research. There is incomplete coverage of some sources, such as church and missionary records, but this is the most useable guide to Indian research. This guide offers record descriptions and case studies to show how some records are used. Many items available at the FHL are discussed.]

Carter, Kent. *The Dawes Commission and the Allotment of the Five Civilized Tribes, 1893–1914.* Provo, Utah: Ancestry, 1999.

Witcher, Curt B., and George J. Nixon. "Tracking Native American Family History." Chap. 14 in *The Source.* Rev. ed. Edited by Loretto Dennis Szucs and Sandra Hargreaves Luebking. Salt Lake City: Ancestry, 1998. [Where to start? This is an excellent introduction to Indian research and includes case studies.]

Canadian

Baxter, Angus. *In Search of Your Canadian Roots: Tracing Your Family Tree in Canada.* 3d ed. Baltimore: Genealogical Publishing Co., 2000.

Merriman, Brenda Dougall. *Genealogy in Ontario: Searching the Records.* 3d ed. Toronto: Ontario Genealogical Society, 1996.

Punch, Terrence M., and George F. Sanborn. *Genealogist's Handbook for Atlantic Canada Research.* 2d ed. Boston: New England Historic Genealogical Society, 1997.

Taylor, Ryan. *Books You Need to Do Genealogy in Ontario: An Annotated Bibliography.* Fort Wayne, Ind.: Round Tower Books, 1996.

Danish

Searching for Your Danish Ancestors: A Guide to Danish Genealogical Research in the United States and Denmark. St. Paul, Minn.: Danish Genealogy Group, 1989.

Smith, Frank, and Finn A. Thomsen. *Genealogical Guidebook & Atlas of Denmark.* 2d ed. Provo, Utah: Stevenson's Genealogical Center, 1979.

Eastern European

Baxter, Angus. *In Search of Your European Roots.* 3d ed. Baltimore: Genealogical Publishing Co., 2001. [Includes research overviews for some countries not found in other guides.]

FEEFHS. Federation of East European Family History Societies. P.O. Box 510898, Salt Lake City, Utah 84151-0898. <http://feefhs.org>. [The Web site contains many references to FHL collections and includes some finding aids and indexes.]

Schlyter, Daniel M. *A Handbook of Czechoslovak Genealogical Research.* 2d ed. Buffalo Grove, Ill.: Genun Publishers, 1990. [Includes what are now the Czech Republic and Slovakia.]

English (also see Great Britain)

Humphrey-Smith, Cecil R., ed. *The Phillimore Atlas and Index of Parish Registers.* 2d ed. Chichester, England: Phillimore & Co., 1995.

Irvine, Sherry. *Your English Ancestry: A Guide for North Americans.* Rev. ed. Provo, Utah: Ancestry, 1993. [Many FHL resources are covered.]

Milner, Paul, and Linda Jonas. *A Genealogist's Guide to Discovering Your English Ancestors.* Cincinnati: Betterway Books, 2000.

Moulton, Joy Wade. *Genealogical Resources in English Repositories.* Columbus, Ohio: Hampton House, 1988 (and *Supplement to Genealogical Resources in English Repositories,* 1992).

Reid, Judith Prowse, and Simon Fowler. *Genealogical Research in England's Public Record Office: A Guide for North Americans.* 2d ed.

Baltimore: Genealogical Publishing Co., 2000. Identifies records also found at the FHL.]

Finnish

Clifford, Karen. "The Best Finnish." *Genealogical Journal* 80, nos. 3–4 (1999): 202–208. [Includes many FHL sources.]

Vincent, Timothy Laitila, and Rick Tapio. *Finnish Genealogical Research.* New Brighton, Minn.: Finnish Americana, 1994.

German

Anderson, S. Chris, and Ernest Thode. *A Genealogist's Guide to Discovering Your Germanic Ancestors.* Cincinnati: Betterway Books, 1999.

Brandt, Ed., et al. *Germanic Genealogy: A Guide to Worldwide Sources and Migration Patterns.* 2d ed. St. Paul, Minn.: Germanic Genealogy Society, 1997. [This edition has significant changes from the earlier edition and covers many countries with Germanic connections.]

Edlund, Thomas Ken. *Die Ahnenstammkartei des Deutschen Volkes: An Introduction and Register.* St. Paul, Minn.: Germanic Genealogy Society, 1995.

Jensen, Larry O. *A Genealogical Handbook of German Research.* 3 vols. Pleasant Grove, Utah: Jensen Publications, 1980–86.

Riemer, Shirley J. *The German Research Companion.* Rev. ed. Sacramento, Calif.: Lorelei Press, 2000.

Wright, Raymond S., ed. *Meyers Orts-Und Verkehrs-Lexikon des Deutschen Reichs.* Rev. ed. 3 vols. Baltimore: Genealogical Publishing Co., 2000. [Gazetteer to over 200,000 towns, cities, hamlets, and other dwelling places in the former German Empire before World War I. The text is in Gothic font. This edition includes a translation of the introduction and a guide to deciphering and using Meyers Orts.]

Great Britain (see also English)

"British 1881 Census Project Nears Completion." *Forum* 7 (spring 1995): 1, 16–18. [Details on the massive project to index the 1881 census of England, Scotland, and Wales; the index may be used at the FHL, among other locations.]

Hunter, Dean J. "The Expanded British Collection at the Family History Library." A series that identifies the repositories at which filming was done, lists what was filmed, and tells how many rolls of film were created for each location. These articles appeared in *Forum*, the quarterly publication of the Federation of Genealogical Societies.

Part I: Vol. 4, no. 4 (winter 1992): 3–5. List of the repositories at which the new filming was done or from which films were purchased. Heavy emphasis on England, some for Ireland, Scotland, and Wales. Details the types of records filmed.

Part II: Vol. 5, no. 1 (spring 1993): 4–7. Details how to access the material and begins the summary of what was filmed.

Part III: Vol. 5, no. 2 (summer 1993): 4–5. Beginning of listing, by county in England, of the new films.

Part IV: Vol. 5, no. 3 (fall 1993): 7–8. Continuance of listing, by county in England, of the new films.

Part V: Vol. 5, no. 4 (winter 1993): 12–13. Completion of listing, by county in England, of the new films.

Hunter, Dean J. "Growth of the British Collection at the Family History Library: 1996 to June 2000." *Forum* (winter 2000).

Pelling, George. *Beginning Your Family History in Great Britain*. 7th ed. Rev. by Pauline Litton. Birmingham, England: Federation of Family History Societies, 2001.

Hispanic Countries

Byers, Paula K., ed. *Hispanic American Genealogical Sourcebook*. Detroit: Gale Research, 1995.

Platt, Lyman D. *Genealogical Research in Latin America and the Hispanic United States*. St. George, Utah: Teguayo Press, 1993.

Ryskamp, George R. *Finding Your Hispanic Roots*. Baltimore: Genealogical Publishing Co., 1997. [Includes much detail on the vast Hispanic resources at the FHL.]

Irish

Grenham, John. *Tracing Your Irish Ancestors*. 2d ed. Baltimore: Genealogical Publishing Co., 2000.

Mitchell, Brian. *A Guide to Irish Parish Registers*. Baltimore: Genealogical Publishing Co., 1988.

Radford, Dwight A., and Kyle J. Betit. *A Genealogist's Guide to Discovering Your Irish Ancestors*. Cincinnati: Betterway Books, 2001. [Includes research on Irish ancestry in Great Britain, the United States, Canada, Australia, New Zealand, and the British West Indies.]

Reilly, James R. *Richard Griffith and His Valuations of Ireland*. Baltimore: Clearfield Co., 2000.

Ryan, James G. *Irish Church Records: Their History, Availability, and Use in Family and Local History Research*. Dublin, Ireland: Flyleaf Press, 1992.

———. *Irish Records: Sources for Family and Local History*. 2d ed. Salt Lake City: Ancestry, 1997.

Italian

Carmack, Sharon DeBartolo. *Italian-American Family History: A Guide to Researching and Writing About Your Heritage*. Baltimore: Genealogical Publishing Co., 1997.

Colletta, John Philip. *Finding Italian Roots: The Complete Guide for Americans*. Baltimore: Genealogical Publishing Co., 1993.

Nelson, Lynn. *A Genealogist's Guide to Discovering Your Italian Ancestors*. Cincinnati: Betterway Books, 1997.

Jewish

Avotaynu: The International Review of Jewish Genealogy. Published quarterly in Teaneck, New Jersey. [It includes how-to articles, record updates, data on archives and libraries, and more related to Jewish research in many countries. It is also helpful for non-Jewish research in these areas, as it frequently refers to FHL sources and filming updates. See chapter four for ordering details.]

Kurzweil, Arthur. *From Generation to Generation: How to Trace Your Jewish Genealogy and Family History.* 2d ed. New York: HarperCollins, 1994.

Mokotoff, Gary, and Warren Blatt. *Getting Started in Jewish Genealogy.* Bergenfield, N.J.: Avotaynu, 1999.

New England

Anderson, Robert Charles. *The Great Migration Begins: Immigrants to New England, 1620–1633.* 3 vols. Boston: New England Historic Genealogical Society, 1995.

Melnyk, Marcia D. *Genealogist's Handbook for New England Research.* 4th ed. Boston: New England Historic Genealogical Society, 1999.

New Netherlands

Epperson, Gwenn F. *New Netherland Roots.* Baltimore: Genealogical Publishing Co., 1994. [Covers mostly seventeenth-century New Netherlanders in this country and aids in tracking them back to their European roots. Heavy emphasis on what's available at the FHL.]

Norwegian

Thomsen, Finn A. *Genealogical Maps & Guide to the Norwegian Parish Registers.* Bountiful, Utah: Thomsen's Genealogical Center, 1987.

————. *Scandinavian Genealogical Research Manual.* Bountiful, Utah: Thomsen's Genealogical Center, 1993.

Polish

Chorzempa, Rosemary A. *Polish Roots.* Baltimore: Genealogical Publishing Co., 1993.

Scottish

Cory, Kathleen B. *Tracing Your Scottish Ancestry.* Baltimore: Genealogical Publishing Co., 1990.

Irvine, Sherry. *Your Scottish Ancestry: A Guide for North Americans.* Salt Lake City: Ancestry, 1997.

Swedish

Johansson, Carl-Erik. *Cradled in Sweden.* Rev. ed. Logan, Utah: Everton Publishers, 1995.

Swedish Genealogical Resources. 2d ed. St. Paul, Minn.: Swedish Interest Group, 1994.

Swiss

Moos, Mario von. *Bibliography of Swiss Genealogies.* Camden, Maine: Picton Press, 1993. [Bibliography of published works related to Swiss families; sections by name and location.]

Wellauer, Maralyn A. *Tracing Your Swiss Roots.* Milwaukee, Wis.: the author, 1991.

Welsh

Hamilton-Edwards, Gerald. *In Search of Welsh Ancestry.* Baltimore: Genealogical Publishing Co., 1986.

Rowlands, John, and others, eds. *Welsh Family History: A Guide to Research.* 2d ed. Baltimore: Genealogical Publishing Co., 1999.

Rowlands, John, and Sheila Rowlands. *Second Stages in Researching Welsh Ancestry.* Baltimore: Genealogical Publishing Co., 1999.

FAMILY HISTORY LIBRARY INFORMATION GUIDES

Additional items are noted in chapter four and not repeated here.

Cerny, Johni, and Wendy Elliott, eds. *The Library: A Guide to the LDS Family History Library.* Salt Lake City: Ancestry, 1988. [This gives you an overview of the holdings; however, a tremendous amount of material has been added since this guide was published. Also on CD-ROM. An update is in progress.]

Hawgood, David. *FamilySearch on the Internet.* Birmingham, United Kingdom: Federation of Family History Societies, Ltd., 1999. [Though this author's guides have an English bent, they are still useful to all researchers.]

———. *IGI on Computer: The International Genealogical Index From CDROM.* Ramsey, Huntingdon, Cambridgeshire, England: the author, 1998.

Meyerink, Kory L. "An Insider's Guide to the Family History Library." *Ancestry* 18 (July/August 2000): 20–23.

Nichols, Elizabeth L. "Family Group Records Collection and Related Records of the Family History Library," *Genealogical Journal* 24, no. 1: 11–27. [The collection is housed in the Joseph Smith Memorial Building.]

———. "The International Genealogical Index (IGI), 1993 Edition." A thorough discussion of the IGI appeared in four consecutive issues of *Forum,* the quarterly of the Federation of Genealogical Societies.

Part I: Vol. 5, no. 4 (winter 1993): 5–10.
Part II: Vol. 6, no. 1 (spring 1994): 4–6.
Part III: Vol. 6, no. 2 (summer 1994): 4–8.
Part IV: Vol. 6, no. 3 (fall 1994): 5–9.

Other articles on the IGI by the same author have also appeared in *Forum*:
"International Genealogical Index (IGI) Updated by Addendum"
    Part I: Vol. 7, no. 3 (fall 1995): 5–8.
    Part II: Vol. 7, no. 4 (winter 1995): 4–6.
"International Genealogical Index Addendum Version 2 (Released 1997)."
    Vol. 10, no. 2, (summer 1998): 1, 14–17.
Parker, J. Carlyle. *Going to Salt Lake City to Do Family History Research*. 3d ed. Turlock, Calif.: Marietta Publishing Co., 1996.
Schaefer, Christina Kassabian. "Your Key to the Vault." *Family Tree Magazine* 1, no. 2 (April 2000): 60–64. [Excellent article on accessing FHL collections through local Family History Centers.]
Simon, Vaughn L. "The Family History Library." *Association of Professional Genealogists Quarterly* 13 (September 1998): 94–95.
Sperry, Kip. "Latter-day Saint Records," *Ancestry* 19, no. 2 (March/April 2001): 28–31.
Warren, Paula Stuart, and James W. Warren. "Genealogy City: Salt Lake City." *Family Tree Magazine* 1, no. 4 (August 2000): 44–49.

FAMILY HISTORY LIBRARY PUBLICATIONS

Most of the FHL publications listed in chapters three and four are not repeated in this section. The Family History Publications List provides title, price, and publication number for many of the Research Outlines, Resource Guides, and forms available from the library. These can be purchased at the library, at FHCs, online, or by mail. (Salt Lake Distribution Center, 1999 West 1700 South, Salt Lake City, Utah 84104-4233.) Fax orders to (801) 240-3685. For phone orders (charged to MasterCard, Visa, or American Express) call (800) 537-5950. [The Family History SourceGuide, available online and in CD-ROM versions, incorporates many of the library publications in a fast and easy-to-use format.]

The Hamburg Passenger Lists, 1850–1934. 2d ed. Salt Lake City: Intellectual Reserve, Inc. 1999.
Roberts, Jayare, comp. *Register of U.S. Lineage Societies*. 2d ed. Salt Lake City: Family History Library, The Church of Jesus Christ of Latter-day Saints, 1990.
Using the Old Scottish Church Records and Parochial Records Index. Salt Lake City: Family History Library, The Church of Jesus Christ of Latter-day Saints, 1998. [Research Outline; FHL publication number 36077000]

GENEALOGICAL RESEARCH GUIDES

Allen, Desmond Walls. *First Steps in Genealogy: A Beginner's Guide to Researching Your Family History*. Cincinnati: Betterway Books, 1998.
Carmack, Sharon DeBartolo. *The Genealogy Sourcebook*. Los Angeles: Lowell House, 1997.

Croom, Emily Anne. *Unpuzzling Your Past: A Basic Guide to Genealogy*. 4th ed. Cincinnati: Betterway Books, 2001.

Eichholz, Alice, ed. *Ancestry's Red Book: American State, County, and Town Sources*. Salt Lake City: Ancestry, 1989. [Overview of sources state by state.]

Greenwood, Val D. *The Researcher's Guide to American Genealogy*. 3d ed. Baltimore: Genealogical Publishing Co., 2000.

The Handy Book for Genealogists. 9th ed. Logan, Utah: Everton Publishers, 1999. [Overview guide to state and county sources. For U.S. counties, lists beginning dates of records, records available, date of county creation, maps, contact addresses, and more. This edition also includes overviews of several foreign countries.]

Hinckley, Kathleen W. *Locating Lost Family Members & Friends: Modern Genealogical Research Techniques for Locating the People of Your Past and Present*. Cincinnati: Betterway Books, 1999.

Hone, E. Wade. *Land & Property Research in the United States*. Salt Lake City: Ancestry, 1997.

Meyerink, Kory L., ed. *Printed Sources: A Guide to Published Genealogical Records*. Salt Lake City: Ancestry, 1998. [Guidebook and bibliography to a wide variety of publications on many topics including states, countries, and ethnic groups.]

Rose, Christine, and Kay Ingalls. *The Complete Idiot's Guide to Genealogy*. New York, N.Y.: Macmillan, 1997.

Szucs, Loretto Dennis, and Sandra Hargreaves Luebking. *The Source: A Guidebook of American Genealogy*. Rev. ed. Salt Lake City: Ancestry, 1997.

LANGUAGE AND HANDWRITING

Evans, Barbara Jean. *The New A to Zax: A Comprehensive Genealogical Dictionary for Genealogists and Historians*. 2d ed. Champaign, Ill.: the author, 1990.

Johnson, Arta F. *How to Read German Church Records Without Knowing Much German*. Columbus, Ohio: Copy Shop, 1980.

Shea, Jonathan D., and William F. Hoffman. *Following the Paper Trail: A Multilingual Translation Guide*. Teaneck, N.J.: Avotaynu, 1994. [Guide to translating records in many languages, including Czech, French, German, Italian, Latin, Lithuanian, Polish, Russian, and Swedish.]

Sperry, Kip. *Reading Early American Handwriting*. Baltimore: Genealogical Publishing Co., 1998.

Suess, Jared. *Central European Genealogical Terminology*. Logan, Utah: Everton Publishers, 1978. [Covers German, Latin, French, and Hungarian terminology in microfilmed records.]

LIBRARIES AND GENEALOGICAL SOCIETIES

Allen County Public Library, 900 Webster St., Fort Wayne, Ind. 46802. Holds all periodicals indexed in PERSI and has extensive genealogy collection. Internet: http://www.acpl.lib.in.us/genealogy.

American Library Directory: A Classified List of Libraries in the United States and Canada, With Personnel and Statistical Data. 53d ed. New York: R.R. Bowker Co., 2000. [Biennial]

Bentley, Elizabeth Petty. *The Genealogist's Address Book.* 4th ed. Baltimore: Genealogical Publishing Co., 1998.

Directory of Special Libraries and Information Centers. 23d ed. 3 vols. Detroit: Gale Group, 1998. [Published irregularly.]

Federation of Genealogical Societies, P.O. Box 200940, Austin, Tex. 78720-0940. Publisher of *Forum.* Phone: (888) 347-1500 (toll free). Internet: http://www.fgs.org.

National Genealogical Society, 4527 Seventeenth St. North, Arlington, Va. 22207-2399. Publisher of *NGS Newsmagazine* and *National Genealogical Society Quarterly.* Internet: http://www.ngsgenealogy.org.

New England Historic Genealogical Society, 101 Newbury St., Boston, Mass. 02116. Publishes *Register* and has extensive genealogy collection. Phone: (617) 536-5740. Internet: http://www.nehgs.org.

Utah Genealogical Association, P.O. Box 1144, Salt Lake City, Utah 84110. Membership organization with quarterly journal and newsletter. The newsletter (*UGA News*) carries information on recent additions to the library. Internet: http://www.infouga.org.

Wisconsin Historical Society, 816 State St., Madison, Wisconsin 53706. Holds many periodicals indexed in PERSI and has extensive genealogy collection. Internet: http://www.shsw.wisc.edu/index.html.

MILITARY

Deputy, Marilyn Jane, et al., comps. *Register of Federal United States Military Records: A Guide to Manuscript Sources Available at the Genealogical Library in Salt Lake City and the National Archives in Washington, D.C.,* 3 vols. Bowie, Md.: Heritage Books, 1986.

Geiger, Linda Woodward. *The Value of WWI Draft Registration Cards and Other WWI Records.* Session F-117, Syllabus, Federation of Genealogical Societies and the Ohio Genealogical Society Conference, 1998. Audiotape available from Repeat Performance.

Neagles, James C. *U.S. Military Records: A Guide to Federal and State Sources, Colonial America to the Present.* Salt Lake City: Ancestry, 1994.

Nelson, Ken, and Marva Blalock, comps. *Register of Federal United States Military Records: A Guide to Manuscript Sources Available at the Genealogical Library in Salt Lake City and the National Archives in Washington D.C.,* Vol. 4. Salt Lake City: Family History Library, The Church of Jesus Christ of Latter-day Saints 1989.

White, Virgil D. *Index to Old Wars Pension Files, 1815–1926.* Rev. ed. Waynesboro, Tenn.: National Historical Publishing Co., 1993. [Also check for abstracts and indexes to Revolutionary War pension and service records and for War of 1812 pension index by the same author.]

MISCELLANEOUS

Carmack, Sharon DeBartolo. *Organizing Your Family History Search: Efficient & Effective Ways to Gather and Protect Your Genealogical Research.* Cincinnati: Betterway Books, 1999.

Clooz: The Electronic Filing Cabinet for Genealogical Records. Ancestor Detective, P.O. Box 6386, Plymouth, Mich. 48170. Internet: http://www.ancestordetective.com/.

Dollarhide, William. *Managing a Genealogical Project.* Baltimore: Genealogical Publishing Company, 1999. [Updated edition with many helpful tips and genealogical forms.]

Humphrey, John T. *Understanding and Using Baptismal Records.* Washington, D.C.: Humphrey Publications, 1996.

Periodical Source Index. (PERSI) Fort Wayne, Ind.: Allen County Public Library Foundation. [Annual indexes since 1986 to articles in thousands of contemporary genealogical and historical periodicals. Also a sixteen-volume retrospective set of published volumes, indexing most U.S. genealogical periodicals ever published and many historical periodicals. Also in CD-ROM and online editions. Internet: http://www.ancestry.com.

Repeat Performance, 2911 Crabapple La., Hobart, Ind. 46342. [Sells audiotapes of taped sessions from FGS Conferences (1991 and later), NGS Conferences (1992 and later), and several regional and state conferences. Internet: http://www.audiotapes.com].

Warren, James W., and Paula Stuart Warren. *Getting the Most Mileage From Genealogical Research Trips.* 3d ed. St. Paul, Minn.: Warren Research and Publishing, 1998.

NATIONAL ARCHIVES GUIDES AND MICROFILM
(Microfilm guides are online at http://www.nara.gov.)

American Indians: A Select Catalog of National Archives Microfilm Publications. Rev. ed. Washington, D.C.: National Archives and Records Administration, 1998.

Black Studies: A Select Catalog of National Archives Microfilm Publications. Washington, D.C.: National Archives, 1984.

Guide to Genealogical Research in the National Archives. 3d ed. Washington, D.C.: National Archives and Records Administration, 2000.

Immigrant and Passenger Arrivals: A Select Catalog of National Archives Microfilm Publications. 3d ed. Washington, D.C.: National Archives Trust Fund Board, 1991.

Szucs, Loretto Dennis, and Sandra Hargreaves Luebking, eds. *The Archives: A Guide to the National Archives Field Branches.* Salt Lake City: Ancestry, 1988.

PASSENGER LISTS AND NATURALIZATION RECORDS

Barss, David. *New York Immigration 1820–1943.* 2d ed. Salt Lake City: Family History Library, The Church of Jesus Christ of Latter-day Saints,

1993. [This compiled finding aid is in a three-ring binder and is shelved in the reference area on the library's second floor. It contains background information as well as FHL catalog printouts for the microfilm indexes and passenger lists in the library collection for the port of New York. It also includes examples of the indexes and passenger lists themselves, as well as references to helpful published sources also in the library collection.]

The Church of Jesus Christ of Latter-day Saints. *U.S. Passenger Lists 1820–: Register of film numbers for passenger lists and indexes of vessels arriving in the United States*. Salt Lake City: Family History Library, n.d. [Located in the same area as the New York finding aid, this three-ring binder contains comparable information for other U.S. ports.]

Colletta, John Philip. *They Came in Ships*. Rev. ed. Salt Lake City: Ancestry, 1993. [An excellent, short guide to researching passenger lists.]

Glazier, Ira A., ed. *The Famine Immigrants: Lists of Irish Immigrants Arriving at the Port of New York, 1846–1851*. 8 vols. Baltimore: Genealogical Publishing Co., 1983–1986. [This is an example of a growing number of passenger arrival list indexes or abstracts. Other ethnic groups represented in these are German, Russian, Swedish, Italian, and Dutch.]

Newman, John J. *American Naturalization Records, 1790–1990: What They Are and How to Use Them*. Bountiful, Utah: Heritage Quest, 1998.

Schaefer, Christina K. *Guide to Naturalization Records of the United States*. Baltimore: Genealogical Publishing Co., 1997. [Emphasis on microfilmed naturalizations (county and federal level) at the National Archives or the Family History Library. The book does not make clear to readers specifically what it includes. As a result, the specifics for some states are excellent, while for others, such as Minnesota, the listings are erroneous and may mislead researchers into thinking filmed county records are not available. For Minnesota all the county-level District Court naturalization records are available on microfilm from the state historical society.]

Tepper, Michael. *American Passenger Arrival Records: A Guide to the Records of Immigrants Arriving at American Ports by Sail and Stream*. Rev. ed. Baltimore: Genealogical Publishing Co., 1993. [This is an update of the 1988 edition. It covers colonial emigration records, finding aids, reference materials, National Archives microfilms, current projects related to immigration research, and more.]

Wilkins, Judith S., Merill Gillette, and David Barss. *U.S. Federal Naturalization Records*. 2 vols. Salt Lake City: Family History Library, The Church of Jesus Christ of Latter-day Saints, 1992. [This register identifies naturalization records from U.S. federal courts that are available at the FHL. Many more microfilmed naturalization records from state, county, and other courts are also available at the FHL on microfilm and at the FHL and other repositories as published abstracts or indexes.]

SALT LAKE CITY AND AREA GUIDES

Adare, Sierra, and Candy Moulton. *Salt Lake City Uncovered.* Plano, Tex.: Seaside Press, 1997. [Not complete, but easy to read and covers some things not in other guidebooks.]

Angus, Mark. *Salt Lake City Underfoot: Self-Guided Tours of Historic Neighborhoods.* 2d ed. Salt Lake City: Signature Books, 1996. [Even if you don't venture far, this guide "reveals the diverse heritage" of a very interesting city, its buildings, and neighborhoods and has excellent maps.]

Duffy, Kate and Bryan Larsen. *The Insiders' Guide to Salt Lake City.* 2d ed. Manteo, N.C.: Insiders' Publishing, Inc., 2000.

Godfrey, Margaret Sandberg. *City-Smart Guidebook: Salt Lake City.* Santa Fe, N.M.: John Muir Publications, 1999.

Salt Lake Visitors Guide. Salt Lake City: Salt Lake Convention & Visitors Bureau, biannual. [The Convention & Visitors Bureau is a very helpful source of information and assistance. Phone (801) 521-2868), write (180 South West Temple, Salt Lake City, UT 84101-1493) or stop by the Visitors Center, just a block south of the Family History Library.]

Weir, Bill and W.C. McRae. *Moon Handbooks: Utah.* 6th ed. Emeryville, Calif.: Avalon Travel Publishing, 2001.

U.S. LOCALITY GUIDES

Bamman, Gale Williams. *Research in Tennessee.* Arlington, Va.: National Genealogical Society, 1993. [Just one of a series of NGS publications about state research. Others include Indiana, Minnesota, Missouri, Oregon, Rhode Island, South Carolina, Texas, Virginia, and Washington, D.C. The NGS *Quarterly* has carried many extensive articles on researching in these and other states.]

Crawford-Oppenheimer, Christine. "Lost in Pennsylvania? Try the Published Pennsylvania Archives," *The Pennsylvania Genealogical Magazine* 40 (fall/winter 1997). [Also a lecture by same author and same title presented (session T-89) at the 1997 NGS Conference in the States in Valley Forge, Pennsylvania. Audiotape available from Repeat Performance.]

Eichholz, Alice, ed. *Ancestry's Red Book: American State, County, and Town Sources.* 2d. ed. Salt Lake City: Ancestry, 1991. [It includes a chapter on each state; however, coverage is uneven.]

Guzik, Estelle M., ed. *Genealogical Resources in the New York Metropolitan Area.* New York: Jewish Genealogical Society, Inc., 1989. [Many New York City–area resources have been filmed.]

Hogan, Roseann Reinemuth. *Kentucky Ancestry: A Guide to Genealogical and Historical Research.* Salt Lake City: Ancestry, 1993.

Iscrupe, William L., and Shirley G. M. Iscrupe. *Pennsylvania Line: A Research Guide to Pennsylvania Genealogy and Local History.* Laughlintown, Pa.: Southwest Pennsylvania Genealogical Services, 1990.

Leary, Helen F.M., ed. *North Carolina Research: Genealogy and Local History.* 2d ed. Raleigh, N.C.: North Carolina Genealogical Society, 1996.

McGinnis, Carol. *Virginia Genealogy: Sources & Resources.* Baltimore: Genealogical Publishing Co., 1993.

Sperry, Kip. *Genealogical Research in Ohio.* Baltimore: Genealogical Publishing Co., 1997.

Steele, Edward E. *Guide to Genealogical Research in St. Louis.* 4th ed. St. Louis: St. Louis Genealogical Society, 1999.

Szucs, Loretto Dennis. *Chicago and Cook County: A Guide to Research.* Salt Lake City: Ancestry, 1996. A thorough guide to research in a large city. Many Chicago and Cook County records are at the FHL.]

Warren, Paula Stuart. *Minnesota Genealogical Reference Guide.* 5th ed. St. Paul, Minn.: Warren Research and Publishing, 2001.

WORKS PROJECTS ADMINISTRATION

Child, Sargent B., and Dorothy P. Holmes. *Check List of Historical Records Survey Publications.* Washington, D.C.: 1943. [WPA Technical Series Research and Records Bibliography No. 7. There are several other federal publications which list WPA publications. Also in reprint edition (Baltimore: Clearfield Press, 1989).]

Hefner, Loretta L. *The WPA Historical Records Survey: A Guide to the Unpublished Inventories, Indexes, and Transcripts.* Chicago: The Society of American Archivists, 1980. [Information on unpublished WPA projects and where the records were located circa 1980. Internet: http://www.archivists.org/ .]

Heisey, John W. *Works Projects Administration: Sources for Genealogists.* Indianapolis: Heritage House, 1988. [Information on both published and unpublished WPA projects.]

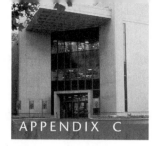

APPENDIX C

Forms

Individual Time Planning Calendar for_____

Note: the shaded areas indicate hours that the Family History Library is CLOSED.

TIME	Wednesday	Thursday	Friday	Saturday	Sunday	Monday	Tuesday	Wednesday
6:00 AM	▓	▓	▓	▓	▓	▓	▓	▓
6:30 AM	▓	▓	▓	▓	▓	▓	▓	▓
7:00 AM	▓	▓	▓	▓	▓	▓	▓	▓
7:30 AM					▓			
8:00 AM					▓			
8:30 AM					▓			
9:00 AM					▓			
9:30 AM					▓			
10:00 AM					▓			
10:30 AM					▓			
11:00 AM					▓			
11:30 AM					▓			
NOON					▓			
12:30 PM					▓			
1:00 PM					▓			
1:30 PM					▓			
2:00 PM					▓			
2:30 PM					▓			
3:00 PM					▓			
3:30 PM					▓			
4:00 PM					▓			
4:30 PM					▓			
5:00 PM					▓			
5:30 PM					▓			
6:00 PM					▓	▓		
6:30 PM					▓	▓		
7:00 PM					▓	▓		
7:30 PM					▓	▓		
8:00 PM					▓	▓		
8:30 PM					▓	▓		
9:00 PM					▓	▓		
9:30 PM					▓	▓		
10:00 PM	▓	▓	▓	▓	▓	▓	▓	▓
10:30 PM	▓	▓	▓	▓	▓	▓	▓	▓

Research Log

Ancestor's name

Objective(s)

Locality

Date of search	Location/ call number	Description of source (author, title, year, pages)	Comments (purpose of search, results, years and names searched)	Doc. number

5/88. Printed in the USA. 31825

Reprinted by permission. © 1999–2000 by Intellectual Reserve, Inc.

Research Log

Research by_____	**Date** _____
Address_____	**Page** _____ of _____ **Research Logs**
_____	**Surname or Individual being researched**
E-mail _____	_____

Repository:	Format: ☐ Manuscript ☐ Microfilm ☐ Microfiche ☐ Book
	☐ Card Index ☐CD ROM ☐ Web site ☐ Computer database
Call Number:	Title/description:
	Author:
	City of Publication:	Publisher:	Copyright date:
	Indexed?	Volume:	Condition:

SEARCH OBJECTIVE:

SEARCH RESULTS: | COPIED?

Research Calendar

Researcher:				Ancestor:		
Locality: State/Country/Town				Time Period:		

Brief Problem Statement:

Search Date	Where Available	Call #	Title/Author/Publisher/Year Or Record Identification Information	Notes	Page #'s

Excerpted from First Steps in Genealogy, copyright 1998 by Desmond Walls Allen. Used with permission of Betterway Books, a division of F&W Publications, Cincinnati, Ohio.

Give Yourself a Tour

Shortly after you arrive at the Family History Library, spend twenty minutes walking through the library. If it's your first trip to the library, walk through to become familiar with the facility. If you've been there before, verify what has or hasn't changed since your last trip.

The first floor lobby area
- ❑ Information desk
- ❑ Orientation room
- ❑ Elevators and stairs, telephones, and information brochures

First floor (U.S./Canada)
- ❑ Bulletin Boards
- ❑ FamilySearch workstations with printers
- ❑ Reference area
- ❑   Reference counter
- ❑   Reference books and finding aids
- ❑ Book area
- ❑ Copy center and attendant window
- ❑   Book copiers: regular, express, and color
- ❑   Stapler, paper cutter, tape, three-hole punch
- ❑   Forms and FHL publications
- ❑ Lockers and coatracks
- ❑ Map cabinets
- ❑ Research tables
- ❑ Snack Room area
- ❑   Vending machines
- ❑   Change machine
- ❑   Postage stamp machine
- ❑ Water fountains and rest rooms

Second floor (U.S./Canada)
- ❑ Elevators, stairs, and telephones
- ❑ Reference area
- ❑   Reference counter
- ❑   Reference books and finding aids
- ❑ Research tables
- ❑ FamilySearch workstations with printers
- ❑ Microfilm and microfiche cabinets
- ❑ Microfilm and microfiche cabinets
- ❑ Copy center and attendant window
- ❑   Film, fiche, and book copiers, stapler, paper cutter, tape, three-hole punch
- ❑   Forms and FHL publications
- ❑   Film rewinders
- ❑ Lockers and coatracks
- ❑ Water fountains and rest rooms

Floor B1 (International)
❏ Elevators and stairs, telephone, bulletin board
❏ Reference area
❏   Reference counter
❏   Reference books and finding aids
❏ FamilySearch workstations with printers
❏ Microfilm and microfiche readers
❏ Research tables
❏ Book area
❏ Microfilm, microfiche, and map cabinets
❏ Copy center and attendant window
❏   Book, film, and fiche copiers
❏   Stapler, paper cutter, tape, three-hole punch
❏   Forms and FHL publications
❏   Film rewinders
❏ Lockers and coatracks
❏ Water fountains and rest rooms

Floor B2 (British Isles)
❏ Elevators and stairs, telephone, bulletin board
❏ Reference area
❏   Reference counter
❏   Medieval section (ask at reference counter)
❏   Special collections (ask at reference counter)
❏   Reference books and finding aids
❏ FamilySearch workstations with printers
❏ Microfilm and microfiche readers
❏ Research tables
❏ Book area
❏ Microfilm, microfiche, and map cabinets
❏ Copy center and attendant window
❏   Book, film, and fiche copiers
❏   Stapler, paper cutter, tape, three-hole punch
❏   Forms and FHL publications
❏   Film rewinders
❏ Lockers and coatracks
❏ Water fountains and rest rooms

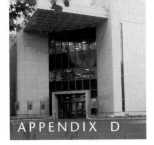

FHL Media Contact Information

Journalists from a variety of media constantly inquire about the Family History Library and the fascination with tracing family history. As polls continue to point out the ever increasing public interest in the search, the news media realize this is a topic for a story. The FHL provides a media kit and also some online media information about the library and genealogy in general. Check the FHL Web site, <http://www.familysearch.org>, and click on "Site Map" to find links to media information. Visiting journalists should also check <http://www.lds.org> for media information.

The FHL offers tours for journalists, and one way to arrange such a tour is to complete a form online. The tour includes a visit to the library, a chance for some one-on-one discussion, information on FamilySearch Internet, and information on the various segments of the search for familiy history. The tour can be directed toward research for a specific state, country, or specialty area, such as military or medical research. The library may be able to refer journalists not traveling to Salt Lake City to contacts in their own area. The library is also able to provide stock photographs and news clips for airing. For more information contact

> Media Relations Staff
> Public Affairs Department
> 15 East South Temple
> Salt Lake City, UT 84150
> Phone: (801) 240-1111
> E-mail: mediahelp@ldschurch.org

Index

Most topics specific to working on-site in Salt Lake City are subentries under the topic Family History Library. Books and articles included in the text and appendixes are usually indexed only by topic, not by title or author. Information pertaining to a country was indexed under that country's name. (If you are looking for information on Danish records, look under Denmark.) We prepared this index with the variety of its readers in mind: researchers at Family History Centers, people living in or traveling to Salt Lake City, genealogists of varied experience levels, the media, FHL and FHC staffs, the Salt Lake Convention & Visitors Bureau, and ourselves as well as others. Our goal is an index that is general enough to help beginners and detailed enough to be useful on-site in Salt Lake City.